Interpreting African American History and Culture at Museums and Historic Sites

INTERPRETING HISTORY

SERIES EDITOR

Russell Lewis, Chicago History Museum

EDITORIAL ADVISORY BOARD

Eloise Batic, Indiana Historical Society
Jessica Dorman, The Historic New Orleans Collection
W. Eric Emerson, South Carolina Department of Archives and History
Tim Grove, National Air and Space Museum
Lorraine McConaghy, Museum of History and Industry, Seattle, Washington
Sandra Smith, Heinz History Center
Ellen Spear, Heritage Museums & Gardens
Larry Wagenaar, Historical Society of Michigan

STAFF

Bob Beatty, AASLH
Charles Harmon, Rowman & Littlefield Publishers

About the Series

The American Association for State and Local History publishes the *Interpreting History* series in order to provide expert, in-depth guidance in interpretation for history professionals at museums and historic sites. The books are intended to help practitioners expand their interpretation to be more inclusive of the range of American history.

Books in this series help readers:
- quickly learn about the questions surrounding a specific topic,
- introduce them to the challenges of interpreting this part of history, and
- highlight best practice examples of how interpretation has been done by different organizations.

They enable institutions to place their interpretative efforts into a larger context, despite each having a specific and often localized mission. These books serve as quick references to practical considerations, further research, and historical information.

Titles in the Series

Interpreting African American History and Culture at Museums and Historic Sites

Edited by Max A. van Balgooy

Foreword by

Lonnie G. Bunch III, Founding Director

National Museum of African American History and Culture

ROWMAN & LITTLEFIELD
Lanham • Boulder • New York • London

Published by Rowman & Littlefield
A wholly owned subsidiary of The Rowman & Littlefield Publishing Group, Inc.
4501 Forbes Boulevard, Suite 200, Lanham, Maryland 20706
www.rowman.com

Unit A, Whitacre Mews, 26-34 Stannary Street, London SE11 4AB

British Library Cataloguing in Publication Information Available

Library of Congress Cataloging-in-Publication Data Available
ISBN: 978-0-7591-2278-9 (cloth)
ISBN: 978-0-7591-2279-6 (paper)
ISBN: 978-0-7591-2280-2 (electronic)

∞™ The paper used in this publication meets the minimum requirements of American
National Standard for Information Sciences—Permanence of Paper for Printed Library
Materials, ANSI/NISO Z39.48-1992.

Printed in the United States of America

Contents

PART III   CASE STUDIES

Foreword

"All the Day, Every Day": Reflections on Thirty Years of Interpreting African American History

LONNIE G. BUNCH III, FOUNDING DIRECTOR NATIONAL MUSEUM OF AFRICAN AMERICAN HISTORY AND CULTURE

ARLY IN my career, I traveled to Nashville, Tennessee, to visit the Hermitage Plantation, the one-time home of Andrew Jackson. While on a tour of the house and grounds, a nervous docent repeatedly glanced at me whenever she mentioned the "servants," her terminology for the enslaved who toiled on the grounds we trod. As the tour progressed, the docent wanted me to understand that Jackson's relationship with the enslaved was more like a family than owner or master. Her proof was the relationship between Jackson and his "loyal servant" Alfred. As we entered the cemetery, she made her case by pointing out how Jackson and Alfred were so close personally that at his death, Alfred was buried by the feet of Andrew Jackson. To the tour guide, their proximity in death spoke volumes about loyalty and friendship. To me, it seemed as if positioning Alfred so close to Jackson's body meant that Alfred was to serve Jackson throughout all eternity.

There is no doubt that much has changed in the interpretation of the African American experience in museum and historic sites. The days when African Americans were viewed only when juxtaposed to the white community or when black men and women were invisible and omitted from the historical narrative are, in most cases, long gone. The study of African American history is now a vibrant and essential part of many institutions that interpret America's past, as evidenced by the important chapters that comprise this significant publication. Yet it is too soon to be satisfied with the progress that has been made: the major challenge museums and historic sites face is the need to centralize the narrative of African American history in a manner that is ripe with meaning, ambiguity, and complexity.

Far too frequently, the interpretation of African American history is still viewed as exotic, ancillary, or a necessary palliative that shows a commitment to, or at least, the recognition of an underserved audience. Rather than being viewed as a separate but equal presentation, the interpretation of this history, this culture must be seen as the quintessential American story: a history that profoundly shapes us all regardless of race or region. African American history, then, is a wonderful lens that illuminates what it means to be an American. Only by viewing the African American experience through this broader framework can we find a new integration that allows all who visit these museums and historic sites to better understand how much American notions of resiliency, freedom, spirituality, and hope were shaped by an African American narrative, and how much of America's national identity has been forged in the fires of the African American experience.

In 1939, historians hired by the Works Progress Administration set about interviewing those who were formerly enslaved. One of those interviewed was Cornelius Holmes, who was enslaved on a rice plantation in South Carolina. When asked if slavery still mattered nearly seventy-five years after emancipation, Holmes replied: "Though the slavery question is settled its impact is not. It is in our politics, in our courts, on our highways, in our manner and in our thoughts—all the day, every day." What a gift it will be when museums and historic sites can help our publics understand that they are shaped, touched, and made better by African American history, all the day, every day. The chapters in this volume give me hope that that day is not too far distant.

Acknowledgments

MS. SANDRA WHEDBEE introduced me to African American history while I was in the sixth grade at Magnolia Elementary School in Upland, California, but it was the National Trust for Historic Preservation that gave me the opportunity to explore it more broadly and deeply through its historic sites and its African American Historic Places Program (funded in part by the Ford Foundation) as its director of interpretation and education. Those years allowed me to meet many of the leaders in the field and learn about their extraordinary work in preservation and interpretation. In turn, this book is a small effort to share that experience with others so that we may together create a more relevant and engaging history for all Americans. Thanks, too, to the American Association for State and Local History for launching this series of books on historical interpretation, and to Mary, my wife, for her continual encouragement and support.

Introduction

MAX A. VAN BALGOOY

"[I]'M NOT AN African American." It's one of the most common reasons why museums and historic sites are reluctant to interpret African American history and culture. Telling someone else's story can be scary. What if I get the facts wrong? What if I say something offensive? Perhaps it would be better if their story was told by their people. Here's the good news: it's not *their* history but *our* history.

African American history contributes to our identity as Americans in the same way as the history of women, immigrants, or Native Americans. Embracing all parts of American history as our own creates the firm foundation from which we can interpret African American history. We know that our history defines us, shapes us, and explains us. Without it, our memory and identity is diminished. Although history does not predict the future, it does explain our current situation and provides meaningful lessons for our lives. History serves as our personal and community memory, helping us analyze and understand the world around us. It's the accumulation of all the deeds and misdeeds, hits and misses, paths taken and rejected that make us who we are today. The more we know about our history, the better we understand today's complex world. If you've spent time with someone suffering from Alzheimer's disease, you quickly become aware of the importance of memory to the person's personality and abilities. When our memories fail as a nation, when our history is incomplete, our assumptions can be flawed and our decisions faulty. How essential it is, therefore, that we interpret the history of our communities and nation holistically, recognizing the stories of all people—including African Americans—who created, affected, and contributed to our United States.

This book suggests ways to improve and enhance the interpretation of African American history at museums and historic sites—and what a rich history it is. Unfortunately, Americans miss most of it. High school textbooks may include a few paragraphs or mention a couple of the leading lights, such as Frederick Douglass and Rosa Parks, but often African American history is distilled to insignificance or pushed into the "blue boxes," the sidebars to the main story. To find meaningful, thoughtful African American history takes some effort, and museums and historic sites can guide the way.

In the sixth grade, a special reward for me was earning some time in our classroom library. Our teacher had stocked the shelves with lots of good books, and I still remember my excitement when I finished a biography of George Washington Carver—this man was amazing! How can I become as smart and creative as him? Tell me more! Looking back now, I suspect that Ms. Whedbee had carefully curated the collection to get us to see far beyond our daily lives (insisting on "Ms." should have been my clue to her reform-minded perspective, but at twelve years old, I didn't notice these things). We can take that same approach in the exhibits, tours, events, and programs at our museums and historic sites, taking confidence in knowing we're sharing a more complete and full history.

Here's more good news: most Americans, not just African Americans, want to know about African American history. Alex Haley's *Roots*, the autobiography turned into an epic television series in 1977, introduced Americans to a history they never knew—and they were spellbound. As museums, we're in an ideal position to build upon this interest. Visitors trust museums more than any other source, including college professors and eyewitnesses, because they expect we provide a balanced interpretation that incorporates various perspectives and uses authentic objects.[1] After graduating from high school or college, adults turn routinely to museums for their education. That's why they see our exhibits, take our tours, visit our websites, attend our events, and buy books in our shops. We're the experts both in the content and in facilitating learning.

African American history does contain difficult, controversial, and sensitive topics—as does all of American history. As history museums and historic sites, we have a great responsibility to share all of the lessons of history, whether it moves through success and failure, tragedy and delight, laughter and sadness. Favoring one without the other can mislead our listeners, giving them only an incomplete understanding of our past and present.

As history organizations, we have an advantage in building understanding—we can look back and describe what occurred, find patterns, examine cause and effect, evaluate choices, and make decisions about the future. Historical interpretation is not simply a recounting of facts. A piano has eighty-eight keys, but to make music, you choose only a few of them. As interpreters we are creating music, selecting those people, places, and events that can best convey meaning and understanding about the past. Interpretation requires us to study, analyze, and select evidence that reveals a significant story, narrative, or lesson. History is not merely for entertainment, but education, and increasingly museums and historic sites are using history to explain current events and inform decisions. African American history has much to teach us.

In 1992, Fred Wilson reinterpreted the collections of the Maryland Historical Society to "provoke new ways of thinking, to encourage critical learning, and to reconnect them to the past viscerally."[2] In the "Mining the Museum" exhibit, he created unexpected combinations of objects and words, such as placing silver repoussé vessels and iron slave shackles together in a vitrine labeled "Metalwork, 1793–1880," that provoked discussions about slavery and race, "opening that sore and cleaning it out so it can heal."[3] The next year, San Francisco Heritage allowed Wilson to do something similar at the Haas-Lilienthal House. These exhibits broke attendance records, generated extraordinary publicity, and were hailed as pathbreaking, but it seems that path was not taken very far. Nevertheless, as this book's bibliography shows, there has been tremendous progress in the last twenty years in many other ways. Philipsburg Manor in New York, Maymont in Richmond, Shadows-on-the-Teche in Louisiana, Conner Prairie Interactive History Park in Indiana, the Power of Place Project in Los Angeles, Harriet Beecher Stowe Center in Connecticut, the Old Courthouse in St. Louis, New York Historical Society, National Museum of American History, Levine Museum of the New South in North Carolina, Portsmouth Black History Trail in New Hampshire, Colonial Williamsburg, and many, many others have launched innovative programs and exhibits that raised the level of interpretation of African American history and culture.

These efforts in reinterpretation have their origins in the 1960s with the rise of the New Social History, which explored the lives of ordinary people and overlooked groups, including African Americans. It was also the decade of the first generation of African American museums (the DuSable Museum, Anacostia Museum, Wright Museum, Studio Museum in Harlem, Museum of the National Center for Afro-American Artists), the formation of the National Black History Museums Conference, the inclusion of the home of Frederick Douglass into the National Park Service, and Congress's consideration of a Commission on Afro-American History and Culture. These achievements can be traced back to the 1870s, when African Americans organized displays, speeches, and performances at the world's fairs and national expositions that remembered their distinctive past and envisioned a better future.[4] In 2016, we'll cross another threshold when the Smithsonian Institution opens the National Museum of African American History and Culture.

This book is another step in a path being laid by many people for nearly 150 years. Although much has been accomplished at museums and historic sites to enhance and improve the interpretation of African American history and culture, we've also learned a great deal and discovered there's still more to be done. This book suggests some future directions.

The first section lays out some of the current challenges in the interpretation of African American history. Amanda Seymour shares her observations of tours and programs at the homes of the first five presidents to provide a baseline for the chapters that follow. The next two chapters by Kristin Gallas, James DeWolf Perry, and Julia Rose help address slavery and other sensitive or difficult topics, which often cause many museums and historic sites to hesitate. They originally appeared as technical leaflets in *History News* and are further expanded as separate books in this series. David Young describes Cliveden's efforts to more fully engage the surrounding neighborhood in African American history, giving his executive director's perspective on the benefits and conflicts.

Michelle McClellan opens the next section on research. Although it's often claimed that it isn't possible to interpret African Americans because there's no information, she shows how much can be learned by examining Dr. Tann's visit to treat the family's malaria, a brief episode in the *Little House in the Prairie* books. William Peterson reminds us to question assumptions in historical interpretation. By conducting original research, he uncovered a mistake made more than a century ago that revealed the enslaved childhood of Sarah Bickford, a business leader in Virginia City, Montana. Lila Teresa Church, Matthew Pinsker, Bernard Powers, D L Henderson, and Martha Katz-Hyman show how research into community, the law, churches, cemeteries, and material culture open up entirely new sources for understanding the African American experience. Lynn Rainville encourages us to consider

Facebook and other social media as ways of conducting research, an approach that can be easily adopted by museums and historic sites.

The final section contains a diverse collection of case studies of successful exhibits, programs, activities, and projects to inspire ideas and provoke discussion. George McDaniel and Benjamin Filene describe how the study of one local place can make big connections to state and national history. Stacia Kuceyeski and Andrea Jones show ways to engage students in history, both inside and outside the museum. Preserving sites associated with African American history is an ongoing challenge, and Jenny Scanlin and Teresa Grimes share some of the urban planning and historic preservation tools they used to protect twentieth-century buildings in Los Angeles. Wendi Manuel-Scott and Sara Howard-O'Brien provide an alternative to preservation in their case study of a now-demolished segregated school in Virginia. Although all of these projects rely on a collaborative approach, it's emphasized in the closing chapters. Robbie Davis reviews the award-winning exhibit on Vietnam veterans at the Heinz History Center and provides a behind-the-scenes view of its development. Robert Connolly and Ana Rea built a relationship between a museum and the local community through an unconventional service learning project (and the chapter itself is a collaboration between the museum director and one of the student leaders). Ellen Griffith Spears and Shelia Washington collaborate as well on their chapter, which describes a grassroots effort to interpret the Scottsboro Boys in Alabama that ultimately led to "full and unconditional pardons" to the three defendants with standing convictions. It's a fitting conclusion to this book because it shows the tremendous impact that museums and historic sites can have when they interpret African American history.

A review of the author biographies shows this book is a collaboration as well: experienced scholars, newly minted graduates, directors, educators, historians, anthropologists, urban planners, African Americans, and non–African Americans. That diversity is intentional because the best interpretation is done as a collaboration to ensure it incorporates multiple perspectives. In interpretation, the process is as important as the product. Learning should occur not just in our visitors but also in our institutions and ourselves as we design and implement programs, exhibits, and tours. Expect change to happen.

Some of those changes can be seen throughout the chapters, although they are more subtle. African Americans are not treated as a homogenous group with the same interests, motivations, and histories but as distinct individuals with names and families. The topics go farther than slavery and civil rights, travel outside the South, look at life in places other than cotton fields and basement kitchens. Not that those topics and places are unimportant to African American history, but it has to move beyond what are quickly becoming clichés of interpretation at museums and historic sites.

During the past two years as I assembled this anthology, I've become increasingly aware of some needs and opportunities in the field. There's a general absence of program evaluation and visitor research to help us measure and increase the impact of the interpretation of African American history, particularly in museums and historic sites outside of Virginia or on topics other than slavery and the civil rights movement. Reviews of exhibits are plentiful compared to tours or school programs, but they typically focus on the scholarly content and very little on the audiences, visitor experience, interpretive methodology, or development process.

Second, and much more difficult to resolve, is the assumption that African Americans are a separate race. Race is an idea developed during the infancy of modern science to explain human differences. History shows us that race is a slippery idea in America, with categories changing rapidly (especially if you are Irish, Italian, Slavic, or Jewish) to justify status in response to political and cultural needs.[5] Because race is socially constructed, it can also be deconstructed—and history organizations can play a crucial role because they can unpack and explain the history of race. I don't suggest that any of this is easy. Indeed, while races do not exist, racism does, but as Frederick Douglass reminds us, "If there is no struggle, there is no progress. Those who profess to favor freedom and deprecate agitation, are men who want crops without plowing the ground, they want rain without thunder and lightning."

Notes

1. Roy Rosenzweig and David Thelen, *The Presence of the Past: Popular Uses of History in American Life* (New York: Columbia University Press, 1998), 89–114.
2. Lisa G. Corrin, *Mining the Museum: An Installation by Fred Wilson* (New York: New Press, 1994), lxx.
3. Corrin, *Mining the Museum*, 34.
4. In *Negro Building: Black Americans in the World of Fairs and Museums* (Berkeley: University of California Press, 2012), Mabel Wilson provides a detailed history of African American history museums from 1870 to 2000.
5. To learn more about the social construction of race, see *Whiteness of a Different Color: European Immigrants and the Alchemy of Race* by Matthew Frye Jacobson (Cambridge, MA: Harvard University Press, 1998) and *The Metaphysical Club: A Story of Ideas in America* by Louis Menand (New York: Farrar Straus Giroux, 2001).

PART I

CHALLENGES AND OPPORTUNITIES

CHAPTER 1

Pride and Prejudice

Interpreting Slavery at the Homes of Five Founding Fathers

AMANDA G. SEYMOUR

MUSEUMS ARE places of significant power: they are sites of knowledge production, presentation, and perpetuation. In fact, they serve as some of the highest-ranking sources of trustworthy historical information outside of the traditional academy.[1] As subsets of museums, historic sites are no exception.

Many homes of prominent historical figures from the American Founding Era have been converted into museums, open for public exploration.[2] Arguably the most popular sites, based on yearly visitation, are the homes of the Founding Era presidents, or Founding Fathers: George Washington, John Adams, Thomas Jefferson, James Madison, and James Monroe. At the homes of these great men, their lives and legacies are celebrated, and the homes themselves serve as important symbols on the American political and ideological landscape (see figure 1.1).

The American Founding Era was, without doubt, an exceptionally important part of the formation of the nation that we know today. While the study and celebration of the Founding Fathers is certainly an integral part of our national culture and heritage, these men were not the only ones who shaped the nation. Traditionally, at the historic homes of these men, the interpretive information presented revolves around the associated Founder, making it seem as though the Founders were the most important, sometimes even the only agents in shaping the fledgling nation.

There were many other people besides the Founding Fathers who lived on their estates, and by extension, actively and equally sculpted the United States. This large group of people did not have the qualities of the hegemonic trifecta of the wealthy white male (middle- and lower-class people, people of color, and women) yet shaped history just as much as the Founders. Though since they were (and are) not part of the privileged group, their histories

Figure 1.1. Monticello, home of Thomas Jefferson (third president of the United States) and hundreds of free and enslaved African men, women, and children. Courtesy of the Thomas Jefferson Foundation at Monticello, photo by Max A. van Balgooy.

are, as a result, not as privileged, well-preserved, or well-presented at these historic house museums.

The particular non-hegemonic group of focus for this study is those that were enslaved during the American Founding Era, and more specifically, those who worked on the plantations owned by the Founders.[3] This entire class of humans was considered chattel—property to be moved and used at the owner's will. Being from the lowest class, the histories of enslaved people have traditionally fallen to the wayside, though there has arguably been an increased interest in exploring and reviving these histories as the New Social History emphasizes the study of "individuals and groups that were marginalized in more conventional historical studies."[4] Even though the New Social History has increased the interest in the "complexity, nuance, and multiple viewpoints" of historical narratives, I will argue that the historical interpretations at the house museums of the Founding Fathers have not fully incorporated the perspectives acknowledged by the New Social History, specifically of those people who the Founding Fathers enslaved.[5]

Because the interpretations of slavery at these historic homes of the Founding Fathers are lacking in nuance and complexity, I will further argue that the interpretations may present a skewed version of history for the visiting public, downplaying the brutality and moral, social, and legal entanglements of the institution of slavery. As a result of this skewed history, where the more shameful details of the Founding Era are downplayed, visitors may come away with an unwarranted, rose-colored view of the Era, which could potentially lead to what I will call a *false nostalgia* for the period.

It is important that this issue be addressed at these particular historic sites (and, by extension, other historic sites that interpret slavery) because a false nostalgia for a time period results in historical amnesia, where the more depressing details of slavery and the people affected by it remain unacknowledged, undervalued, and forgotten. Historical amnesia creates a number of problems, one of which is the undervaluing of the contributions made by those the Founding Fathers enslaved (and their later descendants) in the shaping of the nation as we know it today.

The tours and exhibits at the homes of the first five presidents—Mt. Vernon, Peacefield, Monticello, Montpelier, and Ash Lawn-Highland—demonstrate how historical amnesia and false nostalgia can creep into the interpretation. While these museums are not purposefully distorting history, it can happen due to inadequate research or training, fear of discussing sensitive or unfamiliar topics, or an inability to view the site from the visitors' perspective. This preliminary and superficial study of the interpretations of slavery at these popular historic homes also calls to attention the need for further analysis into the messages that these sites are sending to the visiting public about the African American experience during the Founding Era. For both situations, I will offer some suggestions that can be adapted by museums and historic houses around the country so that they actively and continuously work toward presenting more inclusive, nuanced histories for everyone who had historical ties to the site.

While there is certainly nothing wrong with fondly looking back on a time when communities were smaller and products and lifestyles were more artisanal, it must be remembered that the Founding Era was also a time when it was economically and socially acceptable to own other human beings. This feature of the period is a significant part of why I consider nostalgia for the Founding Era unwarranted. The fledgling nation was not a simpler place, especially not for those who had no rights or control over their own bodies or lives. I argue that the way sites interpret the history of the Founding Era, especially in the interpretation of slavery, can promote the kind of false nostalgia I have described.

Over the course of five years, from 1996 to 2001, Jennifer Eichstedt and Stephen Small conducted a study of 122 sites that were historically plantations but are now open to tourists (what they call "plantation museums") in Virginia, Georgia, and Louisiana. They were interested in the interpretations of slavery at these sites and sought to conduct "a systematic analysis of the strategic rhetorics that are employed by plantation museums to manage, and in most cases confine to oblivion, the system of slavery and the presence of those enslaved."[6] They found that sites generally fell into four categories of interpretation of slavery: (1) symbolic annihilation and erasure, (2) trivialization and deflection, (3) segregation and marginalization of knowledge, and (4) relative incorporation.

Symbolic annihilation and erasure occurs in interpretations that suggest "that slavery and people of African descent literally were not present or were not important enough to be acknowledged."[7] The authors enumerate various interpretive devices that signal symbolic annihilation and erasure, such as perfunctory inclusion of information on slavery, the use of euphemisms when referring to enslaved people or slavery, use of the passive voice in interpretations, universalizing, and making ahistorical statements. Trivialization and deflection comes in a variety of forms: portraying slavery as a benevolent institution; promoting the tropes of the happy or grateful slave, loyalty after emancipation, and untrustworthy slaves; and valorizing whiteness by advancing narratives of the good owner, whites as hard workers, and contemporary whites as "slaves." When sites have separate tours or exhibit areas where slavery is the focus, Eichstedt and Small consider it a display of segregated knowledge, which "limits the exposure that the public has to this knowledge and reinforces the importance and normalcy of learning only a white-centric view of history."[8] Finally, sites that employ relative incorporation "demonstrate that there has been an obvious effort to incorporate issues regarding slavery and those enslaved throughout the interpretive locations that a visitor might attend at a given site."[9]

For Eichstedt and Small, these interpretive devices serve to "tell a story of American history that centers around whites, males, and elites, and that these sites erase or minimize the presence, labor, and lives of enslaved Africans and African Americans."[10] The resulting distortion of the history of slavery can paint an inaccurate picture of the Founding Era and cause false nostalgia. Eichstedt and Small's framework provides the basis for this study on the interpretation of slavery, but I will take the analysis one step further by determining if the respective interpretations of slavery are promoting a false nostalgia for the Founding Era.[11]

While all five sites had a range of issues to be addressed, I focus on *one* interpretive method that was present at each site at the time of visitation followed by suggestions on improving the interpretation to avoid promoting a false nostalgia for the Founding Era.

George Washington's Mount Vernon

During one of my visits to the Upper Yard, where the barracks-style slave quarters are located, there was a period-costumed, first-person interpreter playing the part of George Washington's personal valet, William Lee. He was standing outside of the quarters in a grassy area speaking to a crowd of about fifteen visitors, some of whom would come and go at various intervals, creating a relatively informal situation. What drew my attention to his interpretation and held me there for about twenty minutes was his commentary on how "here at Mount Vernon, compared to other estates, life is better for us slaves."[12] He elaborated on the different areas where Washington showed "compassion" and "humanity" toward those he had enslaved, including the recognition of marriages even though they were not recognized under the law, and his level of care for the enslaved people who became ill.[13]

This first-person interpreter was clearly deploying what Eichstedt and Small call the happy or grateful slave narrative, introduced earlier in the chapter. This narrative was problematic for two main reasons. First, the topic of slavery was actually being used to valorize Washington and bolster his image, fashioning him as more humane and tolerant than other slaveholders during his time. Second, using the happy or grateful slave narrative trivialized the brutal nature of the institution of slavery and could foster racist attitudes, where "people of African descent are seen as childish, simple, and unable to care for themselves."[14] The actor's interpretation was tightly focused around Washington and the image of him being "an enlightened slaveholder."[15]

First-person interpretation, like any other interpretive method, has its benefits and drawbacks. Sharing a personal experience or story can aid in connecting to the past and can, in some cases, foster empathy and understanding of a perspective not previously considered. In terms of slavery and the African American experience during the Founding Era, first-person interpretation could be an especially effective tool, which Mount Vernon was attempting to use. However, William Lee's interpretation would have been much more effective had the interpreter spoken about his own life experiences rather than focusing just on George Washington's conduct and attitude. Perhaps Lee could have shared information about his family, his daily tasks as Washington's valet, his interactions with other slaves on the plantation, or the story of how he became a valet. If that kind of information is unknown, first-person interpretation should be avoided, as it belies the experience of slavery and can create a version of American history to which visitors are more likely to look back with a sense of nostalgia rather than hindsight-fueled caution and sorrow.[16]

John Adams's Peacefield

At Adams National Historic Park, four generations of Adamses are interpreted at four different historic buildings, starting with John Adams (called JA for purposes of clarity). Even though the Adams family never owned slaves, the topic of slavery was still included in the park's interpretation. However, slavery was mostly mentioned in discussions about John Quincy Adams (JQA), given his advocacy for abolition and his association to the *Amistad* case. Even though JA did not own slaves, it is important to include him and his house in this study since he is such a prominent Founding Father, and our collective ideas about the Founding Era are partially shaped by his life and legacy.

There are some fairly common misconceptions about slavery in New England (and the North in general) that I have encountered during my time as an historic interpreter and student of history. Some of these misconceptions may be informed by the fact that JA is one of the most well-known New Englanders of the Founding Era, where he may serve as a representative of all Founding Era New Englanders in the minds of many Americans. That is, because he is one of the more prominent Northerners from the Founding Era, many Americans may believe that his lifestyle was representative of the Northerners of that period. And perhaps because he did not own slaves, the misconception that slavery did not exist in the North is surprisingly common.

There were hardly any mentions of slavery at the National Park. During one visit, when the interpreter was showing the servant's quarters of the Old House at Peacefield, he noted that the Adams family in general was always opposed to slavery but did not share further details on the topic. On another visit, the only mention of slavery was when the interpreter discussed JA and the Constitution: while JA had respect for individual rights (meaning he would have identified more with the anti-slavery side of the aisle), he believed that getting the political factions to compromise was more important, which led to maintaining the institution of slavery.

Overall, the lack of discussion (or as Eichstedt would call trivialization and deflection) about slavery at the Adams National Historic Park was problematic for two reasons. First, it belied the pervasive nature of slavery in Massachusetts and New England during JA's lifetime. Failing to discuss the context of slavery in New England can actually promote the commonly held, though mythical and nostalgic, notion that slavery did not exist in the North. Second, interpreting JA and JQA in the same space increased the chance that visitors conflate their politics, when JA could not necessarily be called an abolitionist while JQA could. Abridging the history of slavery in New England and the incendiary nature of the issue during JA's time was a missed opportunity on the part of the Adams National Historic Park to describe JA's feelings about the institution and the reasons why he did not own slaves, and it may lead to a false nostalgia about JA's historical environment.

Thomas Jefferson's Monticello

Thomas Jefferson as a slaveholder was a common theme in the interpretations at Monticello, and some of the realities and complexities of plantation life were described in the interpretive material: violence, splitting of families through sale or purchase, inter-racial unions, and Jefferson's freeing of only a small fraction of his total slaves upon his death. However, this information was presented with the most detail and nuance in areas and tours on the grounds that many visitors do not engage with or access (underneath the house, on the lane that runs beside the house called Mulberry Row, and on the supplemental Slavery at Monticello tours), which might risk promoting a false nostalgia, given the relative tranquility and less-unsettling topics during the average visitor experience, such as the main house tour. While the topic of slavery was dealt with relatively well at the points where it was discussed, the discourse can become bounded, or segregated, as Eichstedt and Small would call it, if it is not continuously interwoven in all aspects of the interpretive experience, just as slavery was continuously interwoven into all aspects of Founding Era life.

It is thus important that the interpreters incorporate this kind of information into their tours of the main house. As with any site that gives relative interpretive freedom to the tour guides, the tours have incredible variation based on the interpreter. It follows, then, that when it comes to discussing slavery, there is also incredible variation. On some tours, I found that an interpreter might speak about Jefferson's likely paternity of Sally Hemings's children (as is mandated by the interpretive guidelines) and then only bring up slavery again if prompted by a visitor's question.[17] On the other hand, I have been on tours where an interpreter deftly incorporates the topic of slavery on every stop on the tour, engaging the visitors in mindful and sensitive discussions about the topic. The latter is the ideal model for the main house tour: it is important that the connection between Thomas Jefferson's great achievements and his dependence on slave labor is made clearly and often, so as to avoid a perception of the site that may cause a false nostalgia for the Founding Era. Those that were enslaved by Jefferson had just as much of a hand as Jefferson in making the Monticello that visitors see today, and it is important to share that information with visitors to create a more complete historical narrative.

Professional development focused on the facts about slavery is, of course, a necessity at historic plantation sites, but expert training on *how* to thoughtfully and sensitively talk about slavery during interpretation is also needed at these sites. This kind of training should occur with regularity, covering different facets of the interpretation of slavery. It could not only help interpreters with their own presentations but could also promote a wider trend of visitors—and society at large—being more self-reflexive, realistic, and unapologetic about the history of slavery in our country.

James Madison's Montpelier

Montpelier, like Monticello, was noticeably trying to present slavery more realistically and holistically, but they too suffered from segregated knowledge, though in a different way than Monticello.

The only detailed biographical information given about any enslaved person at Montpelier was of Paul Jennings, who was a household slave and eventually became James Madison's manservant. The discourse about Jennings in the orientation film was mostly about how he helped James and Dolley Madison. During the main house tour, in the dining room, there were life-sized cutouts of dinner guests around the table, and the cutout that represented Paul Jennings was standing aside the table, prompting the interpreter to talk about him each time I visited (see figure 1.2). Also, in Madison's bedroom, each interpreter played an audio clip with a voice actor reading a quote by Jennings about Madison's death. Aside from most of the interpretation about Jennings actually spotlighting the Madisons (and promoting Eichstedt and Small's loyal slave trope), Jennings was really the only enslaved person mentioned or studied during the average visitor experience. Underneath the house, there was an interpretive area rich with artistically and thoughtfully produced information about slavery at Montpelier and in a wider historical context, though this information was also segregated (like at Monticello), and it was unclear how many visitors actually engage with and access this information.

While repeatedly giving detail about an enslaved person throughout the visitor experience is an obvious effort on Montpelier's part to incorporate the histories of people aside from the Madisons, it could belie the numbers of enslaved people it required to sustain the plantation, causing a false nostalgia for the site, historical environment, or time period. Just as at Monticello, inclusion of multiple characters in the story of Montpelier, both enslaved and free, could help paint a more truthful and contextualized picture of the site and era, and professional development is an effective tool for successful incorporation of these historical agents into all aspects of the site's interpretation.

James Monroe's Highland

At Ash Lawn-Highland, as it is currently called, the main house tour ended outside, where visitors were encouraged to explore the Service Yard on their own. The buildings in the Service Yard were all of stone structure and painted white, and they were staged with objects

Figure 1.2. An exhibit in the dining room at James Madison's Montpelier. Paul Jennings is depicted standing on the left side. Courtesy of the Montpelier Foundation, photo by Max A. van Balgooy.

to indicate the building's use. Each of the buildings also had interpretive information about the use of the building.

One building, a dwelling, was a one-roomed structure with a sleeping loft, staged to indicate that it housed an enslaved family. The interpretive information failed to mention that this dwelling, with its stone structure and chimney and wooden floors, would have been atypical of the housing for enslaved people at Highland, and perhaps even historically inaccurate—it was reconstructed in 1985 based on a 1908 photograph and little archaeological evidence.[18]

This kind of atypical structure can lead to a false sense of relief on the part of contemporary visitors, who may think, based on the structural amenities, that slavery wasn't all that bad. For proof of this phenomenon, while I was exploring the outbuildings alongside other visitors, I saw a couple leaning over the barrier ropes at the entrance of the dwelling to check if they "at least had fireplaces." It is not difficult to assume that this couple may have walked away from the site with that false sense of relief, which goes hand-in-hand with a false nostalgia.

For a problem such as the one noted earlier, the simple solution is to tweak the interpretive material to reflect the likelihood that the structure was atypical and probably not historically accurate, perhaps with a description of what the building may have actually looked like. Going even further, the interpretive information might include information on how many people may have lived there or what the conditions were like, which would provide a more accurate portrayal of how those that Monroe enslaved may have lived. The less simple (and much more expensive) solution is to research the historical structure and recreate it as it would have been in Monroe's time. Of course, financial situations of the sites must always be taken into account, but it is possible for sites to make small changes to their interpretive material or experience that fit within their budgets to present a more accurate history of slavery at the site. Ash Lawn-Highland's word-processed interpretation plaques could be edited with more sensitive and agent-oriented language while still presenting the facts.

Conclusions

Failing to give a detailed or realistic presentation of slavery at historic sites may keep visitors (subconsciously or otherwise) unaware of slavery's structure, prevalence, and nature, potentially promoting a rosy view of the Founding Era and perpetuating a false nostalgia for the period. I would argue that each of the sites in the study, in their own ways, are culprits of this promotion of false nostalgia. However, each has the potential, also in their own ways, to increase understanding about this complex topic and thus decrease the chance that visitors become nostalgic for the Founding Era.

Finding the balance of presenting a critical history and remaining respectful—but not reverent—to the Founding Fathers is indeed challenging, though possible, for each site in this study. Indeed, while they still have their own challenges, Monticello and Montpelier are good examples of how interpretations can move in a direction of a more holistic approach in the presentation of history.

I have previously suggested solutions to help mitigate the perpetuation of false nostalgia at Founding Era sites, and one of the most readily available solutions is to incorporate more information about those enslaved and/or marginalized within the main tour of the Founder's home.[19] Of course, quality must prevail over quantity. Sensitively and mindfully folding in context and complexity to the presented facts is key to a successful interpretation of slavery.

It is not enough for sites to acknowledge the presence of slavery. The *ways* that slavery is interpreted has direct bearing on the message that the site sends to the public. There is the danger that the topic of slavery may be referenced in many parts of the entire interpretive experience but treated at a relatively shallow degree, making it appear as though the information is incorporated throughout the site. Achieving both breadth and depth should be the goal for the interpretations of slavery at these historic sites.

Incorporating my suggested solutions into the interpretations at these five historic sites may help to clear the path toward a more self-critical perspective of the history of our nation and may eventually translate into a more holistic and fair treatment of all those who call themselves American, both in the past and present. Pride and prejudice need not go hand-in-hand.

Notes

1. Roy Rosenzweig and David Thelen, *The Presence of the Past: Popular Uses of History in American Life* (New York: Columbia University Press, 1998).

2. "American Founding Era" and "Founding Era" are terms I borrow from the University of Virginia Press, describing the time that encompasses both the Colonial and Revolutionary eras.

3. It is true that John Adams did not own slaves, but slavery was still prevalent in Massachusetts and greater New England. Slavery is indeed interpreted at the home of John Adams, which is the primary justification for including his historic home in this chapter.

4. Robert E. Weir, "New Social History," in *Class in America: An Encyclopedia*, ed. Robert E. Weir (Westport, CT: Greenwood Press, 2007), 576.

5. Weir, "New Social History," 576.

6. Jennifer L. Eichstedt and Stephen Small, *Representations of Slavery: Race and Ideology in Southern Plantation Museums* (Washington, D.C.: Smithsonian Books, 2002), 2.

7. Eichstedt and Small, *Representations*, 105.

8. Eichstedt and Small, *Representations*, 170.

9. Eichstedt and Small, *Representations*, 203.

10. Eichstedt and Small, *Representations*, 4.

11. My dedicated field research occurred from 2012 to 2013, and I visited each of the sites in the study at least twice during that time. I attempted to understand and recreate the average visitor experience at each site and investigate how it shapes perceptions and understanding about slavery in the American Founding Era. I modeled my fieldwork on certain parts, but not all, of Eichstedt and Small; that is, visiting sites more than once to appreciate differences in content based on the guide, taking advantage of the varying interpretive experiences offered at each site, and avoiding engagement with interpreters, particularly about slavery, to experience what they call the "regular tour." This study effectively serves as a timestamp of each site's interpretation on slavery during the field research period.

12. Personal observation by author, Mt. Vernon, March 10, 2013.

13. Personal observation by author, Mt. Vernon, March 10, 2013.

14. Eichstedt and Small, *Representations*, 151.

15. Mount Vernon Ladies' Association, *George Washington's Mount Vernon: Official Guidebook* (Mount Vernon: Mount Vernon Ladies Association, 2000), 182.

16. For the pros, cons, and recommendations on first-person interpretation (including the African American experience), see *Past into Present: Effective Techniques for First-Person Historical Interpretation* by Stacy Flora Roth (Chapel Hill: University of North Carolina Press, 1998).

17. Having been employed by the Thomas Jefferson Foundation as an interpreter, I have knowledge of the interpretive guidelines set forth by the management, one of which is that, on every tour, all interpreters must address the likelihood of Jefferson's paternity of Sally Hemings's children.

18. Sara Bon-Harper, executive director of Ash Lawn-Highland, indicated the problem of Ash Lawn-Highland's ahistorical structures at a seminar we both attended in February 2013.

19. Amanda G. Seymour, "Pride and Prejudice: The Historic Interpretation of Slavery at the Homes of Five Founding Fathers" (MA thesis, George Washington University, 2013).

CHAPTER 2

Developing a Comprehensive and Conscientious Interpretation of Slavery at Historic Sites and Museums

KRISTIN L. GALLAS AND JAMES DeWOLF PERRY

INTERPRETING SLAVERY, with its powerful resonances, is a privilege and a great responsibility. For many years, the field has neglected to interpret, interpreted incompletely, or perpetuated myths about the presence and lives of enslaved people at historic sites and museums across the country. We have an obligation to the public to share a comprehensive and conscientious story of the past, especially as studies show that the public considers museums to be their most trusted source of historical information.[1]

As historic sites and museums position themselves to bear witness to America's tragic history of slavery, they should ask about their interpretive experience, "What is *at stake* if visitors leave our site without an accurate, balanced, and sensitive understanding of slavery and its role in our history?"

Over the past thirty to thirty-five years, historic sites and museums have begun to incorporate stories of slavery into their interpretation. Major institutions like the Colonial Williamsburg Foundation and the National Trust for Historic Preservation have led the way in sharing the lives of enslaved people at their sites. However, even today, visits to many southern plantations or antebellum historic house museums, or to northern sites with histories related to slavery, are likely to tell a different story.[2] Here the lives and even physical presence of the enslaved have all but vanished, and the broader political, economic, and social context of slavery is nowhere to be found.

The Tracing Center on Histories and Legacies of Slavery is committed to helping sites and museums work through concerns surrounding the interpretation of slavery to find opportunities to share this important history with visitors. In several years of offering workshops and consulting with historic sites and museums interpreting the history of slavery, we have been struck by the lack of literature offering concrete advice for sites working to rectify the field's shortcomings in this area. As a result, the Tracing Center decided to take a closer look at moving the conversation forward.

Why Should We Interpret the History of Slavery at Our Site?

The United States suffers a form of collective amnesia about much of our history of slavery, especially about its breadth and depth throughout our society and across the country. The historical experience of slavery in the United States goes far beyond the traditional narrative of enslaved Africans picking cotton or cutting sugar cane on large southern plantations; as a result, far more museums and historic sites have a history of slavery to interpret than is commonly acknowledged.

The northeastern United States, for instance, sent out 85 percent of the nation's slaving voyages, while the infamous "triangle trade," and the colonial provisioning trade to slave plantations in the West Indies, were important enough to the northern colonies that President John Adams remarked, "I do not know why we should blush to confess that Molasses was an essential Ingredient in our Independence."[3] Slave-owning itself was far more widespread in the Northeast, Midwest, and West than the public suspects, lasted far longer than is recognized today, and was no less harsh in practice than slavery in the South. The primary economic impetus for the nation's westward expansion, prior to the Civil War, was the demand for foodstuffs for southern slave plantations. Much of the profit from southern cotton production flowed north and west, to commercial centers like New York City and to the textile industry in the North, which became a major economic engine for the nation.

Slavery played an essential role in the history interpreted at a multitude of historic sites throughout the nation, including historic homes, small family farms, commercial centers, and industrial sites, as well as at large-scale plantations. By interpreting this history, we can tell more comprehensive and balanced stories about our sites and of all who lived or worked there, including the voices of the marginalized. Just as importantly, we can expand visitors' understanding of the contributions of slavery, and of the lives of enslaved African Americans, to the political, economic, and social life of the entire nation. Finally, because slavery is a painful chapter in our nation's history, and one fraught with implications for our society today, there is tremendous value in helping our visitors understand that the institution of slavery wasn't merely the responsibility of the South or of a wealthy elite, but was a cornerstone of the nation's economy and society, and an engine of upward mobility for millions of American families.

Figure 2.1. Royall House and Slave Quarters in Medford, Massachusetts, has the oldest surviving slave quarters in New England (on right). Photo by Max A. van Balgooy.

What Makes Slavery Challenging to Interpret?

Our distorted public memory of slavery contributes to making this a challenging history to interpret, as does the fact that history involves the painful invocation of episodes of trauma, violence, and oppression.[4] We believe there are two issues that make the interpretation of slavery, and similarly controversial histories, especially challenging for museums and historic sites: the ways in which this history invokes *contested narratives* and how *racial identity* influences the experience of interpreters and visitors.

Contested Narratives

All people, including site staff and visitors, have identities that define how they see themselves, how they make sense of the world, and how they interact with others. These identities, in turn, are largely based on *narratives*: "It is through narrativity that we come to know, understand, and make sense of the social world, and it is through narratives and narrativity that we constitute our social identities [and] come to be who we are."[5] These accounts include not just personal stories, but also grand historical narratives that are widely shared, on topics such as how the United States came to be, how families have prospered here, and the nation's defining values.[6] People hold multiple identities at once, and thus they can possess narratives simultaneously about their families, their region, their racial or ethnic groups, their social class, and their nation, among others.[7]

In the United States, our public memory of slavery contributes to historical accounts in which slavery plays little or no part, aside from its role in the history of African Americans and of a few wealthy southern plantation–owning families. In the Northeast, for instance, many (white) Americans have identities based on stories in which their families, their region, their socioeconomic class, and the nation as a whole found success without depending much, if at all, on enslaved labor. Instead, their identities rely on stories emphasizing themes such as self-reliance, entrepreneurship, free labor, and individual merit. Many of these narratives incorporate slavery through tales in which ancestors are presumed to have been abolitionists, or to have sacrificed for emancipation during the Civil War. Similarly, historical narratives of those from the Midwest and the West tend to be ahistorically independent of slavery, as well.[8]

Interpreting slavery well means exposing staff and visitors to narratives in which slavery played a much broader role in the history of the nation. Staff and visitors will find themselves contending with narratives that tell how slavery was an essential part of the successes of the northern colonies, and of the northeastern, Midwestern, and western states, and therefore of many white families and institutions which do not see their histories as intertwined with those of slavery at all. This situation sets up a sharp clash between old and new narratives which can cut to the core of a person's sense of identity.

Dismantling old narratives and replacing them with new, and historically more accurate, alternatives may be healthy and productive. But this process can generate resistance, resentment, or outright disbelief, and requires careful thought and sensitive handling for a successful outcome. When people confront information which does not fit within the narratives that inform their identities, they tend to experience "serious mental confusion," "powerlessness, despair, victimization," and other cognitive and emotional difficulties.[9] The process of integrating a new historical narrative into one's identity, and reconciling it with core beliefs and values, is a gradual one, involving fits and starts, and is mostly an unconscious process.[10] It is therefore essential that an interpretive plan and staff training take this process, and its manifestations, into account, and that visitors be given plenty of opportunity to express their cognitive and emotional struggles as they absorb the interpretation.

The Role of Racial Identity

The history of slavery in the United States is not merely a painful part of our shared past, evoking trauma, violence, and oppression. Slavery is also a living history which conjures powerful emotions for many Americans because it raises issues like racial justice, healing, or repair. Confronting this history invokes historical narratives at the core of how many Americans understand their identity—whether on the basis of race or ethnicity, or in terms of family, socioeconomic class, or regional affiliation.

No matter what race or ethnicity we belong to, Americans come with "racial baggage"— preconceived notions about others based on skin color, as well as a stew of emotions such as

Figure 2.2.   Visitors and staff participating in the "Follow the North Star" program at Conner Prairie Interactive History Park, Fishers, Indiana. Photo courtesy of Conner Prairie Interactive History Park.

defensiveness, fear, anger, guilt, shame, or resentment. These emotions can be easily stirred up by the topic of slavery, especially if the topic is explored in depth, made personal, or presented in a way with which we are not already familiar. A site's interpretive plan must therefore take into account the cognitive and psychological challenges for staff and visitors as they encounter this history.

How Do We Proceed?

To gain a better understanding of the state of the field and how we could help museums balance these contested narratives, the Tracing Center conducted a survey exploring needs and challenges in interpreting slavery. Respondents described facing challenges like these:

- "telling the story in a way that fulfills our mission"
- "getting people who are skittish about slavery and 'black museums' in the door"
- "lack of extant built environment"
- "multiple claimants to the 'truth' of the enslaved experience"
- "getting volunteers and staff to discuss slavery on public tours"
- "being sensitive about the issue without sugar coating it"
- "difficult to keep African American interpreters"
- "white resistance"

- "fear of locals"
- "lack of broader context"
- "the board"[11]

Each of these concerns has merit, but they are not insurmountable challenges. As we explored the survey results with our colleagues and leaders in the field,[12] we organized the responses into six categories, a framework to help structure the creation of a comprehensive and conscientious interpretation of slavery. These six categories are: comprehensive content, race and identity awareness, institutional investment, community involvement, visitor experiences and expectations, and staff training. Each of these six components deserves more time and space than we can devote to it here, so we will provide a brief overview of each, as well as a handful of tips.

Comprehensive Content

Comprehensive content starts with the recognition that the history of slavery in the United States is broader and deeper than our public memory generally acknowledges, and that far more historic sites have a historic connection to slavery to interpret than have generally done so. Although briefly mentioned earlier, these issues merit far more inquiry than permitted here, and will generally spur fresh research into the direct and indirect connections of any particular historic site to slavery.

Comprehensive content also includes bringing the history of slavery to life through the power of individual stories, especially those which go beyond traditional slave narratives to reflect the historical agency of free and enslaved black Americans, and here again, the broader context of slavery can be helpful. The stories of individuals who were enslaved can be brought to light with a conscious awareness of the full spectrum of circumstances within which the enslaved found themselves in this nation, including geography, time periods, and occupations. Historical agency, meanwhile, can best be conveyed with a full appreciation of the ways in which slavery was experienced and resisted.

Race and Identity Awareness

We suggested previously that the interpretation of slavery invokes powerful emotions and challenges narratives at the core of identity, for staff and visitors alike. What can be done about this, so that staff can proceed in relative comfort to do their jobs well, and so that visitors can experience interpretation without undue discomfort or resistance?

It's important that staff be given opportunities to explore their own baggage so that they can understand their preconceptions, any gaps in their knowledge, and any emotions that are stirred up when engaging this material, before trying to engage with the public. For staff to confront these sensitive issues requires more than a set of readings or listening to an experienced trainer talk; this process is about both "head" and "heart." The Tracing Center starts by helping staff confront historic myths about slavery, and especially about the role played by slavery in the history of all families in this country. Because this history clashes with widely held narratives, the learning process can generate significant cognitive dissonance.

At the same time, confronting this history and its living legacy raises a powerful stew of emotions. Using facilitated dialogue, as well as media and a variety of exercises, helps staff become more aware of the ways in which race, and the history of slavery, impact their own identities, as well as how to constructively approach their own emotions around slavery and race. Our website (www.tracingcenter.org) offers resources and suggestions for approaching this learning process.

Institutional Investment

When boards and executive teams foster institutional support for the interpretation of slavery, they make it central to planning, secure funds and staffing for relevant initiatives, and create internal and external awareness. Obtaining such support can be especially challenging in the area of slavery, and an institution's staff must be fully committed to the interpretation from top to bottom—trustees to volunteers. The commitment to interpreting slavery must become ingrained into the institution's zeitgeist, which may be a long-term process.

A commitment to the story should be incorporated into the institution's guiding documents. Creating buy-in for a new institutional narrative may be difficult in light of the history, so it's important that organizations do their work to uncover and confront their own issues before they bring the content to their visitors. Taking the time to lay the groundwork by bringing trustees and executive teams on board, to help them to question their own narratives and interrogate their own feelings regarding slavery and race, and to define a shared purpose, can pay dividends in terms of institutional support for executing the interpretive plan.

While undergoing reinterpretation during the 1990s, Philipsburg Manor, an eighteenth-century site within Historic Hudson Valley in New York, retained its existing mission statement, which did not refer to slavery at all. Within that framework, however, staff worked with an African American advisory board to establish specific, written goals for interpreting slavery at the site and in the broader context of the North. These words did more than explain the goals of the reinterpretation process. As Michael Lord, associate director of education, said, "We needed to have these words for the staff to focus ourselves . . . and to understand the direction we wished to go. This was very important as an internal document as much as it was to state our purpose."[13]

Community Involvement

As museum professionals, we know that our community is broadly defined in terms of visitors, educators, scholars, donors, and other stakeholders who support, challenge, and retain an interest in the institution and its mission. Active community involvement makes organizations stronger and institutions more relevant to the wider community and to potential visitors, deepens perspectives, and creates opportunities that are more significant and impactful.

The decision to engage in an interpretation, or reinterpretation, of slavery offers new opportunities to expand your institution's network of community stakeholders. Precisely because the conscientious and comprehensive interpretation of slavery can be controversial, this choice can make your institution more appealing to individuals and groups which may be less interested in traditional historical interpretation—including such traditionally underrepresented visitor groups as young people and people of color, as well as groups focused on contemporary social and political issues, including issues related to race, privilege, and marginalized voices. A robust interpretation of slavery can help your site become a more visible community institution, and a destination for engaging programming connecting to modern concerns and fostering lively public discussion.

Making the involvement of new and prospective community stakeholders a central pillar of your interpretative plan can also help your site address one of the most common concerns in the interpretation of slavery: how institutions can undertake this process with few (or no) African Americans among their board or on staff. Community engagement can provide sources of advice and bring a degree of accountability to your interpretive process. Community partners may include descendants of the enslaved (and of slave owners); local scholars of African American history; churches and other places of worship; and community organizations addressing matters of racial, social, and economic importance. Many historic sites seeking to interpret or reinterpret slavery have been enthusiastically supported by local National Association for the Advancement of Colored People (NAACP) chapters. One Civil War site we visited found that by putting on a play about a divisive historical event involving local white and black residents, they were able to recruit a black director and cast members, garnering the site a substantial increase in input and involvement from the local black community.

Visitor Experiences and Expectations

An often-expressed concern from museums is, "Our visitors don't want to hear about slavery. They've come for an enjoyable experience; slavery will only upset or depress them." Statements like these sell our visitors short. A 2008 study found that a majority of respondents felt that museums do have a role in presenting controversial topics, expressing views such as, "Museums are a public forum for issues that should challenge society." Respondents also felt strongly that museums should allow visitors to offer comments about controversial topics, recommending feedback forms, suggestion boxes, tours, lectures, and discussion groups.[14]

Museums can learn more about their visitors' expectations by conducting a formal front-end study—you have to know where they are in order to take them where you want to go. It's important to note that visitors come with prior knowledge and, as previously mentioned, staff play an important role in helping visitors put the pieces together. Through the active engagement of visitors, our cultural storehouses will be able to tangibly demonstrate the connection between the historic experience of slavery and current issues of race, privilege, and human rights.

Staff Training

Staff involved in the interpretation of slavery don't just need training in order to help guide visitors through the stew of emotions raised by talking about slavery. Staff are likely to struggle with the same conflicting narratives and racial baggage as visitors, and need to embark internally on the same conversations and learning processes we want to train them to have with visitors.

A frank and open dialogue about the concerns of front-line staff is a good place to start.

Devoting time to discussing concerns about visitor reactions is critical to producing confidence in interpreters and assuring them that they will develop the tools to respond competently. Make a list of the outcomes interpreters fear and talk about how to respond if these things occur. Exploring such scenarios together provides interpreters with the confidence that they can manage whatever situation may arise, as well as concrete resources for handling their concerns. During a training session at Monticello, for instance, staff expressed fears ranging from visitor complaints to threats of violence. They then brainstormed a list of resources available for responding to potential issues, including historical research, institutional policies to support staff, and the availability of colleagues for support and security.

In addition to discussing concerns about visitor interactions, it's important to equip staff with skills for delivering the narrative. Interpreters should have a sound understanding of how visitors receive and process challenging historical information.[15] Interpreters should be prepared to individualize and differentiate the stories of enslaved people, ensuring that they are depicted as active historical agents with humanity and individuality—that "slave" is not a one-size-fits-all story. Lack of material culture from the enslaved should not prohibit us from looking at objects traditionally interpreted as about white individuals (for example, dinnerware, or a stagecoach). Instead, ask how these objects would have been used by those who were enslaved. Interpreters should tell emotionally evocative stories about all people who lived or worked at a site, giving visitors equal opportunities to invest emotionally in the lives of the enslaved.

Where Does the Field Go from Here?

"That US slavery has both officially ended yet continues in many complex forms—most notably institutionalized racism and the cultural denigration of blackness—makes its representation particularly burdensome in the United States. Slavery here is a ghost, both in the past and a living presence, and the problem of historical representation is how to represent that ghost, something that is and yet is not."[16]

Presenting the history of slavery in a comprehensive and conscientious manner is difficult and requires diligence and compassion—for the history itself, for those telling the story, and for those hearing the stories—but it's a necessary part of America's collective narrative about our past, present, and future. These details and more are elaborated in our edited volume, *Best Practices for Interpreting Slavery at Historic Sites and Museums* (AltaMira Press, 2014).

Frequently Asked Questions

How do I get started?
We recommend starting a conversation with the institution's management team. What is the institutional objective for fully incorporating stories of slavery and the enslaved at your site? How will you define success through a comprehensive narrative, staff training, and visitor interactions and reactions? Make a plan on how to work through the six components—who will be responsible for what, what will a successful outcome look like, and what is expected of each member of the team.

What if my staff or board rejects our plan?
Be proactive to stave off the possibility of rejection. Anticipate that some people may have difficulty fitting the new historical content into their existing narrative, so prepare your content carefully and provide context. Consider making a plan for the board or staff to go through a learning process and exchange of ideas before they consider what you are proposing. Acknowledge that issues and concerns about race will arise throughout the process—start with facilitated dialogue to get an idea of where everyone is starting from intellectually and emotionally, and where their concerns may lie.

Will interpreting slavery really bring in a diverse audience?

The more diverse the content you represent the better the opportunity visitors have to find relevance to their lives; therefore, a more diverse audience should be attracted to your museum. Makes sense, but it's not so easy. In addition to developing comprehensive and conscientious narratives, exhibitions, and programs, institutions need to build their community connections and reach out to those audiences they want to bring in.

We're not comfortable talking about this information with each other or our visitors—how do we prepare?

We do not want to step unprepared into the minefield of history and contemporary issues of race. In preparation for talking with visitors, staff need to become learners, developing a more comprehensive understanding of the history of slavery, and recognizing how this will challenge narratives at the core of their own identities. Staff will also want to discuss questions and concerns they have about race, and will require resources for learning about race, identity, and privilege, as well as models for how to talk about these issues.

What if a visitor doesn't want to talk about slavery?

A visitor doesn't necessarily need to engage in conversation with an interpreter to process new historical content. Forcing visitors into conversation will likely make them uncomfortable. Train staff to recognize signs that visitors are wrestling internally with difficult new knowledge, including actively resisting or struggling to incorporate ideas being interpreted. The goal is to keep visitors listening and to offer them additional points of entry into the new narrative, so they continue to process and work on reconciling this new information, even long after they leave.

As a white person, can I interpret this history?

It is the responsibility of historic sites to present a comprehensive and conscientious narrative about this essential part of US history. Race should not, and indeed cannot, be a barrier to telling this story. Through facilitated dialogue and engaging with people of other races, staff can come to terms with any anxiety or lack of knowledge. It can also be difficult for black interpreters to present this history—how to represent with dignity and gravitas the horrors of slavery, with which black interpreters are often no more familiar than their white counterparts. For years, however, black history has been filtered through white gatekeepers, largely obscuring the agency of black Americans. By interpreting this history responsibly, both black and white interpreters can bring context and compassion to their subject.

Notes

1. Jose-Marie Griffiths and Donald King, *InterConnections: The IMLS National Study on the Use of Libraries, Museums and the Internet* (Washington, D.C.: Institute for Museum and Library Services, 2008). http://www.interconnectionsreport.org/reports/IMLSMusRpt20080312kjm.pdf.
2. Jennifer L. Eichstat and Stephen A. Small, *Representations of Slavery: Race and Ideology in Southern Plantation Museums* (Washington, D.C.: Smithsonian Books, 2002).

3. John Adams to William Tudor, *The Works of John Adams, Second President of the United States with A Life of the Author, Notes, and Illustrations*, ed. Charles Francis Adams (Boston: Little, Brown, 1856), Correspondence 345 John Adams, letter to Judge William Tudor, August 11, 1818.

4. See Julia Rose, "Three Building Blocks for Developing Ethical Representations of Difficult Histories," *AASLH Technical Leaflet #264* (2013).

5. Margaret R. Somers, "The Narrative Constitution of Identity: A Relational and Network Approach," *Theory and Society* 23 (1994): 606. See also Elizabeth Birr Moje and Allan Luke, "Literacy and Identity: Examining the Metaphors in History and Contemporary Research," *Reading Research Quarterly* 44(4): 427; Anna Sfard and Anna Prusak, "Telling Identities: In Search of an Analytic Tool for Investigating Learning as a Culturally Shaped Activity," *Educational Researcher* 34(4) (May 2005).

6. Abbas Barzegar, "The Persistence of Heresy: Paul of Tarsus, Ibn Saba', and Historical Narrative in Sunni Identity Formation," *Numen* 58 (2011): 209, 212; Heinrich Best, "History Matters: Dimensions and Determinants of National Identities among European Populations and Elites," *Europe–Asia Studies* 61(6) (August 2009); Alexander M. Danzer, "Battlefields of Ethnic Symbols: Public Space and Post-Soviet Identity Formation from a Minority Perspective," *Europe–Asia Studies* 61(9) (November 2009): 1559.

7. Jens Rydgren, "The Power of the Past: A Contribution to a Cognitive Sociology of Ethnic Conflict," *Sociological Theory* 25(3) (September 2007): 226–27; Alistair Ross, "Multiple Identities and Education for Active Citizenship," *British Journal of Educational Studies* 55(3) (September 2007): 287; Somers, "The Narrative Constitution of Identity," 619.

8. It is no coincidence that the nation's public memory leaves out the connections of most American families to slavery. Because historical narratives form the core of our identities, we tend to prefer "tightly constructed," unambiguous narratives, and to select historical facts promoting positive views of groups with which we identify (Rydgren, "The Power of the Past," 233).

9. Somers, "The Narrative Constitution of Identity," 617, 630. See also Sonya Dal Cin, Mark P. Zanna, and Geoffrey T. Fong, "Narrative Persuasion and Overcoming Resistance," in Eric S. Knowles and Jay A. Linn, eds., *Resistance and Persuasion* (Mahwah, NJ: Lawrence Erlbaum Associates, 2004).

10. Rydgren, "The Power of the Past," 232.

11. Tracing Center on Histories and Legacies of Slavery, "Surveys of Historic Site Employees" (unpublished study, 2009–2012).

12. Patricia Brooks, Conny Graft, and Julia Rose helped develop the Tracing Center's workshop on interpreting slavery and contributed to formatting the components of 'Comprehensive and Conscientious Interpretation.'

13. Michael Lord (associate director of education, Historic Hudson Valley), interviewed by Linnea Grim, December 18, 2013.

14. "Exhibitions as Contested Sites: The Roles of Museums in Contemporary Society," a three-year research study (2006–2008) conducted by the Australian Research Council with data from museum visitors in Australia and Canada.

15. For instance, research suggests listeners initially respond to information contradicting their worldview by ignoring information, counter-arguing, or questioning the source. These behaviors are to be expected and embraced, not treated as signs of failure. One way to ease this process for visitors is to avoid telegraphing challenging historical information before presenting a suspenseful narrative. Dal Cin, Zanna, and Fong, "Narrative Persuasion and Overcoming Resistance," 177–78. See also Julia Rose, "Interpreting Difficult Knowledge," *AASLH Technical Leaflet #255* (2011).

16. Michel-Rolph Trouillot, *Silencing the Past: Power and the Production of History* (Boston: Beacon Press, 1995), 146.

CHAPTER 3

Interpreting Difficult Knowledge

JULIA ROSE

I NCREASINGLY, public historians are talking about finding ways to interpret histories of oppression, tragedy, and violence that encourage museum visitors and other audiences to reflect on the roots of society today. Interpretations of traumatic histories ask audiences to acknowledge the human toll and the varied viewpoints enveloped in histories of oppression. Such social justice education demands both emotional and intellectual engagement from audiences; engagement not easily carried out. Museum workers and public historians explain that their audiences often express resistance to hearing about oppression. Why? What makes oppressive history difficult to interpret? Why do museums refer to histories of oppression and violence as "the hard stuff"? What is at stake?

In the middle of the twentieth century, the rise of social history asked us to recognize the contributions and events of the common person. This paved the way for museum workers and other public historians to grapple with long-held biases against researching and interpreting the histories of oppression against minorities, women, and "other" populations, and the pain these groups endured. The long-held tradition of focusing on white, male, majority populations has given way to a genuinely widespread movement to elevate, interpret, and study histories of common persons. The results include contextualized and integrated social histories that recall a complex maze of relationships among historical players, their historical times, and relevant material culture. These histories tend to reveal stories of pride and shame and stories about achievements and afflictions.

Interestingly, social history scholarship not only asks us to find out what happened to marginalized or silenced populations, but also asks us to take on the immense challenge of engaging audiences in interpretations about their traumatic histories. Audiences, including museum visitors, attendees to films and lectures, museum workers, and public historians, are faced with learning about historical traumas. These audiences are learners, and they deserve effective strategies to engage in the learning of histories of oppression.

> "A social scientist cannot change the data, only record and analyze it. The first few 'dirty words' [referring to racial slurs used in interpreting American slavery at a living history site] elicited some nervous laughter in a room of 600 people, but we all got over it. But our issue is can our audience get over it? How can we show them hard issues honestly? Can living history do this, or are we only good for the cheery stuff?" —Association of Living History, Farm, and Agricultural Museums (ALFHAM) listserv, February 2, 2011.

Defining Difficult Knowledge

The hard stuff in museums and other public history venues includes interpretive content about histories of mass violence, racism, enslavement, genocide, war, HIV/AIDS, slavery, and other traumatic events. Educational psychologist Deborah Britzman calls the hard stuff "difficult knowledge."[1] Audiences, visitors, public history workers, and learners in general who wish to avoid, forget, or ignore traumatic histories will turn away from the difficult knowledge that they cannot stand to know or bear to hear. The person faced with learning difficult knowledge that she or he cannot bear to know represses that information and returns to it through expressions of resistance that appear as negativism, irreverence, jokes, and denials.[2]

Traumatic histories can instigate negative responses from all types of learners, making some public history presentations and museum experiences uncomfortable, confrontational, or even appear illegitimate. Responses are unique to each person. Everyone does not have the same level of tolerance for learning histories of oppression, which makes the job of developing equitable and sensitive interpretation strategies for history about difficult knowledge extremely challenging.[3]

Much is at stake. Interpreting difficult knowledge questions how people understand history, and how they have long viewed the world. Exhibits, collections, and historic sites about difficult knowledge can be disruptive and can interfere with a visitor's individual reality. The history of hate or violence can be felt as a confrontation to an individual's sense of morality and pains the individual to accept the history of such horror. The immediate expressions of resistance are signals that an internal learning crisis has formed for that individual. The new difficult knowledge is in conflict with how the learner understands the history. Britzman explains that the learner cannot transcend the internal conflict caused by the difficult knowledge. Instead he or she must work through the internal conflict in an emotional and cognitive process to make sense of the new difficult knowledge. The learner may exclaim, for example, "That is unbelievable!" or "That is not what I read!"[4]

Consider for a moment the internal risk of learning difficult knowledge. Think about the possibility of how learning difficult knowledge can put the learner at risk by disturbing the learner's innermost understanding of himself or herself. Does the history of the Jim Crow South, for example, raise personal questions about how the learner understands race relations and how he or she sees race relations today impacting his or her life? Does the history of preserving a row of slave cabins at Evergreen Plantation in South Louisiana raise emotional feelings in the learner that makes him or her want to change the subject and not talk about nineteenth-century American plantation slavery? Does the learner feel implicated,

Figure 3.1. The double cabin at Magnolia Mound Plantation in Baton Rouge, Louisiana, includes furnished period rooms and an exhibit interpreting the life of enslaved people. Photo by Julia Rose.

self-conscious, or threatened? Do some of our responses to the difficult knowledge lead us to resist a particular interpretation because it is too much to bear? At stake is "my understanding of what I believe to be true." Difficult knowledge can lead to learners resisting information in an exhibit so vehemently that he or she will just shut down and refuse further engagement with the subject, the exhibit, or the presenting institution.

A common discussion among exhibit planners and museum workers is a plea for the interpretation to provide "just the facts" and an interpretation of history that is neutral and not controversial. In reality, a historical interpretation will always come from some particular viewpoint, and facts are always delineated by a history's authors. The task for museum workers and other public historians, then, is to take into account the learning crisis difficult knowledge will invariably incite in some audiences. At stake is the individual learner's comfort and at risk is the individual experiencing a stressful learning crisis that is too much to bear.

How then do museum workers and other public historians approach interpreting difficult knowledge given these insights into the emotive and cognitive powers of difficult knowledge to impede learning and jeopardize an individual's sense of self?

The Five Rs of Commemorative Museum Pedagogy Reception

One strategy for enabling learners in history institutions to engage with difficult knowledge is called "Commemorative Museum Pedagogy" (CMP). CMP provides ample time for the learning process to unfold to allow the learner to work through his or her learning

"Some people believe that ignoring the past or whitewashing it (literally) will allow healing to occur; that we can get on with a just world by simply looking forward from today; that there need be no account of the past, no dredging up of old skeletons, no probing of old wounds. We fundamentally challenge this assertion. We believe that without a full and open discussion of the past, its relation to contemporary inequalities and oppressions, and considerations of how to respond to these historical and contemporary inequalities, true healing cannot take place. Sites that pride themselves as providing history to the masses have an important role to play in this process—either as maintainers of oppressive patterns or as teachers for a just future."[1]

Difficult knowledge about slavery, racism, and other oppressive events contain historical information that comes from an array of empirical sources including artifacts, documents, statistics, dates, and a variety of other rich empirical evidence to construct interpretations. Historical interpretations, however, can be embellished with local lore and shared information that has not been researched. Curators and exhibit planners are responsible for assembling accurate and vetted content to develop interpretations of difficult histories, and must recognize that their interpretations are dependent on the visitors' abilities to make connections to the histories recalled. The actual quality of the impact the empirical content will make on the interpretations depends on the investigated, measured, and relevant choices made by the curators, exhibit planners, and the front-line interpretation workers.

It is understandable that no exhibit, landscape, or building is large enough or complete enough to contain the extent of human suffering and sadness that they commemorate. Authentic interactions with exhibits ask visitors to take the responsibility to deeply consider how these particular spaces, objects, and descriptions represent the injustices inflected on a population. However, at the same time museum workers need to acknowledge to themselves and to their visitors that partial perspectives in historical interpretations are inevitable. The partial nature of historical interpretations asks museum workers and visitors to reflect, question, and research the changing definitions of the past and our understandings about the present that the empirical content collectively stands to represent.[2]

Consider how different perspectives and alternate voices from history can shape and reshape historical facts by highlighting some histories and suppressing other histories. Museum workers can work toward achieving balance in a historical interpretation by including multiple viewpoints. Harris Shettel suggests curators conceptually and physically treat each area in exhibitions from multiple perspectives. Their interpretations about controversial historical events should include thoughtful artifacts, images, and testimonies to illustrate varying viewpoints. While the risk of biases will emerge, testimonies and primary sources have great potential to deepen visitors' learning experiences. The voices of victims, witnesses, oppressors, and the immediate historical responses from the politicians, policymakers, and lawmakers, for example, create a fuller representation of the temporal historical context for the event. Multiple perspectives move historical interpretations toward a more balanced approach to understanding painful histories.[3]

Notes

1. Jennifer Eichstedt and Stephen Small, *Representations of Slavery: Race and Ideology in Southern Plantation Museums* (Washington, D.C.: Smithsonian Institution Press, 2002), 270.
2. Julia Rose, "Three Building Blocks for Developing Ethical Representations of Difficult Histories," *History News* 68, no. 4 (Autumn 2013), *Technical Leaflet #264*.
3. Harris Shettel, "Exhibit Controversy: Can It Be Avoided? Can We Help?" *Journal of Museum Studies* (1997): 268–75.

crisis. CMP is made up of five stages designed to provide a sensitive learning setting. The five stages of CMP are easily remembered as the "5Rs": *Receive, Resist, Repeat, Reflect,* and *Reconsider.* They are all parts of a nonlinear cognitive process for learners to make sense of a disruptive history.[5]

1. Receive

Audiences are likely willing to learn new historical information when they arrive at an exhibit or public history venue. Other than school groups on a field trip, audiences choose to come and spend time reflecting on the historical content in an exhibition or presentation. At the beginning of the experience or presentation, the unknown is how committed each individual is to learning about the history presented. Also not evident is how much each individual feels he or she already knows about the subject interpreted in this venue. Museum workers and public historians can provide welcoming introduction spaces. They can include disclosure statements about the kind of difficult knowledge contained in the exhibit or presentation, and they can inform visitors that subject matter in the exhibit or presentation could be upsetting or controversial.

2. Resistance

Audience members are also learners who will respond to difficult knowledge in unique and personal ways. When new information is perceived as disruptive to the learner's understanding of history, or challenges the learner's sense of self or moral senses, he or she will react by repressing the new knowledge in a negative way. These negative responses are indicative of the individual experiencing a learning crisis. Resistance can be detected through individuals' verbal expressions saying that the difficult knowledge is unpleasant, uncomfortable, false, or not worth thinking about; resistance can be heard in the guise of biases, jokes, or sarcasm. Physical responses are also indicators of resistance such as leaving, attending to minor distractions, or moving quickly through the exhibition. Resistance is indeed a personal response and includes the healthy intellectual responses to contemplate, challenge, and research information and interpretations. Resistance occurs in degrees of internal disruption and is not always an indication of a visitor's lack of knowledge but rather an indication that the difficult knowledge presented is impacting that visitor in a new way. Resistance to difficult knowledge is part of a normal learning process. The phenomenon of resistance includes the most learned visitor and the most inexperienced visitor.

3. Repetition

Learners will begin grappling with information they find disruptive and repeat particular parts of difficult knowledge in a variety of ways. Repetition allows the learner to consider more deeply the content he or she finds hard to accept. The learner can repeat a story again and again aloud or to himself or herself, or ask the same questions, or read a text multiple times—all are parts of the learning process for working through the difficult knowledge.

Learners will likely mix expressions of resistance and repetition. It is important to recognize that the 5Rs of CMP do not necessarily happen sequentially. For example, a learner can move from expressions of disbelief to explaining his or her own personal connections to the history and back to disbelief multiple times.

On one occasion, at a training session at a historical plantation site, museum staff who could not immediately accept a revised narrative that included the history of the site's enslaved community repeated out loud the new slave life information, saying it was unbelievable or was insignificant. Others repeated the portions of the regular tour narrative that they were attached to, or portions that were in jeopardy of being edited if the new slave life histories were incorporated. These staff members did not necessarily refuse resisted knowledge. In many instances, they repeated the conflicting information aloud and reread the new tour narrative and secondary history sources. The museum staff was eager for opportunities to repeat information, as they reflected on the possibility of expanding the current tour to include slave life history.[6]

As learners work through repressed difficult knowledge by way of repetition, each new piece of knowledge has to be fit into his or her internal psychic reality. This rebuilding of the learner's inner world characterizes the successful work of learning difficult knowledge.[7]

4. Reflection

Learners are entitled to sufficient time to reflect on the difficult knowledge they are grappling with on a tour or in a presentation. Opportunities to talk about their thoughts and ask questions are important for people to work through the information they find challenging. Reflection can be entwined with expressions of repetition when the learner continues to repeat information and questions. Not all reflection happens immediately in the museum or on site. Visitors at a historic site, for instance, might ask for more information from a tour guide, reread exhibit labels, purchase books in the gift shop, or pursue more information about the difficult knowledge on their own after they have left. Providing opportunities for conversation or places to sit will encourage learners to reflect on the difficult knowledge or sensitive topics that they are working through.

5. Reconsideration

Learners will offer verbal expressions about how they reconsider difficult knowledge. For example, they might make analogies between the difficult knowledge and another point. "A-ha" moments are a part of reconsidering information that conflict with or challenge existing ideas. Museum workers can also observe reconsideration when learners want to talk about their personal connections to the difficult histories. For example, when walking along the reflecting pool at the Oklahoma City National Memorial, some visitors recount where they were that tragic day in 1995. Not all responses are verbalized, however. Nonverbal evidence of reconsideration include more subtle cues like head nodding, eye contact, note taking, lingering, and continued participation in viewing the exhibit. Reconsideration reveals an audience's further engagement in difficult knowledge.

Figure 3.2. Benches along the paths that connect the historic buildings at the West Baton Rouge Museum in Louisiana provide places for visitors to discuss and reflect on the interpretation. Photo by Julia Rose.

Conclusion

Learners who are engaged in working through difficult knowledge respond, while others simply shut down and refuse further engagement or consideration of the topic. Indifference is one way to resist difficult knowledge. *Each learner who is engaged will find opportunities to repeat and reflect on the information to make sense of the traumatic history, internally or aloud.* This is a key point. The learner actively engaged in learning demands more information and opportunities to think and respond to the difficult knowledge.

A group of high school students on a tour at Magnolia Mound Plantation in Baton Rouge, Louisiana, were led inside a slave quarter dwelling on exhibit. A fifteen-year-old African American young woman refused to continue on the tour and would not enter the two-room, 150-year-old cabin, exclaiming, "I will not go in there, that is not me!"[1]

Note

1. Julia Rose, observation of her students at Magnolia Mound Plantation, Baton Rouge, Louisiana, 2003.

What Museum Workers and Public Historians Can Do

1. **Use CMP as a framework to more effectively engage audiences in difficult knowledge**. The 5Rs give learners time and resources to work through difficult knowledge.
    a. **Reception:** Provide a welcoming introduction that discloses that difficult knowledge is contained in the venue and could be upsetting or controversial.
    b. **Resistance:** Anticipate negative responses from learners and allow them to be aired with the understanding that expressions of resistance probably indicate that the person is experiencing a learning crisis.
    c. **Repetition:** Arrange the learning setting to include avenues to revisit artifacts and displays or to reread information. Make information available to learners to review online or in print to study at their own pace.
    d. **Reflection:** Ask learners if they have questions. Provide opportunities for conversation or places to sit to encourage learners to reflect on the difficult knowledge.
    e. **Reconsideration:** Offer learners opportunities to respond by providing places for them to share their ideas or comments. Offer social action information that is relevant to the theme of the difficult knowledge. Ask learners, "What do you think?"
2. **Design interpretations that encourage empathy from visitors.** Consider including cameos of individuals or groups that recount the traumatic historical journey of one person or a group. Visitors will care about the condition of historical communities and individuals when the interpretation includes rich descriptions of real people who are recognizable as men, women, and children with familial and communal relationships to one another and to the world. Such multidimensional representations work to encourage empathy, moving learners to truly care about historical individuals; herein lay the questions about immorality and injustices that difficult knowledge raises for learners.[1]
3. **Avoid objectifying human experiences.** The words we choose to interpret history can unintentionally create a buffer between the learner and the human suffering entwined in history. Generic and anonymous descriptions make it less painful to talk about violence and oppression. Language can lessen learners' immediate resistances but simultaneously disengage learners from reflecting on the human consequences of the violence or oppression. Avoid words like "slave" or "troops" that objectify the people we intend to interpret by leaving out their names and human attributes.
4. **Recognize that difficult knowledge will generate varying degrees of audience engagement.**
5. **Recognize that engagement in learning difficult knowledge is succeeding when learners show evidence of the 5Rs and demand to know more.**

Note

1. Julia Rose, "Name by Name, Face by Face: Elevating Historical Representations of American Slave Life," *Exhibitionist* 7(2) (Fall 2008): 37–43.

> ## What Museum Workers and Public Historians Should Not Do
>
> 1. Assume your interpretation is neutral.
> 2. Believe facts are unquestionable.
> 3. Believe your audience sees the world the way you see the world.
> 4. Rush your audience to understand an interpretation.
> 5. Ask audiences to "get over it."
> 6. Avoid histories of oppression, violence, or tragedy.

Successful social justice education aims to move learners to respond because responses signal that the learners care. Responses can vary widely among individuals. They range from visitors joining the museum, purchasing books, making contributions to a cause, contributing to a blog or writing an editorial, to less demonstrative actions such as discussing the difficult knowledge with others outside of the exhibition, or perhaps changing one's opinion.

Not all audiences will agree with the information on an intellectual level. That is reasonable for any academic project. However, the key difference between an intellectual challenge to difficult knowledge and resistance to learning is that the learner who is intellectually challenging the content cares enough about the difficult knowledge that he or she continues reflecting on the subject, while the learner who shuts down is unwilling to grapple with the pain raises the difficult knowledge raises for him or her.

Last Word

If we could erase memories that haunt us, would we? Attempts to forget will diminish our capacity for empathy. A challenge for museum workers and public historians is to understand how to impart the histories of oppression and violence in meaningful and sensitive ways that do not shut down audiences' willingness to learn. Historical interpretations of difficult knowledge, framed through CMP, encourage audiences to respond to the histories of oppression and violence enough to care what happened in the past and eventually to demand to know more and respond in the present.

Notes

1. The notion of difficult knowledge is especially useful to museum workers to identify the hard stuff in history that visitors and audiences often challenge, resist, find uncomfortable and avoid, or forsake for more palatable versions of histories. Educational psychologist Deborah Britzman explains that "difficult knowledge" is the hard stuff to earn, especially the traumatic histories of mass violence and oppression. The person who is faced with learning difficult knowledge that she or he cannot bear represses that information and returns to it through expressions of

resistance that appear as negativism, irreverence, jokes, and denials. See Deborah P. Britzman, *Lost Subjects, Contested Objects: Toward a Psychoanalytic Inquiry of Learning* (Albany: State University of New York, 1998).

2. Britzman, *Lost Subjects, Contested Objects.*

3. Julia Rose, "Rethinking Representations of Slave Life at Historical Plantation Museums: Towards a Commemorative Museum Pedagogy" (PhD dissertation, Louisiana State University, 2006).

4. "Working through" is a part of the process of grieving first identified by psychoanalyst Sigmund Freud in his description of mourning. See *Basic Freud: Psychoanalytic Thought for the 21st Century* by Michael Kahn (New York: Basic Books, 2002).

5. Rose, "Rethinking Representations of Slave Life."

6. Rose, "Rethinking Representations of Slave Life."

7. For theoretical explanations on working through new knowledge in the context of loss in learning, see works about the educational theories by Melanie Klein and Anna Freud, including Deborah Britzman, *After-Education: Anna Freud, Melanie Klein and Psychoanalytic Histories of Learning* (New York: State University of New York Press, 2003); and Juliet Mitchell, editor, *The Selected Melanie Klein* (New York: Free Press, 1986).

Suggested Readings

Britzman, Deborah P. *Lost Subjects, Contested Objects: Toward a Psychoanalytic Inquiry of Learning.* Albany: State University of New York, 1998.

Irwin-Zarecka, Iwona. *Frames of Remembrance: The Dynamics of Collective Memory.* New Brunswick, NJ: Transaction Publishers, 1994.

Linenthal, Edward T. *Preserving Memory: The Struggle to Create America's Holocaust Museum.* New York: Penguin, 1995.

Simon, Roger, Sharon Rosenberg, and Claudia Eppert, eds. *Between Hope and Despair: Pedagogy and the Remembrance of Historical Trauma.* Lanham, MD: Rowman & Littlefield, 2000.

CHAPTER 4

Expanding Interpretation at Historic Sites

When Change Brings Conflict

DAVID W. YOUNG

A PROMINENT African American historian was shouted down at a meeting about the President's House, and was called an apologist for rape and a traitor to his race. A black National Park Service interpreter, well known for his walking tours of Underground Railroad history in Philadelphia, was screamed at and called "Uncle Tom" by a crowd in front of the Liberty Bell.[1] The white executive director of a small historic site in a predominantly black section of Philadelphia was summoned to the state representative's office to explain why he was conducting a multigenerational oral history of twentieth-century events in the neighborhood. In my decade as a public historian in Philadelphia, I have witnessed each of these episodes and many others. Nor are these examples only to be found in the "city of brotherly love." Similar stories abound across the country, from academic departments and museum planning workshops to conference sessions and church basements.[2] Historians, museum staff, board members, and others who are just beginning the process of reinterpreting a site's story are often surprised by how heated the process can become and say, "Why didn't anyone warn me?"

Embracing any new history can quickly veer off course, discouraging participants and deflating projects that started with the best intentions. Often public history practitioners who try to interpret the history of minorities find talking about difficult and painful subjects challenging. They may seek other perspectives and rightly involve people from backgrounds different from their own, new kinds of experts, and input from people who are new to the institution. Next steps might include meetings that lead to shouting, staged protests, and hurt feelings with little to show for it. I have seen meetings about worthwhile projects with perfectly nice people descend into heated sessions where competing agendas drown out the opportunity for a discussion of our shared past. And so scarred are the participants that the resentments from the experience linger, only making it harder the next time. Without being aware of some of the obstacles that occur in such projects, a well-intentioned effort may end up feeling somewhere between a cable news shouting match and a heated family argument that makes everyone feel uncomfortable.

It takes a group effort and effective leadership to overcome resistance to change in all kinds of situations. Some of the challenges, therefore, are typical of change at any organization. Meanwhile, history projects involve creative decisions and take place in a context crowded with opinions on how to shape an exhibition, guided tour, or public program. When projects involve difficult history, however, the creative process can be more contentious than any other kind of planning because of the personal nature of what we bring to topics involving memory, heritage, and history.

I work at Cliveden in Philadelphia, which had been a traditional house museum of white heritage; an institution that served as a shrine to the wealthy Chew family that owned the property and to the site's role in the American Revolution (see figure 4.1). In 2008, research into extensive plantation records led the organization to include perspectives of the enslaved workers on plantations owned by the Chew family. Our interpretive planning process brought in experts and activists, including several who had taken part in the President's House project, to advise the organization's embrace of Cliveden's African American history.[3] The meetings we convened convinced me that if one has some inkling of what can take place, it makes it easier to see a contentious process through to results that are some of the most rewarding work that historic sites do. The passions expressed offer a great opportunity to learn from each other, expand our sense of the past, and offer a fuller history to our communities. Listening to and incorporating competing viewpoints can spark a needed transition for historic sites to serve not merely as shrines to the past, but also as forums to contemplate the meaning of history in the present.

Uncover History

Make no mistake; it is understandably hard to talk about the American history of slavery, violence, predatory lending, systemic institutional discrimination, and other sensitive and controversial topics. Consider too that we might be discussing the subjects among people descended from victims talking in the same room as those descended from perpetrators. These factors make it all the more important to understand what can take place. I have seen roadblocks to expanding new history come from both inside and outside an organization. It can come from a board of directors or from colleagues who may be worried about public relations. Such objections stem from a conservative belief that sites do not need to change, when in fact the whole field is continually evolving; in order to remain relevant, interpretation must evolve too. Alternatively, I have seen opposition come from liberally oriented people seeking repair for the sins of the past, even to the point of a specific political

Figure 4.1. Cliveden, a National Trust Historic Site and National Historic Landmark in the Germantown neighborhood of Philadelphia. Photo by Max A. van Balgooy.

agenda, such as financial reparations or gaining electoral support. Their open-mindedness to new history may be limited to the specific point they wish to make. In any case, the views expressed are based in personal emotion, even deep-rooted pain. And it is important to step back and acknowledge the pain and suffering, because that simple step of honoring the difficulty opens people up to consider how painful history can give rise to arguments that do not really dispute facts, dates, or footnotes, but bring us to meaningful historic interpretation.

In history, the things we can agree on are the least meaningful to explore. We can agree *when* the Civil War started and ended, for instance, but *why* it was fought and *how* it ended are bigger issues that each generation wrestles with—and this tension represents the opportunity for history practitioners to explore interpretations that get at larger themes of national and international history. To uncover meaningful history with integrity compels us to embrace African American history—especially subjects that have been too often untold, ignored, or appropriated. Uncovering that history, however, brings emotions to the surface—emotions important enough that some people may use a history project meeting as their first expression of their own pain in public. If the personal pain is not understood, the openly expressed objections can shock participants and grind down efforts to recover as many stories as we can.

In my experience and in talking with other colleagues who have worked on similar projects, the most heatedly expressed passions generally come from four places.

1. Those who approach the subject from a sense of anger.

Sometimes people enter historic interpretation eager to get their own point across, with an almost ideological bent or a specific agenda. Once Cliveden's board and staff decided that we needed to explore the truth of the full story of the site, we invited people from all sorts of backgrounds to help us. Some participants worked with a reparations group, the National Coalition of Black Reparationists in America (N'COBRA), and their representatives stated clearly, "Who are you to tell the story of our people?" The anger of the reparations group's members was rooted in the suffering embedded in their tradition, and they saw their role as defenders of their ancestors' heritage, gatekeepers to historic information about them.

The presence of such a vocal group can lead to two challenges. First the views of people expressing from a point of anger can silence other participants and then be dismissed because others are turned off by the disruption. This leads to the trap of "us and them" thinking and dissects discussions solely into opposing views. Second, when one group is bent on righting wrongs and scoring points, other participants may be marked as messengers of what has been wrong about history, even if they and their ancestors had nothing to do with the transgressions of the past. This can lead to a climate of "shame and blame," silencing people even more. The emphatic energy and passion that such expressed anger can bring to the effort is important, however, because it shows history from perspectives other than our own personal understanding. At Cliveden, for instance, our elderly house tour guides found to their surprise just how much they learned from the reparationist historians: "I had never thought about it like that before."

Among colleagues at other sites like the President's House, we came to understand that people coming from a place of such anger tend to emphasize the brutality and the unfair treatment encountered in the past. By emphasizing how inhumanely people of African descent were treated, their view holds, perhaps we will recognize other people's humanity. In other words, to understand the noble impulse behind the angry pushback meant we could hear facts and viewpoints we had not really considered before. Understanding that sometimes a subject impels people to teach from their deeply held point of view, even if it comes across as angry, may make us more open to learning from them.

2. Those who approach history from a sense of overcoming.

This is a group that is relatively established in their respective community, either through education, upbringing, or economic background. From their point of view, they may want to do the right thing, but not necessarily want to rock the boat. The members of this group want to celebrate accomplishments—showcasing the uplift that ultimately resulted from centuries of struggle. They may express sentiments like, "Can't we all just get along and emphasize how much we have overcome?"

Cliveden is located in the Germantown section of Philadelphia, where there had been a tendency to discuss only the history that commemorated the neighborhood's better days and emphasized its colonial and revolutionary heroes. When we explored twentieth-century history—history that the neighborhood's fifteen historic sites did not normally interpret—we learned new facts and episodes worth exploring. Some were celebratory, like the fact that leading members of the Harlem Renaissance came to the neighborhood in 1928 for an early celebration of "Negro Achievement Week." Some were shocking, such as the Ku Klux Klan also had a large presence in the neighborhood in 1928. One year held alarming contradictions! These discoveries prompted discussion about how such juxtapositions could occur in the same community among neighbors. As more people found out about such contradictions, they wanted to discuss others, including deeply divisive issues like a racially motivated transit strike in 1944, local businesses that practiced discrimination during their lifetimes, and that the neighborhood's Quaker schools did not admit black students until 1945. By finding juxtapositions and discussing them, we come closer to what historians have called a "community of memory"—a group of people (in this case a neighborhood) who agree that they share a cultural heritage and celebrate what is good and openly discuss what is not.[4]

3. Those who approach the subject from a sense of loss.

Some people see the facts of history and the willingness to explore them from new perspectives as a reminder of pain so deeply held they wish to avoid the topic entirely. At a Cliveden board retreat to launch our efforts to interpret the site's connections to plantation slavery, many longtime board members said, "Why are we talking about slavery all of a sudden?" Not only that, when we discussed the subject of Chew family slaveholding with some of the local African American churches in the neighborhood, elderly congregants at the churches expressed the same thing, saying, "People don't want to know about this."

Often people who fall into this group do not know—and may not want to know—the long, cruel history of power, control, and hypocrisy of slavery that cannot be disentangled from American history. While this group crosses many backgrounds, races, and ages, it is important to understand that older members especially, whatever their ethnic or social background, have trouble discussing difficult subject matter. They hope not to make things uncomfortable, a sentiment that may hold for organizations with a long tradition of elitist history, too.

4. Those approaching the project from a sense of skepticism.

Another group that may bring a specific agenda to the discussions emerges from a background of suspicion that these stories are only now just now being told. Their essential question is, "Why haven't we known more about this sooner?" The fact that presenting difficult history is considered bold in the twenty-first century strikes some people in public history as unacceptable. These people see wrongs in the events of the past as well as in the decisions of *how* it has been presented. In other words, they conclude (in many cases rightly) that museums and educational institutions have avoided the truth and swept the subject under the rug for fear that it will shame the institutions. They wish to change the way institutions have defended their own decisions to a process of fuller, inclusive discussions about the history so that decisions are not left up to the institutions but to a larger group willing to share authority.

With so many different points of view strongly held, how is it possible to understand someone else's? It means being open to new perspectives, questioning assumptions and commonly accepted ideas to see them anew. So how do you reconcile so many viewpoints? It depends on where you stand.

Work toward Dialogue

A Zimbabwean proverb states, "Until the lion tells his side of the story, the tale of the hunt will always glorify the hunter." History depends on where one stands at a given time. Each person's viewpoint carries with it important elements of heritage, memory, and history. But does the past have to be so adversarial—like a lion being hunted? What if presenting difficult history—provocative though it might be to some—were a way to prompt discussion?

At Cliveden we encourage people to see others' points of view. During one interpretive planning exercise that involved fifty-seven people of all four backgrounds that I described, facilitators asked everyone to pair off with a stranger and work to construct a timeline of history. On each table was a long sheet of paper representing one century, starting with the 1500s. Working with small groups among strangers, each group went with post-it notes to one table, placing what they thought was a significant event that happened in their century. People added dates of their own choosing—some were key dates in women's history like the Seneca Falls Convention in 1848 or national political milestones, like the ratification of the Constitution. Others added dates of personal import, like when parents migrated to Philadelphia; some noted dates specific to Cliveden history, such as the 1777 Battle of Germantown, the year the museum opened (1973), or when the plantation records were researched (1994). But then other people asked if they could pull out another table, insisting the timeline extend back to the 1400s when Europeans brought enslaved Africans to the New World.

When do you begin? Depending on where you stand, the timeline could begin anywhere. How to categorize dates—by chronology, by topic, by persons? The point of this exercise is that you might get as many good answers as there are people in the room. So which one is right? The ensuing discussion among the participants allowed us to see clearly how much we need one another's perspective to see history more fully. The timeline exercise integrated varied viewpoints to a place where we could discuss competing perspectives as a group.

The President's House exhibitions that opened in 2010 indeed have timelines, but they offer multiple perspectives without an interactive blending. It seems as if one story is told on top of the other. The result suggests a competition for space, continuing the oppositional us/them presentation, rather than an extension of viewpoints. The result was a series of competing shrines to different viewpoints, rather than an open forum for discussion of how they intersect.

The President's House is unique, of course; its presence on Independence Mall in front of the Liberty Bell and its connection to George Washington makes it nationally iconic.[5] At the President's House, a memorial to enslaved Africans in America makes a lasting statement, as it is the first memorial to enslaved people at a federal site. But what about interpreting undertold history at local, smaller sites where the names are less well known? In this case, treading a line between shrine and a forum for discussion can be effective at bringing competing perspectives to gel into a more inclusive interpretation.

Make New Connections

Offering opportunities for people to engage with one another about history is one way to embrace tensions and contradictions, leading to new opportunities for connection. At Cliveden, we found that engagement across agendas, as difficult as it can be, can be demystifying for people both inside and outside the organization, simply by allowing people to be heard. And if people feel they are in an environment that is safe and respectful, they may find themselves ready to tell a fuller story. For Cliveden the challenge was how to tell of the War for Independence *and* the Struggle for Freedom without separating the two. We found that an intentional process—while difficult—makes this possible.

The key to building a safe, respectful atmosphere for making connections across points of view lie in facilitated conversations like the timeline activity. Another example is a program series that emerged from the desire expressed by our public who wanted a chance to weigh in on ongoing research. The *Cliveden Conversations* is an initiative we used that is even more social and allows strangers to discuss history in ways that can feel empowering. As with the timeline exercise, *Cliveden Conversations* has enhanced comfort levels among strangers to discuss the past and perhaps overcome some of their entrenchment.

Like the President's House, Cliveden's planning involved facilitated discussions. Often, facilitated planning sessions use warm-up exercises and getting-to-know activities, but frequently they end with "talking heads" telling us what to think, with little dialogue between attendees. At President's House meetings there was a moderator, who allowed everyone to speak. The meetings still descended into shouting. Conversely, the *Conversations* featured a neutral facilitator (it should be noted, often that person was an organizational psychologist) and used activities to get people out of their own viewpoints to consider those of others. It sounds simple, but the basic act of having a person introduce himself or herself to a stranger began the dialogue and made it easier to engage in discussions of history. And surveys from participants say that the hardest part of the process was getting over the anxiety of a social introduction to a stranger of another race or background.

What resulted was that people were able to consider open discussions about key terms, and a common vocabulary began to expand. It meant that the janitor at the site felt as comfortable expressing her views as the scholar on the board of directors. For instance, a community historian from the reparationist group, who did not have a specific expertise in academic history and might not have been considered a credible expert in some circles, offered her views in ways that allowed us to learn from her without labels attached. We were able to look past credentials and to connect with people as neighbors who are passionate about history and willing to extend their views to find new ways to tell it.[6] The openness to making connections allowed new possibilities for partnerships and opportunities to work with groups from different perspectives, extending the reach and perspective—which was the point of the whole project.

All places are different. What worked or did not work in Philadelphia may not apply in each community. If done well, though, a safe, respectful process to interpret African American history steps back and examines all facts as open to multiple perspectives, includes viewpoints not necessarily incorporated before, and respects the conversation that ensues, welcoming a narrative that emerges without obliterating any one story. And if it is not done at all, it lessens the impact that history can have for civic dialogue to address real issues.

It is altogether fitting that sites embrace centuries of African American history and the layers of stories and meaning ignored by museums for far too long. In fact, I have found that people are eager to talk about difficult subjects in history. Our society desperately needs a vocabulary for understanding the contradictions that lie in our shared past. As preservation historian Ned Kaufmann wrote, "History cannot provide adequate housing, end discrimination, or prevent redevelopment, but it can contribute to the debate that is necessary to achieving these goals."[7] For the good of our society, people should enter the community of memory to assist us in the work we owe to those who have gone before us: to uncover the past, work toward dialogue, and make new connections.

Notes

1. The rediscovery of the story of slave-holding at the President's House led to engagement by members of the public and the U.S. House of Representatives Report 107-564 of 2003 which "urges the National Park Service to appropriately commemorate concerns" of those historical events. The historical commemoration came to be titled "The President's House: Freedom and Slavery in Making a New Nation." This project, located adjacent to the Liberty Bell Center, is a joint cooperation between the National Park Service and the City of Philadelphia. For information, see http://www.ushistory.org/presidentshouse/links.htm.
2. For instance, Thomas Norman DeWolf and Sharon Morgan, *Coming to the Table: The Healing Journey of a Daughter of Slavery and a Son of the Slave Trade* (Boston: Beacon Press, 2012). For international perspectives on interpreting difficult history among diverse stakeholders, see Randall Mason, David Myers, and Marta de la Torre, *Port Arthur Historic Site; Port Arthur Historic Site Management Authority: A Case Study* (Los Angeles: Getty Conservation Institute, 2003); Margaret G. H. MacLean and David Myers, *Gross Ile and the Irish Memorial National Historic Site: A Case Study* (Los Angeles: Getty Conservation Institute, 2003).
3. Philip Seitz and David W. Young, "When Slavery Came to Stay/Transformation at Cliveden," *Museum* 90, no. 3 (May–June 2011): 41–47.
4. Richard Handler and Eric Gable, *The New History in an Old Museum: Creating the Past at Colonial Williamsburg* (Durham, NC: Duke University Press, 1997), 222–35.
5. Gary Nash, "For Whom Will the Liberty Bell Toll: From Controversy to Cooperation," in *Slavery and Public History: The Tough Stuff of American Memory*, James Oliver Horton and Lois E. Horton, eds. (Chapel Hill: University of North Carolina Press, 2009), 75–102.
6. Joseph Cialdella, "A Place of Collaboration: Cliveden and the Merits of Reevaluating a Landmark's Past," *Perspectives on History* (December 2013): 26–28.
7. Ned Kaufmann, *Race, Place, and Story: Essays on the Past and Future of Historic Preservation* (New York: Routledge, 2009), 401.

PART II

RESEARCH

CHAPTER 5

There *Is* a Doctor in the *House*—And He's Black

MICHELLE L. McCLELLAN

L ITTLE HOUSE ON THE PRAIRIE may seem an unexpected entry in a collection devoted to African American history, but literary tourism associated with the "Little House" phenomenon demonstrates how even stories and places primarily associated with traditional (read: white) American history are more complex than they might seem. This chapter explores interpretive challenges and possibilities related to Dr. George Tann, an African American physician who lived near the Ingalls family in southeastern Kansas in 1870. The "Little House" books, an eight-volume series in which Laura Ingalls Wilder recounted her childhood in the Upper Midwest and Great Plains during the 1870s and 1880s, have epitomized the American pioneer experience for generations of readers in the United States and around the world since publication in the 1930s and 1940s. A popular television program loosely based on the books ran on NBC during the 1970s and 1980s, and a myriad of spin-off products, including picture books, paper dolls, and "prequels," appeared in the 1990s. While Wilder fictionalized some aspects of her family's experiences, George Tann was a real person, and Wilder's depiction of him provides an opportunity to enrich our understanding of nineteenth-century African American history. His remarkable life story as a physician who became a homesteader in a racially mixed community on the Great Plains shows that African Americans were not homogenous and that individual stories placed in context can engage visitors in unexpected and very rewarding ways.

As the titles of the books suggest (*Little House on the Prairie*, *On the Banks of Plum Creek*, and so forth), location and setting shape the stories in crucial ways, and readers soon began to investigate their locations as well as visiting Wilder herself at her home in Mansfield, Missouri. Following Wilder's death in 1957, organized commemorative efforts began in Mansfield and in DeSmet, South Dakota, the setting of four books in the original series. Through the 1960s and 1970s, tourism increased in these communities and elsewhere, as other towns realized their Little House connections and the television show brought additional attention. There are now "Little House" destinations in Wisconsin, Minnesota, Iowa, Kansas, and upstate New York, as well as South Dakota and Missouri.[1] Today, the established sites attract up to twenty thousand visitors each year, with many fans traveling to all or at least most of the "Little House" locations. Devoted fans, known as "bonnetheads," document their journeys on blogs and in memoirs and share their enthusiasm through conferences such as "Laurapalooza."[2] American "bonnetheads" are overwhelmingly white and female, and multigenerational groups of mothers and daughters frequently visit sites together. A considerable proportion of tourists are international, following from the popularity of the books and television show in other countries, especially Japan.

While the "Little House" books feature a well-defined sense of place, Wilder did not always provide accurate details regarding the locations or circumstances in which her family lived. As a result, this literary tourism has evolved through the research and boosterism of enthusiastic locals and fans. For decades after the publication of *Little House on the Prairie*, no one knew exactly where this particular little house had been located—including Wilder herself, who had been a very young child when her family lived in it.[3] The Ingalls were squatters there, so no records remain of their filing for or owning land, and clues in the book are contradictory. Researchers during the 1960s identified the family in the 1870 federal census, then correlated census data with subsequent land patent filings to narrow the search. The existence of a hand-dug well on one of the likely plots seemed to offer definite evidence for the location of the Ingalls home, evoking as it did a lengthy account in the book where Laura's father ("Pa") laboriously dug a well with the help of a neighbor.[4]

When it was identified as a Little House site, owners of the property had been unaware of the Ingalls connection, but they agreed to have a marker placed there. Community groups constructed a cabin on the grounds during the 1970s, and two other buildings have been moved to the site: a one-room schoolhouse and a tiny post office. Picnic tables, some interpretive signage, and a gift shop (initially in the post office, now in the nearby twentieth-century farmhouse) completed the scene. Many visitors, especially devoted fans who have read the books multiple times, come to the site with specific expectations shaped by Wilder's lyrical descriptions and by Garth Williams's detailed illustrations. The existence of the well and the replica cabin built and furnished to match descriptions in the book reward fans with a gratifying sense of recognition.

Yet this tableau assimilated the Ingalls family into a standard narrative of white, western settlement. The structures that were moved to the site—a school, a post office, even a hitching post—evoke a pioneer village. No member of the Ingalls family set foot in these buildings, although the schoolhouse was built in 1871. The mother of the current owner of the property taught in that school;[5] in this way, the building links the site with present-day identities. The tangibility of the buildings and the familiar narrative they conjure give them considerable interpretive weight. The risk is that the story they convey—one of settlement, persistence, and ownership—can literally and figuratively overshadow the details of the Ingalls' experience, including the multiracial situation in which they lived.

Wilder's books, especially *Little House on the Prairie*, have been criticized, even banned from school libraries, for their depiction of Native Americans. While some of her descriptions and the views she attributes to particular family members and neighbors regarding Indians are deeply offensive to present-day readers, her overall portrayal is actually more complex than it initially appears.[6] While her mother ("Ma") expresses fear and hatred toward Indians, for example, her father often articulates respect for their local knowledge and skills and insists repeatedly to his wife that Indians should be judged as individuals. As she was writing this book, moreover, Wilder referred to it as "the Indian juvenile" (juvenile meaning that it was a book intended for children).[7] This name suggests that for her, Native Americans were central to the story. Today, signage at the site explains that the Osage Indians signed a treaty relinquishing this land, and Michelle Martin, the current site director, has reached out to Native American communities for programming and collaboration.[8]

Signage at the site also mentions Dr. George Tann, who treated the family when they became ill with malaria. In a chapter called "Fever 'n' Ague," Wilder describes how her family became incapacitated by fever and chills.[9] She paints an alarming scene in which neither parent is able to respond when her sister cries repeatedly for water. Herself very ill, Laura crawls across the floor to bring her sister a dipper of water before collapsing back into bed. Laura then comes out of a kind of delirium to see a disembodied black face, who gives her medicine. Sleeping again after that, she awakens to see a neighbor woman, Mrs. Scott, tending to the family. Then the doctor returned: "And he was the black man. Laura had never seen a black man before and she could not take her eyes off Dr. Tan.[10] He was so very black. She would have been afraid of him if she had not liked him so much." In addition to medicine, Dr. Tann dispensed good humor, talking and laughing with Laura's parents, who wanted him to stay even longer. With many settlers ill, however, the doctor had to depart. He had discovered the Ingalls family when he was alerted by the family dog Jack as he passed by: "It was a strange thing that Jack, who hated strangers and never let one come near the house unless Pa or Ma told him to, had gone to meet Dr. Tan and begged him to come in." Mrs. Scott credited the doctor with saving the family's life: "What would have happened if the doctor hadn't found them, she didn't know."

Wilder's portrayal of Dr. Tann's physical features, emphasizing how different he is from anyone she has seen before, may trouble modern readers, but the tone and style of these passages are consistent with the descriptive mode and observational point of view of the youthful narrator throughout the book. Importantly too, she renders him in very positive—even heroic—terms, as he appears suddenly from out of nowhere to cure them, and even the dog recognizes his kindness and skill. He is the most well-educated person the Ingalls encounter in the entire book series, with the possible exception of clergy, and he is the only doctor Wilder mentions by name. Garth Williams's illustration of this episode depicts Dr. Tann in more formal attire than Pa generally wears, holding a doctor's bag and standing at the foot of Ma and Pa's bed. While readers might be surprised to encounter a black person on the prairie, let alone one who is a professional and plays such an important and intimate role for the family, Wilder does not explain his presence except to say that he was "a doctor with the Indians." His expertise and status as a healer allow him to move among different racial groups. Perhaps surprisingly, his ministrations to Indians have not tainted him such that white settlers would shun his services. Nor does Ma's animosity to Native Americans extend to him. At least as presented in *Little House on the Prairie*, Dr. Tann stands outside the familiar Indian-settler dynamic. For white settler families like the Ingalls, Indians were frightening if majestic. Dr. Tann, on the other hand, was engaging and admirable.

Visitors to the site who are unfamiliar with the book may be taken aback at the mention of Dr. Tann, given both common perceptions of who settled the frontier and present-day demographics of southeastern Kansas. Indeed, casual fans whose knowledge is based on the television show sometimes expect "Doc Baker," the white TV character.[11] But devoted readers are already acquainted with Dr. Tann when they come to the site. While some of the secondary figures in Wilder's books are composites or have fictionalized names, George Tann existed much as he is described, suggesting that Wilder found him compelling and important enough to depict accurately. Subsequent readers and fans have found him similarly fascinating, turning to primary sources to learn more just as they did to locate the Ingalls family. Unfortunately, no known photograph of Dr. Tann has been identified—yet.[12] As is not uncommon in local history, a substantial proportion of the available information about Dr. Tann's life comes from legal records—in his case, they are related to land holdings, medical licensure, and the complicated disposition of family property. Historians must use caution that such an evidence base does not skew the story of his life toward the problems he faced. Dr. Tann also had a complicated personal life; he left a wife and child behind in Pennsylvania, in circumstances that remain obscure. Not surprisingly, there has been resistance in relaying this information to an audience of "Little House" fans that includes many children and families. Concern about compromising his reputation as a local hero may also constrain interpretive choices in disseminating those biographical details to a wider public.

Despite these challenges, we know enough about Dr. Tann to interpret him in context. He is listed in the 1870 federal census just before the Ingalls family, indicating that he lived quite near their home. According to the census, he was a thirty-four-year-old physician who had been born in Pennsylvania. He lived in Kansas with his parents, both of whom had been born in Pennsylvania as well, and the household also included a thirteen-year-old girl described as a "domestic servant." Dr. Tann was thus the same age as Charles Ingalls, although their family arrangements were quite different. Perhaps the two men became friends, as the affinity they displayed in their brief encounter in *Little House on the Prairie* suggests. Kansas State Historical Society librarian Eileen Charbo, who initiated the census research in the 1960s, published a compilation of primary materials about Dr. Tann and news articles describing her findings in 1984.[13] Informal oral histories that Charbo accumulated consistently convey the esteem in which Dr. Tann was held, for his medical skill and for his generosity in caring for all, regardless of race or ability to pay. While the Ingalls family lived in Kansas for only one year—and the replica cabin at the site freezes them in that moment of 1870—Dr. Tann extends well beyond that period, as he remained in the area until his death in 1909. Signage at the site explains that he is buried in the town of Independence, about thirteen miles away (see figure 5.1). The current site director estimates that a slight majority of visitors to the site also go to the cemetery in town.[14] Dr. Tann's gravestone offers a tangible connection to the world of *Little House on the Prairie*, simultaneously fostering a fuller understanding of local history than the Ingalls family can provide.

Dr. Tann's career trajectory illuminates important aspects of American medical history. By placing him in a larger context, historians can fill in the gaps to better understand his life and use him to explain the opportunities and challenges that African Americans faced in the nineteenth century. No record has been found of his formal training; like many nineteenth-century doctors, he probably learned through apprenticeship. Directories identified him as

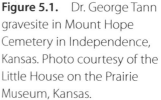

Figure 5.1. Dr. George Tann gravesite in Mount Hope Cemetery in Independence, Kansas. Photo courtesy of the Little House on the Prairie Museum, Kansas.

an "eclectic" physician, a recognized method of practice that drew heavily on botanical remedies but also used a variety of techniques drawn from other approaches (hence the term "eclectic"). By the early twentieth century, however, Dr. Tann, like other doctors in this era, faced ever more restrictive requirements as medical practice and education were increasingly standardized and regulated. Dr. Tann moved his practice a short distance over the state line to Indian Territory (which later became the state of Oklahoma), setting up clinics and constructing a convalescent home for patients who needed extended care. Meanwhile, his wife (he married again in Kansas during the early 1870s) and children remained in Independence while he maintained the farm. Locals explained this arrangement as a way for his family to avoid the racial segregation they would have faced in Indian Territory/Oklahoma, and it may also have been a response to more stringent licensing requirements in Kansas.[15] Eventually, Dr. Tann was required to take an exam to continue practicing, even in Oklahoma. Although extant correspondence indicates his willingness to take this exam, there is no evidence that he ever did, and he apparently retired from practice despite his decades of experience.[16]

In this process, Dr. Tann was probably not targeted because of his race, but this standardization disproportionately affected practitioners who were racial minorities or women of any race, because they were much more likely to have been explicitly excluded from institutions that offered formal medical education.[17] Today at the site, the cloakroom of the schoolhouse has been repurposed as a nineteenth-century doctor's office, complete with chemical compounds. A large panel gives an overview of Dr. Tann's life, using *Little House on the Prairie* as the source.

Finally, Dr. Tann challenges visitors' expectations not just of mythic pioneer history but also of standard markers in African American history. Dr. Tann was never enslaved, and he never lived in the South. Nor were he and his parents part of the well-documented Exoduster movement, an organized migration of African Americans from states of the former Confederacy to Kansas, where they established all-black towns.[18] The Tann family arrived in Kansas ten years before that movement began and they came from Pennsylvania. Wilder depicts him as a singular figure, a rendition which makes him especially memorable for readers. Interpretation at the site can highlight his distinctiveness as an individual *and* underscore the importance of context in understanding his true significance.

The *Little House on the Prairie* site—and the fascinating figure of Dr. Tann specifically—show that historic figures and historic places can retain different meanings for tourists compared with local residents. Elderly neighbors still recall their parents or grandparents talking about "Old Doc Tann,"[19] but his presence in living memory is fading. Furthermore, community knowledge of him would not lead automatically back to *Little House on the Prairie*. Local residents who are aware of him can assess his meaning through what they know of race relations in southeastern Kansas during the intervening decades. Visitors to the Little House site, on the other hand, learn of him because of his connection with the Ingalls family and understand him through that lens. By placing Wilder's depiction of Dr. Tann in multiple contexts—additional biographical details culled from primary sources; community history and local race relations; the professionalization of medicine; and wider patterns in African American history—the "Little House on the Prairie" site can contribute enormously to visitors' understanding of American history. Dr. Tann's life and career, and especially his commitment to Native Americans and the esteem in which he was held by his neighbors of all races, provide a critical corrective to too-common assumptions that all pioneers were white and that violence always dominated race relations on the American frontier.

Notes

1. William Anderson, *The Little House Guidebook* (New York: HarperTrophy, 2002) includes detailed descriptions of the sites as well as brief overviews of how each was established and early tourism. Interview with Anderson, March 2013.
2. The Laura Ingalls Wilder Research and Legacy Association (http://beyondlittlehouse.com), sponsor of the Laurapalooza conference, is one example of an active fan community.
3. Wilder was born in 1867, making her only three years old when her family actually lived in Kansas, as the 1870 census confirms. She is presented as slightly older in the published version of *Little House on the Prairie* than she was in real life.
4. Eileen Miles Charbo, *A Doctor Fetched by the Family Dog: Story of Dr. George A. Tann, Pioneer Black Physician* (Springfield, MO: Independent Publishing, 1984) is a compilation of primary sources about George Tann and brief essays written by Charbo. Evelyn Thurman, *The Ingalls-Wilder Homesites* (Bowling Green, KY: Kelley Printing, 1992), 10–13.

5. Interview with Michelle Martin, site director, March 2014.

6. Michael Dorris, "Trusting the Words," in his *Paper Trail* (New York: HarperCollins, 1994), 268–81. Ann Romines, *Constructing the Little House: Gender, Culture, and Laura Ingalls Wilder* (Amherst: University of Massachusetts Press, 1997), especially chapter 2, "Indians in the House: A Narrative of Acculturation."

7. John E. Miller, *Becoming Laura Ingalls Wilder: The Woman behind the Legend* (Columbia: University of Missouri Press, 1998), 205.

8. Interview with Martin.

9. Laura Ingalls Wilder, *Little House on the Prairie* (New York: Harper & Brothers, 1935), 191–92.

10. Wilder spelled his name with one "n."

11. Interview with Martin.

12. Interview with Martin.

13. Charbo, *A Doctor Fetched by the Family Dog*. Although this publication is now out of print, in 2013 Susan Thurlow researched and produced *Dr. George Tann, Black Frontier Physician* in collaboration with her children. At the 2012 Laurapalooza conference (Mankato, Minnesota), Thurlow explained her motivation as a desire to connect the Little House books more directly with her adopted children, who are African American.

14. Interview with Martin.

15. Interview with Martin.

16. Charbo, *A Doctor Fetched by the Family Dog*.

17. Paul Starr, *The Social Transformation of American Medicine* (New York: Basic Books, 1992), chapter 3.

18. Nell Irvin Painter, *Exodusters: Black Migration to Kansas after Reconstruction* (New York: Knopf, 1977).

19. Interview with Martin.

CHAPTER 6

Finding Sarah Bickford

WILLIAM PETERSON

VIRGINIA CITY and Alder Gulch, Montana, are one of Montana's most visited attractions and the site of one of the largest gold strikes in the American West. That history is complete with unparalleled stories of vigilantism, vicious territorial politics, epic failures, and of course, legendary successes. As the Curator of Interpretation for the Montana Heritage Commission in Virginia City, Montana, my job was to relate those stories to the visiting public with as much truth as possible. One of the legendary successes was Sarah Bickford, and it seemed there were several competing versions of her story. As with all great journeys, historical or otherwise, it starts with unanswered questions. I wanted to find the real Sarah Bickford to answer the nagging questions we had about this African American woman's past. Where did she come from? Who were her parents? Did she have siblings? What was her early life as a slave like? What did the town she grew up in look like? What did she do after the Civil War?

At the time of her death in 1931, Sarah Bickford owned the one of the most important businesses in town: the Virginia City Water Company, which supplied the water vital to the small mountain town. Her success, however, could not have been predicted from her early life.

Born a slave in the South around 1850, she was known as Sarah Blair, named for the family that owned her. Freedom came when she was a teenager, and she grabbed the opportunity to start a new life two thousand miles away on the western frontier. In exchange for her passage west, she cared for the children of Judge John Luttrell Murphy of Knoxville, Tennessee, who was appointed to the Montana Territorial judiciary system in Virginia City. Soon after her arrival in the winter of 1870, Sarah married William Brown, started a family, and opened a restaurant. She had two boys and a girl by this marriage, but tragically, disease took her husband and children within a dozen years. In 1883, Sarah started a second family with Stephen E. Bickford, a white man from Maine, and had a son and three daughters, and then went on to to become a successful business owner.

It's a thrilling story that could be told like a Hollywood movie at the house where Sarah lived for the last forty-three years of her life, however, there was little known about Sarah's earlier history. I wanted a richer interpretation, with the kinds of details that would resonate with modern audiences and increase attention on an important but overlooked person. There were also other nineteenth-century African American residents in Virginia City whose stories, if we could find them, might help us paint a more complete picture of the community. My goal was to find a way to tell these stories, yet my department had little manpower and almost no funding to support such a program. My quest to flesh out the details of Sarah's life led to interesting partnerships, academic adventure, and ultimately a greater understanding of a small community of African Americans who were mostly invisible in the interpretation of Virginia City's storied past. The process we used can be easily adopted by other museums and historic sites.

As a firm believer in the old adage "do your own research," the first step is surveying all the known literature and published material available on Sarah's life through library catalogs and journal databases. Next, identify all primary sources that can be found locally, such as archival records located in the local library or historical society and legal and official documents held by county, state, and national government. Finally, conduct Internet and long-distance research via telephone to determine if the same types of documents are available in nonlocal sources. In Sarah's case, we focused on Tennessee because of her early life there. All of these sources require some skepticism and careful evaluation for accuracy and bias. You also need to be continually open to new leads, even if they're a result of a mistake, as we found in our research.

Since 2007, the Montana Heritage Commission has partnered with the Public History Program at Washington State University (WSU) to conduct Public History Field Schools in Montana. This program leveraged state historical and physical resources with the academic faculty and students of WSU's graduate program. Previous field schools focused on research were mostly academic in nature, but in 2009 it was adapted for public interpretation. With the assistance of WSU professor Orlan Svingen and doctoral student Laura Arata, I received a Partnership-in-Scholarship Grant from the National Trust for Historic Preservation to conduct the research on the African American community in Virginia City, teach a field school course around the research, and produce several interpretive panels for installation at various relevant sites in Virginia City.

While the Internet and digital life have made this historian's world smaller, I still find value in place-based research. After consulting with my colleagues at the American Association for State and Local History and the Tennessee Historical Society, both based in Nashville, it became clear that I needed to further my research at the East Tennessee Historical Society and the Knox County Library in Knoxville. While census records are widely available online, libraries and archivists can only supply short periods of preliminary research for scholars. Also, librarians and archivists cannot anticipate where documents might lead a researcher. Research in Tennessee also provided the context for Sarah's life as a slave and in the years following emancipation. Did the places where she lived and worked still exist? What businesses did her owners pursue? Were they active in the community? This kind of information enriches the story of Sarah Bickford.

That brief, four-day research trip turned out to be unbelievably productive. One of the most exciting discoveries came from a mistake made more than a century ago. While in Tennessee we were able to pin down several key details of Sarah Bickford's life, including such basics as her owners and place of birth. Prior to the end of the Civil War, census records in slave states consisted of two forms: Schedule 1 for free white people, and Schedule 2 primarily for slaves. As I sat in the quiet reading room of the East Tennessee Historical Society archives scanning the Blair census listings, some curious handwritten notations caught my attention. The enumerator had written, "8 year old mullato slave girl owned by the Blairs"[1] on Schedule 1 of his census forms instead of listing the slaves on Schedule 2. Realizing his mistake, he then scratched the information out and wrote "See Schedule 2" in the margins (see figure 6.1). It dawned on me that instead of looking at the names of the Blairs per se, I was looking at the names of the Blairs' slaves. Specifically I found Sarah Bickford and the people that she would have considered her family! My joy at discovering something I had long been seeking was quickly tempered by the reality of slavery and what it might have meant for this child.

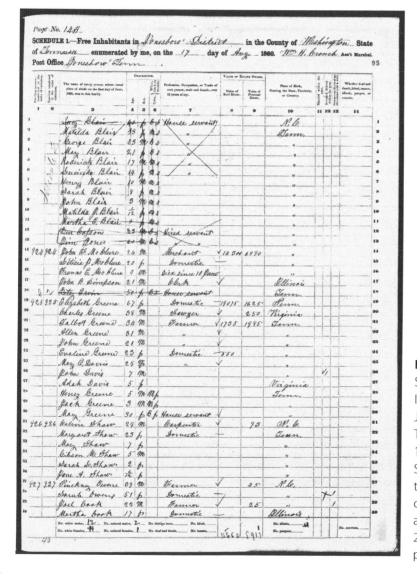

Figure 6.1.

Schedule 1, Free Inhabitants of Jonesboro District, Tennessee, August 17, 1860, page 148, United States Census. The first thirteen names are crossed out with an annotation, "Schedule 2," which lists enslaved persons.

We also located buildings owned by John Blair, likely inhabited by Sarah and her family before the end of the Civil War in 1865, and uncovered more information about other members of Sarah's family. This trip also forever laid to rest the question of Sarah's birthplace as Tennessee and that she adopted the last name of her aunt and uncle, Nancy and Isaac Gammon, at the end of the Civil War.[2]

Upon our return to Montana, preparations began for the field school with students arriving from WSU and from a new partner in the program, the University of Wisconsin, Eau Claire (UWEC). Professor John W. W. Mann, a WSU alumni, saw the practical value of the field school for his students and quickly signed on for the three-week course. Both graduate and undergraduate students from WSU and UWEC were turned loose in Virginia City to conduct extensive research of local sources which ranged from county records to documents in Virginia City's Thompson-Hickman Library.

The students' enthusiasm coupled with their research skills made some rather startling discoveries that completely changed our interpretation of Sarah Bickford. Following their natural curiosity, the students looked in probate records under Sarah's married name of Brown. Through that simple, yet previously untried approach, they turned up the most important new evidence regarding Sarah's life. These records clearly indicated that Sarah's first husband was named John, not William, and that she had lost him not to disease but to divorce. The 1880 divorce proceedings included testimony on her unhappiness and physical abuse. Sarah's preference to describe the loss of her first husband to disease provides an ideal topic for interpreting gender roles and social expectations that still resonates today.

At the end of the field school, the students and faculty spent three days in a small cabin in Virginia City to develop the interpretive text for a series of wayside panels based on their research. They not only examined Sarah Bickford but also Minerva Cogswell, Parthenia Sneed, and Jack Taylor, other African Americans who once resided in Virginia City. The interpretation that emerged revealed a small, seemingly integrated community of African Americans in Virginia City. They owned businesses on Main Street, and as in the case of Sarah Bickford provided vital services to the whole community. Once completed, we sent the text and graphics to the sign production company, and in August 2011, the interpretive panels arrived back on site for installation (see figure 6.2).

The production of the interpretive panels required strong partnerships to attract funding. While the Montana History Foundation continuously supported the programs of the Heritage Commission, for this project we expanded support by creating a community-wide interpretive program with a variety of partners, all of which are recognized on the final signage. At the time, the cost of full-color, high-pressure laminate signs and bases cost about $600 including installation. Sponsors and partners on the project paid for all of the costs of every sign except for salaries and overhead. Site staff and university faculty provided guidance and supervision, but the work was largely accomplished by students. The universities provided their students with real-world experience on a public history project that has tangible and lasting results. Additionally, WSU, UWEC, the Montana History Foundation, and other sponsors now have their names and logos visible throughout a popular tourist destination in southwestern Montana.

The key components of this project are easily replicable in communities all over the country. Doing your own research is critical to the success of any historical interpretive

Figure 6.2. "The Remarkable Sarah Bickford," an outdoor interpretive panel in Virginia City, Montana. Photo by Janna Norby.

program, and each generation of historians will discover new information as new sources and methods emerge. Students are a wonderful way to engage your community, so seek partnerships with amenable schools and faculty members, even if they're located in another state. While I was lucky to have an established relationship with WSU, I believe that most schools would be willing to join similar projects with a local, regional, or state historical agency.

Funding is an ongoing challenge, and while I was fortunate to receive a special grant from the National Trust for Historic Preservation, I did have to find other sources of financial support. By creating wayside interpretive panels, we provided sponsors with something physical and highly visible that could strengthen the relationship between them and the community. We calculated the cost of each interpretive sign and sold sponsorships for individual and groups of signs. Full-color logos could be easily incorporated into the final signs without disrupting the design. Businesses liked this approach because they could easily recognize it as publicity and advertising instead of charity.

What started as this historian's typical curiosity and quest for answers became a grand collaborative effort. Students and teachers both learned as much as the other. Through Sarah Bickford, we provided students with real, hands-on learning experiences. Academically, there was more produced through this research and field school than discussed here, but at a later conference presentation, Professor John W. W. Mann summarized the experience best through his comment, "when students cry because a class is over, you have done something very right."[3]

Notes

1. 1860 US Census and "Finding Sarah Gammon Bickford," http://www.sarahbickford.org/documents.html. Last accessed March 31, 2014.
2. "Finding Sarah Gammon Bickford," http://www.sarahbickford.org/. Last accessed March 31, 2014.
3. John W. W. Mann, "The Public History Field School," Montana History Conference, Helena, Montana, October 2011.

CHAPTER 7

Documenting Local African American Community History

Some Guidelines for Consideration

LILA TERESA CHURCH

IF THE DOCUMENTATION of local African American community history is on your history organization's agenda, how will you begin such an undertaking? Some key questions posed to archivists regarding this subject may inform your organization's understanding of the process. Consider, for example:

- What approaches do African American and majority-white repositories use to document local African American communities?[1]
- What factors influence how archivists of all races/ethnicities document local African American communities?
- What materials are needed to document local African American communities?
- What aspects of the history and culture of local African American communities are history organizations documenting most extensively?
- What model would ensure an adequate collection for documenting local black communities?[2]

The Ethnic Communities Archival Documentation Project (ECADP) completed at the University of North Carolina at Chapel Hill during 2008 examined these questions, among others. Informants for the study were selected from the four major geographical regions of the United States. Twenty-nine archivists from twenty-four states and one nonstate area comprised the study's population. Among this group were eighteen females of African

American, white, and other ethnic identities. Eleven males also participated, including both African Americans and whites. The twenty-nine participants represented twelve African American and seventeen majority-white repositories.

These facilities were situated at nine historically white educational institutions, five historically black educational institutions, two national research centers, two African American museums, three public libraries, and eight state or regional historical societies of varying sizes. The findings and recommendations from this study serve as the basis for these documentation guidelines and provide a set of best practices.

Strategies for Documenting Communities

There are several approaches to documenting the history of local African American communities through primary source materials. Among those that have been used with proven success are strategies to:

- Extend outreach.
- Gain trust among donors.
- Seek out and obtain materials relevant to the collecting missions and policies that particular repositories abide by.[3]

The first two strategies enable archivists to establish a rapport with African American communities and vice versa. The latter places a special focus upon the development of local African American collections, rather than entrusting this history to serendipity or occasional documentation activities.

Step 1: Outreach

The outreach strategies are recognized across the archival profession. They are applicable for all history organizations in documenting the history of local black communities as well as those of other ethnic identities. These strategies may take the form of educational outreach, various types of programs and services that your archive provides for the benefit of the communities you serve, and whatever steps you take to publicize your facility and its holdings, particularly your African American collections.

Educational Outreach

There are two angles from which to approach educational outreach. First, provide information concerning the importance of African American archival materials and the need to deposit them at appropriate facilities. Second, educate donors about your museum or historic site and the services you provide.

If educating prospective donors about archival materials and their importance is your focus, bear in mind that the average person—regardless of ethnicity—may know little about what comprises such collections. Begin by providing insights into the mysteries that sometimes surround the nature of collections and the kinds of items they contain. Explain that personal letters, photographs, clippings, church programs, and other historical documents are collectible because of their informational content. Relate how influential groups and individuals; places of significance; social, cultural, political, and business institutions; particular movements and historical periods; and past events in local black communities figure into these traces that must be preserved for the future. Shed light upon the ways in which researchers and scholars use primary sources to generate secondary sources and reconstruct certain aspects of cultural memory. Call attention to books, documentaries, exhibits, and other works that relied on archival collections to investigate community history. Consider it an extra bonus if you can identify scholars or programs who used *your* collections to study *your* community.

Also, point out the physical nature and sometimes fragile condition of historical materials and provide educational outreach on their importance. African American materials are no less susceptible to the risks of damage and destruction than those of any other ethnic group. Stress the urgency to donate collections while still in as good a physical state as possible. Make donors aware that these one-of-a-kind sources are irreplaceable once they are gone or damaged beyond the point of conservation. To make your point, show examples of the rapid disintegration that can occur over time due to climatic changes with items such as newspapers, scrapbooks, and other paper-based materials.

In addition to talking about the makeup and importance of African American archives, take advantage of times during which you can showcase your collections, such as exhibits, opening receptions, open-house events, or special tours for groups and donors. Including local African Americana in exhibits is a highly effective tool for showing the context in which these materials among your holdings can facilitate the exploration of larger themes or issues.

During the course of your conversations with donors, you will likely encounter some African Americans who express the belief that their personal papers have no value to

Figure 7.1.   Hubbards Hill farmer John Edward Stevens with his horses in Nelson County, Virginia. Collection of Lila Teresa Church.

researchers. Individuals who have lived through times when neither they nor their history were respected or prized in the eyes of the wider society may use this view as justification for not donating materials to a museum or archive. This does not mean, however, that these prospective donors have no personal perceptions about the value of their own history. Your aim is to convey to them why their materials are valuable to your history organization and why your facility is the right choice as a place to house them.

Most of your efforts to provide education about the importance of materials will be geared toward people expected to have a collectible history reflecting their social, cultural, political, and professional contributions over extended periods. You may be pleasantly surprised, however, to see what benefits arise from extending educational outreach to younger age groups in a community. Over the long term, and years after first learning about the importance of preserving the past, some of these individuals may eventually settle upon your museum or historic site when they are ready to donate and deposit their papers.

Find ways to encourage younger age groups from local African American communities to participate in appropriate activities at your institution. In doing so, you foster members of this generation to grow up with an awareness of history and its importance, rather than waiting until a later time in their lives. Consider forging alliances between your organization and other educational institutions. Invite school groups to visit and explore the possibilities of working on joint projects involving some of your collections. Consider providing internships for African American college students with an interest in archival careers. Informants participating in the ECADP pointed to the need for larger numbers of African Americans working in the archival profession. Capturing the interest of children and youth can potentially build momentum for all efforts to strengthen the documentation of local history.[4]

Utilize the second approach to educational outreach to disseminate information pertaining to the history, development, and mission of these facilities. Undoubtedly, you will discover prospective donors have little, if any, knowledge about the importance of archives and collections storage. Explain why your facility was established and describe its operations. Discuss not only the services you provide but the resources available for that purpose. If your mission provides specifically for documenting local black history, be sure to let donors know that as well. Share information about the general procedures that go on behind the scenes when you and your staff set out to solicit and acquire collections. Shed light on the steps that you follow to process, arrange, describe, and make materials available for use. Convincing donors of your ability to care for historical treasures may become a deciding factor in whether or not they surrender their papers to your facility or any other.

As you impart information concerning how your organization cares for materials, also offer some basic guidelines for prospective donors to follow at home to preserve and protect historical items in their possession. Because some archives have not yet acquired many materials, what you say may go a long way in helping prospective African American donors come to a wider appreciation of the value of materials tucked away in their private collections. Not every opportunity to promote the virtues of your museum or historic site will result in the immediate acquisition of collections. In some instances, view educating prospective donors about your institution and archival preservation as a way to plant seeds of goodwill that may subsequently spring forth with a yield in your favor.[5]

When you discuss the appropriateness of your facility, its mission and collecting focus, physical location, and available services, consider whether your museum or historic site is the right fit for the collections, needs, and expectations of the donor. *Do not hesitate to suggest other facilities for prospective donors.* Above all else, be sure to encourage them to deposit their materials *somewhere*, rather than maintaining them in homes, offices, garages, and other structures that may accelerate deterioration and risk loss by theft or fire.

The findings of the ECADP suggest that using educational outreach to gain entrée to African American communities may require more effort for archivists at some majority-white repositories than their counterparts at African American facilities. How long a museum or historic site has operated and collected African American materials may factor into winning donor confidence. Where the matter of confidence is concerned, there should be no surprise to find that African American repositories often have a considerable edge. Unlike other institutions with abbreviated collecting histories or rather recent interests in African Americana, these facilities are generally known for their commitment to preserving black history.

Programs and Services Outreach

However you elect to extend outreach through programs and services, you are likely to recognize some areas of overlap between these and the approaches utilized for educational outreach. Lectures, events, and programs may aid in establishing contact with significantly large numbers of African Americans gathered in one place at the same time. Viewing items in exhibit cases can generate enormous pride among donors from whom they were acquired as well as other visitors. These materials can help a community reconstruct its cultural memory during the course of an exhibit (and beyond). Satisfied donors can provide some of your best advertising to help promote your organization, its collections, and services. Consider what may happen when visitors come upon certain items pertaining to key individuals from the black community whom they know and respect. This sometimes prompts interest by persons who would not otherwise part with their papers to seriously think about following suit by donating their collections and, perhaps, providing financial and other kinds of support. Aside from making lasting impressions upon visitors and donors, the scope, design, and character of exhibit installations speak to your museum's or historic site's commitment to preserving local African American history.

The opening of exhibits and the acquisition of new collections are opportunities to celebrate and publicly recognize and thank donors and other supporters for their contributions to repositories. These events have the potential to attract visitors who might not otherwise frequent a particular facility and can sometimes result in leads to other important African American collections.

Lectures and panel discussions not only welcome the community's presence and participation, but they stimulate intellectual curiosity. Take advantage of these kinds of programs to foster ongoing social, cultural, and educational exchanges between scholars and the communities they investigate.

Programs that your facility may sponsor at certain community-based sites can also go a long way toward cultivating a rapport with black communities. Be open to the idea of establishing and maintaining affiliations with entities such as churches, schools, community centers, and the like. Presenting public lectures at these venues creates opportunities to continue your educational outreach efforts to share your archival facilities, collections, and the importance of including local African Americana therein. Using community venues may also prove beneficial where African Americans are sometimes reticent to visiting history organizations, particularly those characterized by past racial policies and discriminatory practices.

If there are rooms or spaces available for public use, invite hosting African American community groups and organizations to sponsor programs at your site. This outreach promotes interaction and provides insights into local history and culture. Keep an eye out for programs through which groups and organizations focus upon issues of historic preservation. In *Place, Race, and Story*, Ned Kaufman writes about the benefits that result when historical organizations and community groups find common ground to work on preservation-related projects that are centered outside of repositories.[6] Similarly, Sharon Carlson sheds light on approaches that historical organizations may use to extend outreach across ethnic boundaries through archival programs and projects aimed at documenting local history in her article, "Documenting the Experiences of African Americans, Native Americans, and Mexican Americans: Archivists Partnering with Oral Historians."[7]

Even if your facility cannot serve as a host site for outside activities, do not pass up opportunities to attend programs that individuals and groups present at their own venues. Some white archivists participating in the ECADP recognized that this increased their visibility to community members. They also felt that "continually receiving frequent invitations from various community groups over the course of time indicated a measure of their acceptance by community members."[8]

Some of the services that you can provide in conjunction with programs may include public talks about the work of your organization and its African American holdings; introductory workshops on caring for family photograph and documents; offers to serve as an official museum or historic site for various business, social, and cultural entities; and assistance to groups and organizations for making preservation copies of historical records. Providing the latter service may present opportunities to make copies of important caches for inclusion in your own museum or historic site's holdings. Subsequently, your museum or historic site may even acquire some of the collections that you identify through the course of providing services to local communities.[9]

Publicity Outreach

There are at least four types of sources to consider for extending outreach through publicity and keeping the communities you serve apprised of your museum or historic site's efforts to document local black history:

1. local newspapers
2. electronic media, brochures, and materials generated by your facility
3. African American churches
4. information distributed through the courtesy of other repositories[10]

Figure 7.2. Hubbards Hill families gather for Sunday service at Little Zion Baptist Church in Nelson County, Virginia. Collection of Lila Teresa Church.

Budgets will often determine the frequency of advertising your services through certain media. Whenever possible, therefore, contribute articles and feature stories about your facility, exhibits, collections, new and ongoing projects, and your interest in acquiring African American materials. Make a special effort to target black newspapers, regional magazines, and community newsletters published in your vicinity. Using a combination of print and electronic media, including website and social networking, makes it possible to extend outreach over a wide area. Whatever news and updates you provide will help to bring your institution and its efforts in the public eye and create favorable impressions upon residents and organizations in a community.

Extending outreach to communities through local African American churches is both economical and effective. The cost, if any, will likely be far less than media that rely upon advertising to generate revenue. Some churches may willingly include announcements about your museum or historic site and its programs and services in their weekly bulletins or newsletters. A number of churches have special committees that focus upon documenting their own history. Take advantage of opportunities to become known to members of these committees and offer guidance as appropriate for the preservation work they are doing. Go a step further and establish a rapport between your organization and officials of the clergy and their congregations. Ministerial staff members often have considerable influence and may help garner support for historical documentation initiatives and programs that you provide for the community's benefit.

Materials such as bookmarks, brochures, and related materials generated by museums make excellent takeaways to distribute at your site, other venues in local communities, and beyond. Call attention to the strengths of your collections, such as noted personalities, organizations, and businesses from local African American communities. Finally, extend your outreach to other facilities across the museum, library, and archival profession and share news about your organization and recent additions to your holdings.

Step 2. Gain Trust

Gaining donor trust ranks high among the strategies necessary for documenting the history of local African American communities. Ultimately, you must persuade donors to give up the treasures they hold near and dear. How you accomplish this has much to do with your organizational affiliation and position as a staff member or volunteer.

The reputation that your facility forges as a museum or historic site for African Americana and providing scholars with access to these materials can help win donor confidence. Repositories such as historically black educational institutions oftentimes have a considerable advantage. From the beginning, these facilities have demonstrated a commitment to preserving the African American past (unlike some majority-white repositories with a more recent interest in this history). Donors often judge a facility's trustworthiness based upon agreements you make to safeguard and ensure appropriate use of materials. Timeliness in honoring such agreements also figures into how your organization earns trust.[11]

Your reputation as a professional or volunteer historian is equally important as that of the organization you represent. You gain the trust of prospective donors as they get to know you through your interactions with a community. Make an effort to cultivate personal relationships with donors from whom you have already acquired collections; members of friend groups, advisory boards, and community networks; civic leaders; and ordinary people. They can become advocates for you as well as your museum or historic site and facilitate introductions to wider circles where collectible materials are found. Aside from the work you do on behalf of your organization, consider becoming involved with activities and organizations in various communities. Educational outreach also doubles as a trust-building strategy well suited to helping you earn a community's trust.

Regardless of your ethnicity, you should expect certain challenges in your quest to gain trust—they are par for the course. Be prepared to elucidate why you and your museum or historic site are interested in local African American history and explain how collections will be used. Some donors may even probe for evidence of your knowledge and expertise as a historian. Many African Americans believe they should entrust the preservation of their history exclusively to African American institutions. Past experiences of being exploited, undervalued, and disrespected often fuel this thinking, thus making it somewhat more difficult for African American and white archivists at majority-white repositories to gain trust in certain instances. The loyalty of black historians can also come into question if community members perceive them as collecting and seizing African Americana and placing it under the control of non–African American institutions. Be prepared to go the extra distance to overcome the hurdles you encounter. Devote as much time as needed to talk with donors and consider meeting them at locations of their choosing, rather than at your institution. Make known your initial interest through a personal visit instead of sending a letter to prospective donors. Some African American historians may find themselves taking on the role of "mediators because their duties seem partly aimed at reconciling the trust between majority-white repositories and some African American communities."[12] Equally important to the steps you take to gain trust is being recognized as a member of a community, rather than an outsider, and this is often essential to African American donors from a racial standpoint.

Step 3. Solicit and Acquire Materials According to Missions and Policies

Mission statements and collecting policies are probably not thought of as documentation strategies in the traditional sense, but they may be implemented as such. After all, they do not offer guidance on how to navigate a black community and preserve its cultural heritage. These strategies may be viewed as expressions of your facility's commitment and intent to develop collections. They serve as the impetus for other strategies used to extend outreach and gain a donor's trust.

Missions and policies may be formal or informal in nature. Neither version guarantees success, but each can contribute significantly to the development of collections. Some repositories with no formal missions or policies held some of the largest collections of local African Americana identified through the ECADP. These collections were generally found among facilities with missions that encompassed wider geographic areas that included important local history. Meanwhile, formal missions give this history a higher priority for ongoing collection development efforts. There are also several ways to proceed when your facility does not operate with a formal mission. For example, you may elect to focus upon larger designated geographic regions that automatically include local African American communities with relevant materials. "You may also pursue such materials through various targeted documentation initiatives, and sometimes in direct response to news and announcements concerning the availability of papers pertaining to previously undocumented groups and individuals."[13]

Whereas mission statements may broadly articulate that an institution strives to develop local African American holdings, collecting policies can provide greater specificity for what should be sought. Without such a policy, individual archivists may make decisions regarding the collection of materials they deem relevant. Some collections developed through this manner may be very worthwhile, but questions can arise regarding their depth and coverage of important subject areas. The documentation is not always concentrated or consistent, however, sometimes leading to gaps in collections.[14]

Factors That Influence Documentation Initiatives

Although archivists have devised appropriate strategies for documenting local African American communities, this task is not without its challenges. The ECADP participants identified six such factors, some of which seemingly have a domino effect. Insufficient staffing support, for example, impacts all aspects of the work required to cultivate donors and develop collections and make them accessible. The effect of funding shortages may result in a lack of staff resources, preclude repositories with smaller budgets from acquiring collections that other archives acquire through purchases, prevent the expansion of physical space, and adversely affect the services museums and historic sites provide. Those most affected by limited staffing and funding shortages are African American and other ethnic archivists. Limited space to house growing collections is a common challenge in the archival world. This stymied the efforts to expand the overall size of local African American holdings. As a consequence, some informants place restrictions on new acquisitions by refusing donations or returning materials to donors because of a lack of space to house them.

Competition for local African American primary sources may arise between institutions, regardless of their ethnic identity. Majority-white repositories sometimes have an edge because they have the means to purchase collections priced beyond affordability for African American archives. The number of repositories involved in documenting the black history in the same local community can also spark competition.

Aside from competing for materials, some historians are confronted with shortages of collectible materials. This comes to light in situations where the evidence of history is lost or destroyed or community members are unwilling to donate their papers to a museum or historic site. Finally, the issue of race is an impediment for some majority-white repositories, particularly ones that do not "have a great reputation in the African American community because of race relations."[15]

Materials Needed to Document Communities

Whoever and whatever makes history in local African American communities dictates what museums and historic sites should consider documenting. This undertaking requires the cooperative efforts of many such facilities to construct the ensuing narrative. All areas of black life and history need to be documented. Some areas, or rather topics, have received more treatment than others, but by and large, black history is still virgin territory.[16] Richard Cox's "Framework for Documenting Localities" identifies the following topical areas as a guideline:

> agriculture; arts and architecture; business, industry, manufacturing; education, environmental affairs and natural resources; labor; medicine and health care; military, politics, government, law; populations; recreation and leisure; religion; science and technology; and social organization and communication.[17]

Aspects of History Documented Most Extensively

Local black history belongs not just to the communities where it may be found, or solely to African Americans. This is the history of states as well as the nation and the world, and it transcends many boundaries to link us in our humanity. African American and non–African American history organizations, by all indications, are making strides in documenting this history. Some of their holdings include materials pertaining to the arts, entertainment, sports, law, medicine, education, fraternities and sororities, religion, politics, business, industry, social activism, the civil rights movement, community service organizations, and numerous occupations and professions. Approximately half of the repositories in the ECADP also included oral history collections among their local African American holdings. There is evidence to suggest that some repositories may have an easier time acquiring history in this format than other kinds of materials typically included among archival collections. There is no surprise that documentation initiatives at most facilities included in the ECADP seemed to follow traditional collecting patterns, concentrating mainly upon notable and influential personalities. The study found that archivists at some of these repositories are also making considerable headway documenting the history of people who are less well known but equally significant for their contributions to local history.[18]

Conclusion

The sheer number of local African American communities across the United States with important and collectible history is daunting. Preserving this treasure is an undertaking that requires the participation and collaboration of donors, historians, and history organizations, both African American and non–African American. Proven strategies enable institutions to succeed in this endeavor, but adequate funding is critical to these efforts. What matters most, however, is the reputation of historians, both paid and volunteer, and the organizations they serve.

A Model That Ensures Adequate Collections

An ideal model for successfully documenting local African American communities is one that provides adequate support for the work of historians and organizations involved in this endeavor. Such a model consists of two tiers, the upper describing various strategies to document local African American history. These include extending community outreach, gaining community trust, and the solicitation and acquisition of appropriate materials. Their impact and effectiveness comes from the support provided through resources that comprise the model's lower tier: administrative support, funding, archival staff, and facility space. Internal as well as external decision making of administrative personnel may impact the existence and availability of other resources in the lower tier. In addition, funding determines the availability of staffing and space resources.[1]

Note

1. Ibid., 151–52. Church, *Documenting African American Community Heritage.*

Notes

1. The terms "majority-white" and "non–African American" denote history institutions founded and operated to collect, preserve, and interpret the history of a primarily white community or audience.
2. Lila Teresa Church, *Documenting African American Community Heritage: Archival Strategies and Practices in the United States* (PhD diss., University of North Carolina at Chapel Hill, 2008), 168–69.
3. Church, *Documenting African American Community Heritage*, 169.
4. Church, *Documenting African American Community Heritage*, 113.
5. See Bettye Collier-Thomas, "Present Programs and Future Needs" in *Black Bibliophiles and Collectors: Preservers of Black History.* Another useful source is Douglas Kalajian, "Preserving Local Black History" in *The Palm Beach Post.* Both of these writings shed light on the circumstances surrounding immense quantities of African American historical materials not included in repository holdings and the reasons why donors hesitate to relinquish control of them.
6. Ned Kaufman, *Place, Race, and Story: Essays on the Past and Future of Historic Preservation* (New York: Routledge, 2010), 252–56.
7. Sharon Carlson, "Documenting the Experiences of African Americans, Native Americans, and Mexican Americans: Archivists Partnering with Oral Historians," in *Librarians as Community Partners: An Outreach Handbook,* ed. Carol Smallwood (Chicago: American Library Association, 2010), 129–32.
8. Church, *Documenting African American Community Heritage*, 117.
9. Church, *Documenting African American Community Heritage*, 117–18.
10. Church, *Documenting African American Community Heritage*, 120.
11. Church, *Documenting African American Community Heritage*, 134.
12. Church, *Documenting African American Community Heritage*, 140.
13. Church, *Documenting African American Community Heritage*, 147.
14. Church, *Documenting African American Community Heritage*, 148.
15. Church, *Documenting African American Community Heritage*, 160.
16. Bettye Collier-Thomas, "Present Programs and Future Needs," in *Black Bibliophiles and Collectors: Preservers of Black History,* ed. W. Paul Coates, Elinor Des Verney Sinnette, and Thomas C. Battle (Washington, D.C.: Howard University Press, 1990), 160.
17. Richard J. Cox, *Documenting Localities: A Practical Model for American Archivists and Manuscript Curators* (Lanham, MD: Society of American Archivists and the Scarecrow Press, 2001), 130.
18. Church, *Documenting African American Community Heritage*, 152–53.

Resources on Documenting Local African American Community History

Carlson, Sharon. "Documenting the Experiences of African Americans, Native Americans, and Mexican Americans: Archivists Partnering with Oral Historians." In *Librarians as Community Partners,* edited by Carol Smallwood, 129–32. Chicago: American Library Association, 2010.

Church, Lila Teresa. "Documenting African American Community Heritage: Archival Strategies and Practices in the United States." PhD dissertation, University of North Carolina at Chapel Hill, 2008.

Collier-Thomas, Bettye. "Present Programs and Future Needs." In *Black Bibliophiles and Collectors: Preservers of Black History*, edited by W. Paul Coates, Elinor Des Verney Sinnette, and Thomas C. Battle. Washington, DC: Howard University Press, 1990.

Cox, Richard J. *Documenting Localities: A Practical Model for American Archivists and Manuscript Curators*. Lanham, MD: Society of American Archivists and the Scarecrow Press, 1996. Paperback edition 2001.

Kalajian, Douglas. "Preserving Local Black History." *Palm Beach Post*, February 1, 2003. http://www.racematters.org/preservinglocalblackhistory.htm.

Kaufman, Ned. *Place, Race, and Story: Essays on the Past and Future of Historic Preservation*. New York: Routledge, 2010.

CHAPTER 8

Interpreting the Upper-Ground Railroad

MATTHEW PINSKER

I have never approved of the very public manner in which some of our western friends have conducted what they call the underground railroad, but which I think, by their open declarations, has been made most emphatically the upper-ground railroad.

—Frederick Douglass, *Narrative of the Life of Frederick Douglass* (1845)

AT THE VERY outset of the twenty-first century, historic preservationists scored a rare victory for African American history during a public showdown with major commercial developers in Lancaster County, Pennsylvania. They forced multi-million-dollar plans for a new convention center to be altered and space to be created to protect an underground cistern that was thought to have been used by radical abolitionist Thaddeus Stevens while hiding runaway slaves.

The problem with this political victory, however, was that it was based on a shaky point of historical interpretation. Stevens certainly helped runaways, sometimes perhaps even as a local "stationmaster" in the terminology of traditional Underground Railroad lore. Yet by far his more significant contributions to the cause came as an attorney, in real fugitive slave cases which had both national and enduring significance. Yet if preservationists had fought merely to protect the war room of a great fugitive lawyer in the antebellum era buildings that contained both his law offices and residence without also highlighting that mysterious cistern in the rear of the complex, they would have surely failed in their efforts. The archaeologists who had investigated the alleged hiding place never really proved much about any particular escapes connected to that cistern, but they managed nonetheless to capture public imagination in the way that the most popular stories about the Underground Railroad have always done.[1]

In other words, they were probably right for the wrong reasons. People expect high drama in their tales of nineteenth-century freedom seekers. They want to hear all the elusive details about coded quilts and songs, secret passageways, whispered warnings, and nighttime flight. The possibility of the old, feisty, half-crippled abolitionist peering into the darkness of a hollowed-out cistern only seemed to confirm what everybody in Lancaster thought they knew about the great underground resistance movement.

The challenge for modern-day interpreters of the Underground Railroad is to puncture some of those myths without diminishing otherwise sincere public interest in the story. That is a tricky proposition, though it has been made far easier in recent years by an outpouring of first-rate scholarship and through a series of determined efforts at preserving a wider range of African American public history associated with the destruction of slavery.[2] It is now possible—for the first time really—to share a fully nuanced and national portrait of the overlapping, mixed-race networks that helped people escape from bondage, and to appreciate those often-complicated individual stories within the context of the larger legal and political effort to destroy slavery in the United States. The result might not seem quite as dramatic as uncovering a secret code or some hidden escape route, but it does offer the startling realization that active resistance to slavery was remarkably open in certain sections of the country and supported by an aggressive phalanx of lawyers, financiers, and propagandists who deserve greater credit for their skill and determination. Frederick Douglass worried that the "upper-ground railroad" would undo them all, but it turned out to be a prime factor in the antislavery movement's ultimate success.

Since American enslavement was a particularly brutal form of human tyranny, it is sometimes hard to convey just how much the law actually mattered in defining the peculiar institution. Yet there should be no doubt that the slave system demanded extensive statutory and judicial support—and so did the effort to undermine it. You simply cannot—or should not—discuss slavery-related historic sites without at some point setting them in the context of American law. Practically every colony in British North America, for instance, had some kind of fugitive statute prohibiting both runaway slaves and indentured servants from freeing themselves.[3] Yet there was always a strong element of backcountry resistance to this form of patriarchy from the lowlands or Eastern elites. Thus, the issue of fugitives from service remained a perennial problem for colonial masters who complained bitterly about the lack of enforcement for the rules. This was the contested legal tradition which helped inform the notable (and awkwardly phrased) fugitive clauses which the Founders inserted into both the Northwest Ordinance and the US Constitution during the summer of 1787.[4]

Such is also the context necessary to understand the short, divisive history of fugitive slave laws in the United States. There were only two federal statutes, 1793 and 1850, both controversial and each which proved to be utter failures. The first law emerged out of a 1791 kidnapping case from Washington County in western Pennsylvania. Pennsylvania wanted to extradite three Virginians accused of seizing one of its free black residents, but Virginia declined to do so in the absence of a clear federal statute executing the provisions of the Constitution's fugitive clause. The result, after much debate, was a new law that authorized a general interstate extradition process, and then also provided loosely for rendition procedures that would apply to what the statute still delicately referred to as "persons escaping from the service of their masters" or "fugitives from labor."[5] Just as the Constitution had avoided the term "slavery" or "slave," so eventually did both federal fugitive "slave" laws—neither of which actually used that word.

It is fair to describe the 1793 rendition process as loose, because the brief statute (less than seven hundred words) simply authorized the "agent or attorney" of an aggrieved master to "seize and arrest" fugitives wherever he found them and to take them to "any Judge" or "any Magistrate" at federal, state, or local court, in order to obtain an unspecified "certificate" that would provide "sufficient warrant for removing the said fugitive." Moreover, anyone who knowingly harbored fugitives or intentionally obstructed the rendition process was then subject under federal law to a civil procedure that might result in up to $500 in fines, without any jail time.[6]

From the perspective of slaveholders, this was a bad law made even worse by national and international trends working against them. By the 1790s, it was clear that domestic slavery was becoming an almost entirely sectional phenomenon. Northern states had begun a process of gradual abolition, and their representatives had been fighting successfully to keep slavery out of northwestern territories. Then a series of international events such as the Haitian Revolution (1791–1804), Mexican abolition (1829), and British Empire abolition (1833) combined to stoke the sensation that southern slave states were becoming ever more isolated and vulnerable, especially to the problem of slave escapes into nearby free soil.[7] Even the dramatic expansion of slavery into the American Southwest following the introduction of the cotton gin only served to fuel this impression. Since nothing provoked runaways faster than the break-up of their families, the exploding domestic slave trade of the early nineteenth century actually encouraged more escapes.[8] Moreover, since so many of those broken families came from the slave-exporting border region, Upper South states such as Kentucky, Maryland, and Virginia were compelled to work furiously just to keep up with the runaway problem. They attempted to implement their own ever more ambitious regime of "slave-stealing" statutes.[9]

Northern states passed their own laws, too, but more as a kind of sovereign defense mechanism than as enforcement measures. The problem as they saw it was that antebellum slave-catching agents frequently ignored the niceties of people's legal status and too often ended up kidnapping free blacks (such as with the famous case of Solomon Northup from New York). Though northern states rarely demonstrated any concern for the civil rights of their antebellum black residents, these kidnapping episodes provoked a serious states' rights backlash. What resulted was the emergence of personal liberty laws, which were anti-kidnapping statutes adopted by various northern states beginning in the 1820s and which had the effect of frustrating implementation of the federal fugitive slave code.[10] Surprisingly few fugitives were successfully returned back to the South after the 1830s (at least by legal means), and hardly any northern antislavery activists ever faced even the comparatively weak civil punishments threatened by the 1793 statute.

Abolitionists capitalized on these developments during the 1830s and 1840s by publicizing the successes of what they were just then starting to call the "Underground Railroad." By the same token, almost every instance of futility associated with the federal fugitive system became an opportunity for proslavery extremists to argue angrily that southern rights were being trampled upon. That is why US senators Andrew Butler (D-SC) and James Mason (D-VA) proposed sweeping revisions to the federal fugitive rules in January 1850, and why their proposals ultimately became an essential component of the so-called Compromise of 1850. The deal which passed Congress in September included a new, much tougher fugitive slave law as part of a series of measures designed to pave the way for California's admission to the union as a free state.[11]

The 1850 fugitive slave law was the notorious one, made infamous by its harsh provisions which included a new class of federal commissioners who were to be paid more for rendering accused fugitives to the South than if they chose to acquit ($10 versus $5), the denial of any opportunity for accused fugitives to testify on their own behalf, and punishment for anyone who knowingly harbored fugitives or obstructed rendition now with up to $1,000 in fines and potential imprisonment for as long as six months. The statute also went out of its way to expose anyone who aided and abetted fugitives to even further civil damages. This was certainly the type of enforcement system white southerners had always wanted, but it turned out yet again to fall short in their reality.[12]

This frustration for white southerners often gets obscured by the heated propaganda of the sectional crisis. It has been too easy to assume over the years that laws on the books equaled realities on the ground. Yet despite its notorious reputation, the 1850 fugitive law was hardly any more effective in reigning in runaway slaves than its predecessor. During its twelve years of effective operation, the 1850 statute generated only around 350 cases, about a third of them in Pennsylvania and none in New England after 1854. The hated law provoked such an embittered reaction that some northern states, such as Wisconsin, actually tried to nullify it. The US Supreme Court, dominated by proslavery southerners such as Chief Justice Roger Taney, fought back by attempting to address the dubious constitutionality of state personal liberty laws. On two major occasions, the court ruled against these anti-kidnapping statutes—*Prigg v. Pennsylvania* (1842) and *Ableman v. Booth* (1859)—but neither ruling seemed to quell any of the state-based resistance to fugitive rendition in the North.[13]

One of the surest ways to appreciate the depth of this legal controversy is to return to old Thad Stevens and his law office. In late 1851, attorney Stevens helped organize a successful defense for more than three dozen men who had been accused of committing treason against the United States for their role in protecting four runaway slaves. The fugitives had crossed over into Lancaster County, Pennsylvania, from Baltimore County, Maryland, during the late 1840s, where they had found help from a local black self-protection society and from sympathetic white farmers in the otherwise quiet rural community.[14] On September 11, 1851, however, an armed federal posse caught up with them and a shootout ensued, known locally as the "Christiana Riot." The resistance at Christiana provoked heated national attention because the Maryland slaveholder who traveled with the federal marshals, Edward Gorsuch, was actually killed, and (at least according to southern newspapers) had his body mutilated afterward by vengeful ex-slaves. The fact that the charge was treason and not any violation of the new federal fugitive slave law only serves to demonstrate just how inflamed the situation had become by the early 1850s. The first year of the new law's operation had been thoroughly problematic. On the one hand, dozens of fugitives had been rounded up and returned to the South, though to howls of outrage from the antislavery press, but on the other hand there were also ominous examples of open, sometimes violent resistance to the federal law in places such as Boston (Shadrach Minkins) and Syracuse, New York (William Henry, a.k.a. "Jerry"). The Christiana riot was the most violent of these early confrontations over the new statute and had a profound effect on collapsing sectional relations.[15]

To begin, all of the runaways from Christiana escaped successfully, aided by a wide network of northern supporters (including Frederick Douglass, then in Rochester, New York) who helped remove the young men and several of the leading rioters to Canada. Left behind, however, were thirty-eight local men, some white but most free black residents, charged with levying war against the US government (still to this date the largest group charged with treason in American history). These accused rebels received generous support and ultimately free legal counsel paid for by the antislavery community to help with their custody and the federal trial which was held in Philadelphia in late November and early December 1851. Stevens and the other defense lawyers succeeded in making a mockery of the government's case, exposing perjury among some federal witnesses and ultimately compelling even the presiding judge (Supreme Court justice Robert Grier) to acknowledge in his charge to the jury that the high threshold for treason had not been met. The jury subsequently acquitted the first defendant (a white man named Castner Hanway) within about fifteen minutes and eventually prosecutors released the others. Nobody ever went to jail for the murder of Edward Gorsuch.[16]

Naturally, such an outcome sent shockwaves across the already agitated South. Editorial and political outrage was palpable and had far-reaching consequences in ways not always immediately apparent. An enslaved family from St. Louis, for example, discovered that their fate was almost inextricably bound up in the politics of resistance to the fugitive law even though they had never run away from anything. In 1846, Dred and Harriet Scott had sued the widow of their deceased owner in Missouri court, anxious to secure freedom for themselves and their young daughters, Eliza and Lizzie, after they had been held for years as slaves in northern territory. They won, at first, but then found their legal victory reversed on appeal to the state supreme court in *Scott v. Emerson* (1852), a decision which threw out decades of Missouri precedent for such "freedom suit" cases. The state chief justice did not invoke the Christiana episode by name in the opinion, but he was explicit about blaming what legal scholars describe as the breakdown of comity, or interstate legal relations, commenting darkly, "Times now are not as they were."[17] An even more provocative example of unintended consequences from Christiana came in the form of a bitter memory lodged in the mind of an aspiring Maryland actor who was then attending school with Edward Gorsuch's now-orphaned son, Tommy. During the Civil War, John Wilkes Booth would later recall the killing of his schoolmate's father as one of his litany of examples of northern aggression against southern honor.[18]

Yet despite all of this, the Christiana Treason Trial has been forgotten, at least in the popular memory, along with dozens of other notable fugitive slave cases. This is a crucial mistake. Beyond their obvious significance at the time, these legal battles also have the advantage for modern-day interpreters of having generated a small mountain of documentary evidence—witness statements, trial notes, newspaper accounts, and polemical pamphlets—that fully attest to the wide range of openly defiant activities undertaken by the so-called Underground Railroad. In recent years, scholars have employed evidence from these trials to remarkable effect, producing rich, engaging accounts of Christiana and many other pivotal episodes.[19] The net effect of this literature is to render the antebellum sectional battle over fugitives in more realistic terms, and to appreciate how power shifted above the Mason-Dixon Line and the Ohio River. Enslaved people and their allies were still often embattled minorities in the North, but they were by no means powerless, and the law—at least state law—was quite often on their side. Anyone who interprets historic sites that concern the resistance to slavery should be aware of these materials and should consider using them to help document the reality of the public fight against slaveholders.

The great antebellum fugitive cases also provide some fascinating glimpses into the covert side of antislavery activities. During the testimony for the Christiana Treason Trial, for instance, it was revealed that antislavery activists in Philadelphia had developed a remarkably effective spy network that allowed them to monitor the movements of federal marshals. In fact, it was a spy for the Philadelphia Vigilance Committee who had warned the four runaways holed up in Lancaster County that their master and his federal posse were coming after them, and it was that warning which made the entire resistance effort possible.[20]

Northern vigilance committees represented the organized core of the Underground Railroad. They acted essentially as self-protection societies located in various communities and populated mostly by black men, though their ranks also included a fair number of white men and women of all colors. Nineteenth-century committees of vigilance existed to combat lawlessness in American communities wherever effective municipal police force had not yet developed.[21] For free blacks, their vigilance movement emerged during the 1830s, first in New York, but then across a host of northern cities, such as Philadelphia, Boston, and Detroit, and aimed squarely at defeating the kidnapping rings that were harassing members of their community.[22] Yet from the beginning, these vigilance committees also helped runaway slaves, never hesitating to presume that anybody they helped was either born free—or meant to be free.

The story of the Philadelphia Vigilance Committee offers a good example of how antebellum vigilance networks operated. The mixed-race group had a variety of names and iterations in the period between 1837 and 1861, but was led primarily by either Robert Purvis, a prominent mixed-race businessman, or William Still, a hardworking free black clerk born in New Jersey. For most of its existence, the committee operated as a kind of adjunct to the Pennsylvania Anti-Slavery Society, a largely white-led abolitionist group that formed during the mid-1830s as part of William Lloyd Garrison's movement for immediate agitation against slavery. Abolitionists found especially fertile recruiting ground around Philadelphia because of the concentration of both free blacks (the nation's second largest urban black population after Baltimore) and some especially feisty antislavery Quakers. Philadelphia vigilance activists maintained regular communication with other committees across several northern cities and with supporters in both Canada and Great Britain. The group also had secret contacts in slave territory, particularly throughout Delaware, District of Columbia, Maryland, and Virginia. Thus, despite having a full-fledged organization, complete with officers, publicity agents, fundraisers, and various attorneys on retainer, the vigilance committee also served as the covert hub for the mid-Atlantic network that provided aid to escaping slaves.[23]

All of their "underground" activity can be easily documented, however, because the Philadelphia Vigilance Committee kept careful records. Today, these once top-secret escape journals, which typically detail the names of fugitives and agents, experiences of ex-slaves, routes used for escapes, and even the associated costs, are now fully accessible online. Anyone who wants can view operational letters, whether directing the transport of "four large and two small hams" (tongue-in-cheek code for four adults and two children) or requesting reimbursement for replacing worn-out shoes that had been provided to none other than Harriet Tubman.[24] Nor do such records exist just for Philadelphia and its environs. Massachusetts high school students have helped digitize expense records and other documents from the Boston Vigilance Committee. Antislavery editor Sidney Howard Gay kept a detailed journal for his vigilance activities in New York, the subject of an important new monograph from historian Eric Foner. Antislavery newspapers, now digitized from what Frederick Douglass called "our western friends" (meaning abolitionists in places such as Michigan and Ohio), contain periodic but quite specific tallies of fugitive traffic passing through their committees.[25]

There were certainly northern individuals and families who kept their involvement in the resistance movement secret and who deliberately avoided keeping records or joining formal committees—but they were probably in the minority. This is such an essential and widely misunderstood point that it deserves particular scrutiny. Northern defiance of slaveholders was never popular or easy, but it was usually open. Even those who aggressively broke federal law did so with an impunity that seems to have been lost in modern translation. There does not appear to have been a single northern Underground Railroad operative who was killed while helping slaves escape—at least not if he or she remained in the North. No major vigilance leaders spent any significant time in prison, and hardly any ever faced serious legal jeopardy. There were a few passing exceptions, occasional arrests, and sporadic attacks, but they only serve as a reminder that the northern rule was a near total absence of effective punishment for anyone aiding and abetting runaway slaves.

The contrast in the South could not have been greater. Anyone who got caught helping slaves escape below the Mason-Dixon Line could expect the harshest form of legal or extralegal retribution. In 1844, a territorial court in Florida ordered one defendant, a brave but hapless ship captain who had transported some fugitives once, to have his hand branded "SS," for slave stealer. One captured underground operative in Kentucky spent literally decades of his life in prison. The famous story of Henry "Box" Brown perhaps best illustrates the stark dichotomy between northern and southern punishments. Brown was a Virginia slave whose friends literally shipped him in a box from Richmond to Philadelphia in March 1849, under the auspices of the Philadelphia Vigilance Committee. Brown survived the journey, and his escape quickly created a national sensation. Yet neither James McKim, head of the Pennsylvania Anti-Slavery Society (where the box was delivered), nor William Still, the organizer, received any punishment for their role in the affair. The only officials who came after them were representatives of the Adams Express Company who sternly warned against attempting any more such shipping adventures. Sadly, however, one of the men who had helped crate Brown up in Richmond was caught, convicted, and ultimately forced to serve nearly seven years in the Virginia state penitentiary.[26]

Scholars of the Underground Railroad have been working diligently to recapture the nuances of these regional differences. Some of the best recent work in the field has involved what might be considered microhistory of particular antislavery communities. We now have rich studies of fugitive aid networks in places such as New Bedford, Massachusetts;

Oberlin, Ohio; Ripley, Ohio; southcentral Pennsylvania; Washington, D.C.; and several others.[27] Taken together, they help create a national tapestry that situates the Underground Railroad more completely than ever before in the story of rapidly changing nineteenth-century American life. The new work enables modern-day students to appreciate the variety of institutions which contributed to the underground movement—not only churches and antislavery societies, but also barbershops, factories, (real) railroads, shipping companies, newspapers, and even the telegraph. The term "Underground Railroad" was a metaphor from the great market, transportation, and communications revolutions of the early nineteenth century. We need to remember and interpret it in that context, too.

We also need to do better in situating the Underground Railroad within the story of the Civil War. The fugitive crisis of the 1850s was just as relevant to the coming of the war as the territorial crisis, and yet it occupies a lesser role in standard accounts of the antebellum period. The rendition of Anthony Burns, the last fugitive returned from New England before the Civil War, occurred during the same week in May 1854 as the final passage of the Kansas-Nebraska Act. Both events received overwhelming coverage in the newspapers of the day. Yet American history textbooks and state history standards are far more inclined to omit the rendition of Burns and the violent reaction by the Boston Vigilance Committee (they killed a federal marshal) than the presidential ambitions of Stephen Douglas or the explosive controversies over "Bleeding Kansas." When southern states issued resolutions justifying their decisions to leave the Union in 1860 and 1861, they were just as likely to invoke violations of the fugitive slave law as any other single factor.[28]

Almost every major slavery-related controversy from the period had a direct connection to the fugitive problem. John Brown, for example, was an Underground Railroad operative who went out to the Kansas Territory during the mid-1850s. He had labeled his vigilance effort in western Massachusetts the "League of Gileadites," but in Kansas, he simply called his men an army. Yet his violence in both Kansas and at Harpers Ferry owed more to the vigilance community than most modern students realize. Brown recruited both men and money from vigilance operatives in the North. They helped supply and support him during his final years as an antislavery terrorist. Then after his execution, it was William Still who hosted Mary Brown at his home in Philadelphia and James McKim who helped her gather the body from Virginia and return it for burial in New York. Later during the Civil War, vigilance committee veterans such as Still, Harriet Tubman, and Thomas Wentworth Higginson helped organize and lead black recruits for the Union army. Others, such as McKim, helped educate wartime runaways, known as "contrabands" through various relief associations. Underground Railroad operatives quite literally contributed to the destruction of American slavery at every stage of the process.[29]

These interpretive admonitions should not be hard to accept for anyone who works at Underground Railroad sites or simply cares about African American historical preservation. The idea of connecting the story to a wider context is just common sense. Physical locations always serve to underscore the importance of place and geography in the understanding of history. Anyone with site experience knows that it is impossible to successfully interpret a historic structure without considering its wide-ranging social, economic, and political connections to specific communities and eras. Yet the allure of Underground Railroad mythology has been so powerful over the years that too much of this context has been washed away in the spirit of celebrating heroic individual actions. During the first generations of post–Civil War memory those heroes were often white, usually Quaker, and invariably acting in the shadow of recollected, grave antebellum dangers. Beginning with scholar Larry Gara's groundbreaking revisionist study, *The Liberty Line* (1961), however, modern interpreters have been more inclined to focus on the heroism of the fugitives or freedom seekers themselves and to downplay the role of the northern abolitionist network. Thus, by the late 1990s, an important scholarly work such as *Runaway Slaves* (1999) by John Hope Franklin and Loren Schweninger could dismiss the Underground Railroad as "shrouded in myth and legend," devoting only two index entries to the topic within an otherwise comprehensive monograph.[30]

It was probably no coincidence that the same year in which Franklin and Schweninger passed judgment on the sad state of Underground Railroad scholarship, Oprah Winfrey was able to popularize a book about quilt codes that historian David Blight eventually blasted as "a myth, bordering on a hoax."[31] When scholars ignore important subjects, other interpreters occupy the void. The book, *Hidden in Plain View* (1999), purported to explain through the oral tradition of one African American family from North Carolina how coded squares sewn into slave quilts were used to convey information about secret escape routes.[32] Over the years, especially since the mid-twentieth century, there have been many such loose claims about codes embedded within songs, quilts, or rural customs, but trained historical researchers have never been able to find corroborating evidence for this folklore. Instead, quite often, as in the case of Oprah's quilt story, they can find signs of profiteering at work. Oprah certainly had no intention of perpetuating a hoax, but that was arguably the result.

By the same token, three years later when preservationists in Lancaster County invoked the discovery of a mysterious cistern to justify halting plans for a massive convention center project, they were not intending to misrepresent history. They thought, as many did (and still do), that Underground Railroad operatives in the North existed almost totally in secret, relying on a hidden network of "safe houses" and secret passageways to protect themselves and the people they aided from persecution by the tyrannical power of slaveholders. Folks in Lancaster might well have been correct about the cistern, but they did not understand or even imagine the open defiance of the "upper-ground railroad" that existed in antebellum America, and which is only now becoming more apparent to scholars. It is imperative, however, that anyone who aspires to shape the public understanding of how slavery in America got destroyed considers this new scholarship, and attempts to challenge some of the more popular myths about this vital struggle.

Of course, scholars make mistakes, too, and almost never fully agree with each other regardless. There will always be more to discover about such complicated and elusive subjects. Thankfully, there has been a concerted effort in recent years to promote both greater preservation and more sophisticated interpretation of the Underground Railroad. In 1998, Congress adopted the National Underground Railroad Network to Freedom Act, which has so far generated documentation for hundreds of sites, facilities, and programs associated with the general effort to help runaway slaves. Each year, the National Park Service also now convenes an impressive scholarly conference on the Underground Railroad.[33] Many states have commissioned studies and engaged in their own renewed preservation efforts. Individuals have helped, too. In 2004, Oprah Winfrey donated one million dollars to help launch a National Underground Railroad Freedom Center in Cincinnati, and while the museum has sometimes struggled in a tough economic climate, it is still standing.[34]

So, too, is the new Stevens-Smith Historic Site in Lancaster, despite being literally wedged inside the hotel and convention center complex. It turns out that the compromise which preservationists and developers forged in 2002 was unusual. They agreed to preserve only the façade of the Stevens law office as part of the actual convention center, and then planned to make an interpretive museum somewhere inside that would feature the cistern and the story of Stevens and his longtime mixed-race housekeeper (and perhaps soul mate), Lydia Hamilton Smith. That was the plan anyway. The façade has since been restored and the convention center is open, but there is no museum. Local preservationists now admit they will not even be able to begin fundraising for such an ambitious venture until 2020.[35] For now, the public can peer at the cistern through a glass window in the lobby. Or determined tourists of the Underground Railroad can drive about thirty minutes away through the winding rural roads of southern Lancaster County to encounter a state historical marker on what is now an Amish farm. The blue-and-gold sign indicates the nearby location of the once-notorious Christiana riot. It is not enough, surely, but at least, after so many decades of myth-making, it is all finally above ground.

Notes

1. For detailed analysis of the convention center showdown in Lancaster, featuring the contributions of the archaeologists, see Fergus M. Bordewich, "Digging into a Historic Rivalry," *Smithsonian Magazine* (February 2004), http://www.smithsonianmag.com/history/digging-into-a-historic-rivalry-106194163/?all, and Kelly M. Britt, "Archaeology—The 'Missing Link' to Civic Engagement? An Introspective Look at the Tools of Reinvention and Reengagement in Lancaster, Pennsylvania," in *Archaeology as a Tool of Civic Engagement*, edited by Barbara J. Little and Paul A. Shackel (Lanham, MD: AltaMira Press, 2007), 151–72. The actual report from the archaeologists can be found online via the Digital Commons at Buffalo State; see James A. Delle and Mary Ann Levine, "Excavations at the Thaddeus Stevens and Lydia Hamilton Smith Site, Lancaster, Pennsylvania: Archaeological Evidence for the Underground Railroad," *Northeast Historical Archaeology* 33 (2004), http://digitalcommons.buffalostate.edu/neha/vol33/iss1/10/.
2. This chapter will detail numerous examples of the emerging scholarship, but the best overview of the topic probably comes from a collection of essays edited by David W. Blight, *Passages to Freedom: The Underground Railroad in History and Memory* (Washington, D.C.: Smithsonian, 2004).
3. See the classic study by Marion Gleason McDougall, *Fugitive Slaves, 1619–1865* (Boston: Ginn, 1891), http://www.gutenberg.org/files/34594/34594-h/34594-h.htm.
4. Northwest Ordinance (1787), Article VI: "There shall be neither slavery nor involuntary servitude in the said territory, otherwise than in the punishment of crimes whereof the party shall have been duly convicted: Provided, always, That any person escaping into the same, from whom labor or service is lawfully claimed in any one of the original States, such fugitive may be lawfully reclaimed and conveyed to the person claiming his or her labor or service as aforesaid." US Constitution (1787), Article IV, Section 2: "No Person held to Service or Labour in

one State, under the Laws thereof, escaping into another, shall, in Consequence of any Law or Regulation therein, be discharged from such Service or Labour, but shall be delivered up on Claim of the Party to whom such Service or Labour may be due."

5. See chapter 4 in Paul Finkelman, *Slavery and the Founders: Race and Liberty in the Age of Jefferson*, 2nd ed. (Armonk, NY: M. E. Sharpe, 2001), 81–104.

6. See full text of the 1793 statute under Acts of Congress, February 12, 1793, from Annals of Congress, 2d Congress, 2d Session; *A Century of Lawmaking,* American Memory Project, Library of Congress, http://memory.loc.gov/cgi-bin/ampage?collId=llac&fileName=003/llac003.db&recNum=702.

7. Numerous works describe the unfolding of emancipation in the Atlantic world and its impact on the southern slaveholding worldview. One of the best recent summaries comes from David Brion Davis, *Inhuman Bondage: The Rise and Fall of Slavery in the New World* (New York: Oxford University Press, 2006).

8. Scholars now estimate more than two million domestic slave transactions in the decades before the Civil War. See Walter Johnson, *Soul By Soul: Life Inside the Antebellum Slave Market* (Cambridge, MA: Harvard University Press, 1999), 17.

9. According to editors from the Maryland State Archives, that state for one "continually adjusted its laws concerning fugitives." See a useful summary of those changes across the eighteenth and nineteenth centuries at "Legacy of Slavery in Maryland: An Archives of Maryland Electronic Publication," http://slavery.msa.maryland.gov/html/antebellum/histlaw.html.

10. Thomas D. Morris, *Free Men All: Personal Liberty Laws of the North, 1780–1861* (orig. pub. 1974; Union, NJ: Lawbook Exchange, 2001). See also Carol Wilson, *Freedom at Risk: The Kidnapping of Free Blacks in America, 1780–1865* (Lexington: University Press of Kentucky, 1994).

11. See Fergus M. Bordewich, *America's Great Debate: Henry Clay, Stephen A. Douglas, and the Compromise That Preserved the Union* (New York: Simon & Schuster, 2012), 126–27.

12. See full text of the 1850 statute, passed on September 18, 1850, at The Avalon Project, Yale Law School, http://avalon.law.yale.edu/19th_century/fugitive.asp.

13. Though he reaches somewhat different conclusions about how to interpret these facts, see Stanley W. Campbell, *The Slave Catchers: Enforcement of the Fugitive Slave Law: 1850–1860* (New York: W. W. Norton, 1970) for statistical details. Congress did not officially repeal the Fugitive Slave Law until June 28, 1864, but its enforcement was almost nonexistent from the second year of the Civil War.

14. There are some conflicting accounts about the exact number and identities of the runaways from Gorsuch's plantation, but according to the most reliable accounts, there were four young men, all in their mid-twenties: Noah Buley, Nelson Ford, George Hammond, and Joshua Hammond.

15. The best scholarly account of Christiana comes from Thomas P. Slaughter, *Bloody Dawn: The Christiana Riot and Racial Violence in the Antebellum North* (New York: Oxford University Press, 1991). For a good description of the national aftermath of the 1850 fugitive law, see Fergus M. Bordewich, *Bound for Canaan: The Underground Railroad and the War for the Soul of America* (New York: Amistad, 2005). It's worth noting that in later paperback editions of this well-written survey, the publisher altered the subtitle to read: "The Epic Story of the Underground Railroad, America's First Civil Rights Movement."

16. For the full text of the Christiana Treason Trial, see James J. Robbins, *Report of the Trial of Castner Hanway for Treason* (Philadelphia: King and Baird, 1852), http://deila.dickinson.edu/slaveryandabolition/title/0120.html.

17. For a useful summary of the Dred and Harriet Scott case in the Missouri courts, see "Missouri's Dred Scott Case, 1847–1857," Missouri State Archives, http://www.sos.mo.gov/archives/resources/africanamerican/scott/scott.asp. For a fascinating new biography of Harriet Robinson Scott full of insights about slavery and the law, see Lea VanderVelde, *Mrs. Dred Scott: A Life on Slavery's Frontier* (New York: Oxford University Press, 2009).

18. Booth mentioned the killing of Gorsuch in his recently rediscovered draft speech manuscript prepared in Philadelphia in December 1860. See John Rhodehamal and Louise Taper, eds., *"Right or Wrong, God Judge Me": The Writings of John Wilkes Booth* (Urbana: University of Illinois Press, 1997), 55–69.

19. See Slaughter, *Bloody Dawn* (1991) as well as some of the following superb monographs (by publication date): Gary Collison, *Shadrach Minkins: From Fugitive Slave to Citizen* (Cambridge, MA: Harvard University Press, 1997); Albert J. Von Frank, *The Trials of Anthony Burns: Freedom and Slavery in Emerson's Boston* (Cambridge, MA: Harvard University Press, 1998); H. Robert Baker, *The Rescue of Joshua Glover: A Fugitive Slave, the Constitution, and the Coming of the Civil War* (Athens: Ohio University Press, 2006); Mary Kay Ricks, *Escape on the Pearl: The Heroic Bid for Freedom on the Underground Railroad* (New York: William Morrow, 2007); Steven Lubet, *Fugitive Justice: Runaways, Rescuers, and Slavery on Trial* (Cambridge, MA: Harvard University Press, 2010).

20. Slaughter, *Bloody Dawn*, 126.

21. For a good discussion of "vigilance" as a nineteenth-century concept, see Richard Maxwell Brown, *Strain of Violence: Strain of American Violence and Vigilantism* (New York: Oxford University Press, 1975), 114–18.

22. There are very few good studies of the northern vigilance committees and their leaders, but there is finally a first-rate biography of David Ruggles, the movement's founder. See Graham Russell Gao Hodges, *David Ruggles: A Radical Black Abolitionist and the Underground Railroad in New York City* (Chapel Hill: University of North Carolina Press, 2010). Other notable vigilance leaders, such as Robert Purvis and William Still (Philadelphia), George DeBaptiste (Detroit), and Lewis Hayden (Boston), currently lack serious adult biographies. There is, however, a wonderful resource for primary sources related to the movement from C. Peter Ripley, ed., *The Black Abolitionist Papers: Vol. IV, The United States, 1847–1858* (Chapel Hill: University of North Carolina Press, 1991). All five volumes of the *The Black Abolitionist Papers* are also now available in full-text searchable database format via ProQuest.

23. For general background, see articles by Joseph A. Borome, "The Vigilant Committee of Philadelphia," *Pennsylvania Magazine of History and Biography* 42 (1968): 320–52, and Larry Gara, "William Still and the Underground Railroad," *Pennsylvania History* 28 (1961): 33–44, http://ojs.libraries.psu.edu/index.php/phj/article/view/22779/22548. For a compelling first-person account, see William Still, *The Underground Railroad* (Philadelphia: Porter & Coates, 1872), http://deila.dickinson.edu/slaveryandabolition/title/0088.html.

24. See a good searchable full text of Still's memoir at "Slavery and Abolition in the US," Dickinson College Archives, http://deila.dickinson.edu/slaveryandabolition/title/0088.html. To view the actual page images of the vigilance journal, visit the Historical Society of Pennsylvania, http://hsp.org/history-online/digital-history-projects/pennsylvania-abolition-society-papers/journal-c-of-station-no-2-william-still-1852-1857-0. To view directly the letter concerning the "four hams" and Harriet Tubman's worn-out shoes, go to the Underground Railroad Digital Classroom, http://housedivided.dickinson.edu/ugrr/letter_may1856.htm and http://housedivided.dickinson.edu/ugrr/letter_dec1854.htm.

25. For the Boston Vigilance Committee, see Account Book of Francis Jackson, PrimaryResearch. Org, http://primaryresearch.org/account-book-of-francis-jackson. Eric Foner's forthcoming study of the Underground Railroad in New York is tentatively entitled *Gateway to Freedom* (W. W. Norton, in press). Various antislavery newspapers have been digitized and are currently available behind subscription paywalls, but increasingly students can also find freely available examples through the wonderful "Chronicling of America" project by the Library of Congress: http://chroniclingamerica.loc.gov, or also from the research engine at the House Divided Project at Dickinson College, http://hd.housedivided.dickinson.edu/node/9588.

26. Jonathan Walker was the ship captain who received "The Branded Hand" in Florida (later immortalized by a John Greenleaf Whittier poem and a striking 1845 daguerreotype; see Massachusetts Historical Society, http://www.masshist.org/database/viewer.php?item _id=154&pid=15). Calvin Fairbank was a Methodist minister from New York who was arrested twice in Kentucky for aiding runaway slaves, ultimately serving over seventeen years in prison; see Randolph Paul Runyon, *Delia Webster and the Underground Railroad* (Lexington: University Press of Kentucky, 1996). The finest account of Henry "Box" Brown (and the fate of Samuel A. Smith, his friend who was arrested in Richmond), comes from Jeffrey Ruggles, *The Unboxing of Henry Brown* (Richmond: Library of Virginia, 2003).

27. New Bedford, MA: Kathryn Grover, *The Fugitive's Gibraltar: Escaping Slaves and Abolitionism in New Bedford, Massachusetts* (Amherst: University of Massachusetts Press, 2001). Ripley, OH: Ann Hagedorn, *Beyond the River: The Untold Story of the Underground Railroad* (New York: Simon & Schuster, 2002). Southcentral PA: David G. Smith, *On the Edge of Freedom: The Fugitive Slave Issue in South Central Pennsylvania, 1820–1870* (New York: Fordham University Press, 2013). Oberlin, OH: Nat Brandt, *The Town That Started the Civil War* (New York: Dell, 1990). Washington, D.C.: Stanley Harrold, *Subversives: Antislavery Community in Washington, DC, 1828–1865* (Baton Rouge: Louisiana State University, 2003).

28. Stanley Harrold helps detail the case for integrating the fugitive crisis within the coming of war story in *Border War: Fighting over Slavery before the Civil War* (Chapel Hill: University of North Carolina Press, 2010). To view the secession documents directly and to see the emphasis on violations of the fugitive law, go to "Declarations of Secession," The Avalon Project from Yale Law School (http://avalon.law.yale.edu/subject_menus/csapage.asp).

29. The best recent biography of John Brown does a good job of detailing his vigilance connections. See David S. Reynolds, *John Brown: Abolitionist* (New York: Alfred A. Knopf, 2005). For an insightful depiction of how the "contraband" issue both preceded and helped lead to emancipation and ultimately abolition, see James Oakes, *Freedom National: The Destruction of Slavery in the United States, 1861–1865* (New York: W. W. Norton, 2013). Useful online resources for these topics also include the Emancipation Digital Classroom, http:// housedivided.dickinson.edu/sites/emancipation and Visualizing Emancipation, http://dsl .richmond.edu/emancipation.

30. A good example of the early "pro-Quaker" historiography comes from Wilbur H. Siebert, *The Underground Railroad: From Slavery to Freedom* (New York: Macmillan, 1898), http://deila. dickinson.edu/slaveryandabolition/title/0090.html. Larry Gara's groundbreaking study was originally published in 1961 but has since been reissued in paperback: *The Liberty Line: The Legend of the Underground Railroad* (Lexington: University Press of Kentucky, 1996). John Hope Franklin and Loren Schweninger, *Runaway Slaves: Rebels on the Plantation* (New York: Oxford University Press, 1999), 336n.

31. David Blight quoted in Noam Cohen, "In Douglass Tribute, Slave Folklore and Fact Collide," *New York Times*, January 24, 2007, http://www.nytimes.com/learning/teachers/featured_articles/20070124wednesday.html.

32. Jacqueline L. Tobin and Raymond G. Dobard, *Hidden in Plain View: The Secret Story of Quilts and the Underground Railroad* (New York: Doubleday, 1999).

33. See National Underground Railroad Network to Freedom homepage, http://www.nps.gov/subjects/ugrr/index.htm.

34. For some examples of recent state context studies freely available online, see Matthew Pinsker, "Vigilance in Pennsylvania: Underground Railroad Activities in the Keystone State, 1837–1861," http://www.phmc.state.pa.us/Portal/Communities/PublicHistoryPrograms/AfricanAmerican/UGRRContextStudyPinsker.pdf or Raymond Paul Zirblis, "Friends of Freedom: The Vermont Underground Railroad Survey Report," http://www.vermontcivilwar150.com/imgs/history/FriendsofFreedomcopy.pdf. William A. Weathers, "Oprah Gives Freedom Center $1M," *Cincinnati Enquirer*, July 9, 2004, http://www.enquirer.com/editions/2004/07/09/loc_artbrf.09.html.

35. Jack Brubaker, "Restoration on Hold at Stevens Home," Lancaster Online, September 12, 2013, http://lancasteronline.com/news/restoration-on-hold-at-stevens-home/article_0e73b634-7258-535c-95a1-5b0bdb38a929.html.

CHAPTER 9

Churches as Places of History

The Case of Nineteenth-Century Charleston, South Carolina

BERNARD E. POWERS JR.

EVEN THE most casual stroll through the streets of peninsular Charleston reveals history's palpable impact on the shape of life in the contemporary city. South Carolina's oldest urban place, Charleston, has been known as the "Holy City" because of the many church steeples that still dominate the cityscape. More than mere architectural features, in critical ways Charleston's religious institutions map its social, political, and cultural complexity. As a British settlement, the Anglicans constructed St. Philip's in 1683, but within three years French Huguenot immigrants established their church. In 1749 Beth Elohim Synagogue was established by the growing Jewish population, and in the late eighteenth century, Methodism arrived with the construction of Cumberland Street Church in 1786. As the nineteenth century unfolded, Charleston's first Catholic cathedral, St. John the Baptist and St. Finbar, opened in 1854, and St. Matthew's German Lutheran Church was completed in 1872.[1] Each of these important institutions and the populations they represent contributed to the emerging social mosaic of the state's largest nineteenth-century city. Africans and their descendants comprised an important part of that mosaic also; they constituted the majority population until the twentieth century, and their presence shaped and challenged the city in significant ways.

For African Americans, just as for other groups, the church was a fundamental institution. In fact, given the strictures that governed black life, the role it played was even more critical in shaping their unique history. The church and religiosity offer the most significant means for understanding the nineteenth-century experience of black Charlestonians. In many important ways in both slavery and freedom, the church experience, while vital unto itself, also laid the groundwork for advancement in secular areas of life. This way of thinking about the African American experience is not limited to the nineteenth-century South, though. Some of the same issues or variations of them and modes of investigation can also be used to explore the experiences of African Americans in other locations and times.

In the colonial era and particularly before the Great Awakening of the eighteenth century, slaveholders often had reservations about exposing their slaves to religious teaching. For some there was a lingering fear that religious conversion might require emancipation, others believed that religion would make their workforce lazy, and finally, some simply dismissed the notion that slaves could understand Christian precepts in any meaningful way.[2] However, by the 1830s, in response to abolitionists' criticism and in conjunction with the proslavery argument, attitudes toward promoting religion among the slaves changed dramatically. Now increasingly religion was seen as a means to create a more docile, pliant, and productive labor force; the southern mission to the slaves was the outgrowth of this new receptivity to Christianity. The Methodists were leaders in the new plantation missions, but the Baptists, Presbyterians, and even Episcopalians all expanded their efforts among the slaves.[3] Slaves in urban locations like Charleston already had unusual exposure to churches, and the new dispensation ensured access to an even higher level of religious activity.

There are several reasons why the study of the church is essential for any examination of antebellum African American life. During the era of slavery, Protestant churches served as the major vehicle for promoting acculturation among the African and African American populations. Through participation in Christian worship services the enslaved population acquired aspects of Anglo-American secular culture such as language, family values, and clothing styles.[4] With regard to religious values though, there is an important caveat. While it is clear that over time Africans and their descendants increasingly became Christians (especially in cities), they did not simply imbibe the brand of faith and teachings their owners promoted. Certainly their faith rejected what Frederick Douglass once characterized as "slaveholding religion," by which he meant the use of religion to justify the crime of slavery. Also, Charleston's slaves and free blacks practiced a Christianity that differed from that of their owners. As African people they infused Christianity with the spiritual values and beliefs that derived from their own religious heritage. The end product can be best described as Afro-Christianity, which was an amalgam of traditional Christian tenets, combined with African-derived beliefs and practices. As just a few examples, Black Carolinians generally retained strong beliefs about the connection between metaphysical and corporeal worlds, the ability to communicate with spirits, spiritual possession, and worship through a dance-like ritual known as the ring shout.[5] The elements of Afro-Christianity varied regionally and over time; they were most prevalent in the countryside but were also prominently displayed in cities. It is important for historic sites to explore the often distinctive character of African American religiosity in order to explain the complexities of acculturation and social change.

The institutional role of the church provided additional structure around which black Charlestonians organized their lives. During this time the church was widely accepted as the community's chief moral arbiter, and when conflicts arose between members or when a member was suspected of untoward behavior, such cases could lead to a church investigation and even a trial. Church minute books and registers which are organized chronologically are the usual sources for this kind of information. They identify church leaders and religious or moral issues under discussion, and sometimes they contain the proceedings of church trials and the resolution of special requests brought by members. For example, when the slave Perry Peak, formerly of Alabama, was sold to Charleston, he came before the Committee on the Colored Members at First Baptist Church to request permission to marry. He had a "wife" in Alabama and thus his request, because "there was no probability of his ever going back, or her coming here." By obtaining church approval, members could avoid the serious charges of immorality. One black woman would have undoubtedly profited from following this lesson. When her husband deserted her, she simply found another one, but she was subsequently brought up on morals charges. The church report described her infraction as "serious" and continued, "If she had come to the church with a statement of her wrongs before entering upon a second marriage she might have received such advise [sic] as would have prevented the necessity of excluding her from its fellowship." The ultimate disposition of this case is unclear, but the gravity of such matters is borne out by the slave Diana's situation. In 1829 she applied to be received into membership at Circular Congregational Church "after 4 years exclusion for adultery."[6]

The church was also an important forum for cultivating black leadership skills. In 1822 Charleston's Methodist churches were divided into seventy racially segregated classes, and the black members had their own black class leaders. These leaders were both slave and free, and there were cases of slaves serving as leaders for free blacks. The black class leader was essentially a liaison between the membership, the white lay officials, and the minister. They had responsibility for regularly maintaining contact with their members and particularly for overseeing their spiritual and material conditions. At First Baptist Church, black leaders also served as intermediaries between the rank-and-file membership and the church's official Committee on Colored Members.[7] African Americans generally gravitated to the Baptist or Methodist churches, and undoubtedly one of the main reasons for this was that those denominations afforded black men an opportunity to exercise authority as leaders.[8]

The church also provided an opportunity for slaves to acquire literacy, and this will be surprising, given what so many already know about slavery. The South Carolina slave code of 1740 prohibited slaves from learning to write but placed no restrictions on reading. While most slaves were illiterate, it would not have been unusual to find some who were otherwise, particularly in the early nineteenth century. When examining the spiritual condition of black probationary members of the Circular Congregational Church, Reverend Benjamin Palmer commented on how well candidates knew the catechism but also on their literacy status. There were a number, like the slave Susannah, who was described as "learning to read," or the more advanced Tenah who already "reads."[9] However the rise of the abolitionist movement, the threat of slave rebellion at home, and the actual Nat Turner slave rebellion soon led to a policy change. In 1834 the state legislature placed new restrictions on African American literacy. Beginning in 1835 the law prohibited anyone from teaching a slave to read or to write, but also now, for the first time, made it illegal for free blacks to teach one another reading or writing.[10] The new provisions meant that free blacks like Catherine McNeal, who reportedly had kept a "school in Geo. Matthew's yard," were now prohibited from doing so.[11]

In addition to their command of literacy, church records provide other data that can assist the historian to construct a biography of an individual. The antebellum congregations generally contained both slaves and free blacks. So John Hall was a free black who attended the Circular Church, but he was originally a Methodist. He was married, but his wife attended St. Philip's Episcopal Church. In another case, Rebecca Burk was married to John Cotonnot, a free person of color. Her father, Adam, purchased his own freedom, Rebecca's freedom, and that of another daughter. Sometimes the level of information provided affords an unusually intimate and personal view of the historical subjects. For example, Circular Church records reveal why probationary members decided to lead more godly lives and seek to join the church. Some individuals simply had undefined "trouble" in their lives and sought divine comfort and the succor of the church. In other cases the record is specific. Violet's source of "trouble" was that she was "sold in Virginia from her relatives and brought to this city." In Rhina's case the catalyst was "her master's death." Sometimes it may have been seeing the error of one's ways that drove the desire to reconnect to the church. That seems to have been the case with Rose, who, according to church reports, "evidences reformation from frolicking, and melioration of temper."[12] Regardless of the reason, church affiliation filled a vital need for Charleston's African American population. In important ways church records can chronicle both the secular and sacred aspects of African American life, and museum professionals who consult them will find information that allows for a more complete portrayal of individuals and communities.

The institutional church could also be the means through which dissent and resistance were displayed; Charleston witnessed the display of both in the early nineteenth century. When Charleston's white church officials decided it was necessary to more intrusively regulate the affairs of black Methodists, those members, led by the free black Rev. Morris Brown, staged a mass exodus from the denomination in 1817. Then the following year they established a branch of the African Methodist Episcopal Church (AME). These acts were remarkable for their audacity because in a single stroke, black Methodists cast off white authority and then affiliated with a northern abolitionist denomination, controlled by free blacks in Philadelphia, and all this in the heart of the slaveholding South![13] Not surprisingly, black Charlestonians could never win approval from authorities to maintain this church, and in fact, on several occasions its members and leaders were harassed and even arrested for holding unauthorized meetings in violation of the slave code. It was harassment of the church that contributed to an even more radical response by some of the church's members and leaders.[14]

In 1822, the Denmark Vesey slave conspiracy was discovered in Charleston. Vesey was a free black who had formerly been enslaved, a carpenter by training, and a leader in Charleston's African Church, as the AME church was locally known. He organized a group of slaves, several of whom were African Church members, in a plan to rebel by arming themselves, setting fires around the city, and then helping as many as possible to escape the United States to Haiti. In encouraging his supporters and attempting to persuade others to participate, Vesey is alleged to have used the Bible as a justification.[15] This conspiracy never matured into a rebellion because informants alerted the authorities, who arrested Denmark Vesey, other chief conspirators, and anyone suspected of participation. After a series of trials, thirty-five men were hanged including Denmark Vesey, and thirty-seven were sentenced to transportation outside of the country. Municipal authorities used the Vesey conspiracy as the pretext to destroy the African Church in fall 1822, and that same year the state legislature began enacting a series of laws to repress the black population. Now free black men would be required to have white guardians to vouch for their good character, and when out-of-state ships visited the port, any free blacks or "persons of color" on the crew would have to be confined in jail until the ship departed. The state also began to fortify an area in the upper part of the city where in 1841 the South Carolina Military Academy was located.[16]

The official trial records of the Vesey conspirators are among the most important documents to grow out of the conspiracy. Obviously such a record, created for the purpose of marshalling evidence against the accused, has to be used with great caution. However, as a source of information for exploring the city's black community, it is vital. As the country's major center for the Atlantic slave trade, Charleston's black population contained a significant African population but also highly acculturated free blacks and those at various stages of acculturation between these two extremes. In fact, Gullah Jack, one of the conspiratorial leaders, was an African conjurer whose metaphysical power was both respected and feared in Charleston. Conversely, though, the record shows the important role that biblical scriptures played in galvanizing support. Many of those who comprised the nucleus of the conspiracy were privileged slaves and skilled artisans who frequently hired their time out to others. In a major port city, these men were also privy to information about the larger world, and so it is not surprising that Haiti, where Vesey had once lived, figured significantly in the planning.[17] Even though Vesey's plot remained an unrealized conspiracy, it cast a long shadow over the city, which helped fuel apprehensions that eventuated in the American Civil War.

The four-year-long conflict that threatened to rend the nation asunder and the era of Reconstruction which followed ushered in the most creative and challenging period in the history of African American churches. Just as blacks were physically liberated by the Emancipation Proclamation and the Thirteenth Amendment, they transformed their lives in other important and unprecedented ways. Historians now more than ever before appreciate emancipation as a process that unfolded over time rather than an event occurring at one specific point in time.[18] For sure the end of bondage meant that the people were no longer slaves, but that's all it meant with certainty. Now the freedmen had to take positive initiatives to make the otherwise abstract concept of freedom mean something; through action they had to give freedom concrete form and substance. Once invested with citizenship, the men entered the body politic and expanded their rights through voting and holding office. While they played a role in repairing the nation's fractured political and legal bonds, African Americans conceived of new opportunities on other fronts. They dramatically transformed their spiritual lives by deserting their former churches and sometimes even joining new denominations. In the Baptist church these initiatives were based solely on local decisions, but the more hierarchically organized denominations such as the Northern Methodists, African Methodists, and Northern Presbyterians dispatched missionaries to encourage and assist the freedmen to change denominations.

The way the process unfolded in the African Methodist Church was particularly compelling and significant for South Carolina. In the spring of 1863, this church was the first black denomination to dispatch missionaries to the state following the advance of the Union army. When they landed at Hilton Head and began their work ministering to the freedmen, these men became the first AME ministers in the state since closure of the African Church in Charleston in 1822.[19] Charleston finally fell to Union forces in February 1865, and three months later, several additional AME missionaries converged on the city and officially reestablished the denomination in the state in May. Despite the unsettled conditions in the city, by the end of October, Charleston African Methodists had raised enough money to begin construction of their first church. This was Emanuel AME Church, the congregation of which was built on the remnants of those that remained from the original antebellum African Church (see figure 9.1). Based on this distinguished lineage, it is affectionately called "Mother" Emanuel and is the oldest church in the denomination south of Baltimore.[20] The AMEs weren't the only beneficiaries of the freedmen's change in congregational affiliation, and northern Methodists and Presbyterians as well as Congregationalists all appealed to the freedmen's allegiance.

At this time church affiliation was a particularly weighty matter and not to be undertaken lightly. Reginald Hildebrand, who studies this phenomenon in the post–Civil War era, observed that with this decision the former slaves were "redefining themselves as free people." Thus their choices were "just as significant as selecting a surname or deciding where to live and work." Many churches have minute books and other records that show how such grave decisions were made. Since black Baptists attended multiple white churches in Charleston, after the war they had to decide whether they would remain separate or form

Figure 9.1. Emanuel AME Church after repairs, Charleston, South Carolina. Margaretta Childs Archives at Historic Charleston Foundation.

a single church. After much deliberation they decided to "fight the Devil of Secession" and be guided by the "unbroken unity of the Nation." On May 9, 1865, these men agreed to form Morris Street Baptist Church, the city's first congregation of black Baptists.[21] Some black Episcopalians were faced with a similar decision. In late 1849 white Episcopalians constructed Calvary Episcopal Church for slaves who could not be accommodated in their congregations. Most free blacks attended other churches, though. So with the postwar exodus from white churches, antebellum free blacks had to decide whether to now affiliate with Calvary or start a new church. They opted for the latter and created St. Mark's Episcopal Church; by doing so they preserved their somewhat unique status as "formerly free."[22]

With new ways of making a living, accumulating wealth, and learning, Charleston's post-emancipation black community experienced an accelerated rate of socioeconomic differentiation. The church played an important role in this process by introducing a wholly new group, the professionally trained minister. Francis Cardozo was the community's most highly educated minister. A free black Charlestonian before the war, he was trained at the University of Glasgow and in British Presbyterian seminaries. Richard Cain, a leading AME minister, was educated at Wilberforce University, and Benjamin F. Randolph of the northern Methodists attended Oberlin.[23] These men were not only symbolic of the new educational elite, they furthered it by promoting the colleges their denominations sponsored and other institutions of higher education. The northern Methodists chartered Claflin College in Orangeburg in 1869, and in 1881 the AME Church started Allen University in Columbia.[24]

Class differentiation was also apparent among the different church congregations. One way to examine this phenomenon is to scrutinize church membership lists and lists of officers, in conjunction with other sources such as census and tax records, to determine their occupations, property accumulation, and educational levels. In post-emancipation Charleston, generally the Baptist and Methodist congregations were comprised of former slaves who were employed in the full range of manual occupations from unskilled to artisanal. The members were not likely to own real property and had little savings. However, there certainly were exceptions. Centenary Methodist Episcopal Church was one of the city's elite churches and counted a number of Charleston's most wealthy black families among its membership. Almost half of its officers were considered members of black Charleston's upper class.[25]

Whether at the helm of Charleston's new churches or simply as part of the city's religious community, black ministers comprised a layer of leadership heretofore unknown and impossible. As servants to both their secular and sacred communities, some ministers either established or edited Charleston's first African American–oriented newspapers. Reverend Benjamin F. Randolph edited the Charleston *Journal* in 1866 and Richard H. Cain was editor and proprietor of the *Missionary Record*, which disseminated community information and served as an outlet for the local AME church.[26] Ministerial leadership after the Civil War was most visible in the realm of politics as a number of these men sought and held offices through which they promoted community interests. For example, reverends Cardozo, Cain, and Randolph were all elected to the 1868 South Carolina Constitutional Convention, which rewrote the state's antebellum constitution. They all exhibited a keen interest in education, and Reverend Cardozo served as chairman of the education committee. One of the most important provisions of the new constitution was for a statewide system of public education.[27] At the constitutional convention, Richard Cain was instrumental in persuading his colleagues to establish a land commission which would be responsible for assisting the freedmen and others to purchase land. Reverend Cain was subsequently elected to the state senate where he assisted in organizing that state agency. Unfortunately, its successes were limited; nevertheless South Carolina was the only state to use governmental authority in this way to assist the landless.[28]

In an important sense the overarching theme of African American history is the quest for freedom; however, that notion is defined and its definition has changed with time and space. Regardless of its definition, though, the church and religiosity have played central roles. In the antebellum years, churches afforded slaves an opportunity to learn to read and maybe even to write. Certainly it was here that Afro-Christianity offered hope for a new dispensation and challenged southern society's efforts to legitimize racial oppression. Sometimes men sought to subvert the slaveholding system by the force of arms and found justification in the Bible. Most other leaders sought less radical means to serve their people within the framework of the church. A new social order came about through civil war and emancipation, which unlocked the church's greatest potential. It provided freedmen with new denominational choices, leaders, educational opportunities, and means of acquiring status. As renowned church scholar C. Eric Lincoln has noted, the church, particularly in this era, was the "cultural womb of the black community."[29] Through the vehicle of the church and religion, museums and historic sites can explore the contours of the black community in a broader and deeper manner. By understanding the church in this foundational time period and place, we are better equipped to appreciate the role it would assume as a transformative force during the twentieth century and in other places.

Notes

1. Walter J. Fraser Jr., *Charleston! Charleston!: The History of a Southern City* (Columbia: University of South Carolina, 1989), 11, 82; F. A. Mood, *Methodism in Charleston* (Nashville: Stevenson and Evans, 1856), 29, 34–39; Jonathan H. Poston, *The Buildings of Charleston: A Guide to the City's Architecture* (Columbia: University of South Carolina, 1997), 208, 386.
2. John Blassingame, *The Slave Community: Plantation Life in the Antebellum South* (New York: Oxford, 1979), 71–72; George F. Jones, "John Martin Boltzius' Trip to Charleston 1742" *South Carolina Historical Magazine* 82 (April 1981): 93.
3. Albert J. Raboteau, *Slave Religion: The "Invisible Institution" in the Antebellum South* (New York: Oxford, 1978), 152–75; Blassingame, *Slave Community*, 82–84.
4. Blassingame, *Slave Community*, 71, 94–95, 104.
5. Frederick Douglass, *Narrative of the Life of Frederick Douglass, An American Slave* (Boston: the Antislavery Office, 1845), 118–25; Sterling Stuckey, *Slave Culture: Nationalist Theory and the Foundations of Black America* (New York: Oxford, 1987), 12–13, 17–20, 256–57; Margaret Washington Creel, *"A Peculiar People': Slave Religion and Community-Culture among the Gullahs* (New York: New York University, 1988), chapter 9.
6. Minutes and Register of First Baptist Church Charleston County, 1847–75, October 16, 1848, January 16, 1849, First Baptist Church, Charleston (hereafter FBCC); Benjamin M. Palmer's

Pastor's Minute Book, Circular Congregational Church Membership Records, Vol. 2, 1814–36, 34, Circular Congregational Church, Charleston (hereafter CCC).

7. Record of Colored Members of the Methodist Episcopal Church, Charleston South Carolina, 1821–1880, 27–28, 109, Trinity Methodist Episcopal Church, Charleston; Minutes and Register of First Baptist Church Charleston County 1847–75, Entry for January 14, 1851 (FBCC).

8. Janet D. Cornelius, *When I Can Read My Title Clear: Literacy, Slavery, and Religion in the Antebellum South* (Columbia: University of South Carolina, 1991), 22–23.

9. A. Leon Higginbotham Jr., *In the Matter of Color: Race and the American Legal Process* (New York: Oxford, 1978), 196–98; Benjamin M. Palmer's Pastor's Minute Book, Circular Congregational Church Membership Records, Vol. 2, 1814–36, 32 (CCC).

10. Daniel A. Payne, *Recollections of Seventy Years* (Nashville: A.M.E. Sunday School Union, 1888), 27.

11. Benjamin M. Palmer's Pastor's Minute Book, Circular Congregational Church Membership Records, Vol. 2, 1814–36, 33, (CCC).

12. Benjamin M. Palmer's Pastor's Minute Book, 32–34.

13. The AME Church is the first independent denomination of black Methodists, the origins of which date to 1787. Originating in Philadelphia, the denomination was formed as a reaction to discrimination in the Methodist church and also to give African Americans greater control over their church affairs. See Carol V. R. George, *Segregated Sabbaths: Richard Allen and the Rise of Independent Black Churches, 1760–1840* (New York: Oxford, 1973), 49–57, 111; Douglas Egerton, *He Shall Go Out Free: The Lives of Denmark Vesey* (Lanham, MD: Rowman & Littlefield), 110–11, 121.

14. Peter Hinks, *To Awaken My Afflicted Brethren: David Walker and the Problem of Antebellum Slave Resistance* (University Park: Pennsylvania State University), 26–27; Egerton, *He Shall Go Out*, 112, 121.

15. Egerton, *He Shall Go Out*, 74–75, 87, 116–17, 135–37; S. Robert Starobin, *Denmark Vesey: The Slave Conspiracy of 1822* (Englewood Cliffs, NJ: Prentice Hall, 1970), 31, 100.

16. Egerton, *He Shall Go Out*, 200, 213, 221; Starobin, *Denmark Vesey*, 149–51.

17. Starobin, *Denmark Vesey*, 31, 41–43, 100.

18. Reginald Hildebrand, *The Times Were Strange and Stirring: Methodist Preachers and the Crisis of Emancipation* (Durham, NC: Duke University, 1995), xiv.

19. Payne, *Recollections*, 159, 161; *Christian Recorder*, June 27, 1863.

20. Payne, *Recollections*, 162–63; *Southern Christian Advocate*, November 2, 1865; Minutes of the South Carolina Annual Conference of the A.M.E. Church 1876, 9; http://www.emanuelame-church.org/churchhistory.php, accessed May 2, 2014; George, *Segregated Sabbaths*, 92.

21. Hildebrand, *The Times*, xvii; Morris Street Baptist Church Minute Book, May 9, 1865, Morris Street Baptist Church.

22. Robert F. Durden, "The Establishment of Calvary Protestant Episcopal Church for Negroes in Charleston," *South Carolina Historical Magazine* 65 (April 1964): 67, 82–83; Charleston *Courier*, November 17, 1865.

23. Eric Foner, *Freedom's Lawmakers: A Directory of Black Officeholders during Reconstruction* (New York: Oxford, 1993), 35, 39, 175.

24. Joel Williamson, *After Slavery: The Negro in South Carolina during Reconstruction 1861–1877* (Chapel Hill: University of North Carolina, 1965), 191, 231.

25. Bernard E. Powers Jr., *Black Charlestonians: A Social History 1822–1885* (Fayetteville: University of Arkansas, 1994), 214–15.

26. *Christian Recorder*, October 13, 1866, October 16, 1869.

27. Williamson, *After Slavery*, 218–21.

28. Bernard E. Powers Jr., "'I Go to Set the Captives Free': The Activism of Richard Harvey Cain, Nationalist Churchman and Reconstruction-Era Leader," in Randy Finley and Thomas A. DeBlack, eds., *The Southern Elite and Social Change* (Fayetteville: University of Arkansas, 2002), 50–51.

29. C. Eric Lincoln and Lawrence H. Mamiya, *The Black Church in the African American Experience* (Durham: Duke University, 1990), 8–9.

CHAPTER 10

Imagining Slave Square

Resurrecting History through Cemetery Research and Interpretation

D L HENDERSON

MORE THAN 150 years ago, a fourteen-year-old boy known only as "John" was the first African American in Atlanta to be buried in the city cemetery's "Slave Square." John's listing in the cemetery records is the only documentation that has been identified regarding his short life and death.[1] He was born in Fayette County, Georgia, and his cause of death is listed as "complicated diseases," a term indicating that young John suffered from a number of medical issues. The cemetery record also includes the name of John's slaveholder, who arranged for his interment. On Saturday, February 10, 1853, John was buried in grave number 1, row 1 south, but this geographical reference matches no known coordinates in the cemetery today. Slave Square no longer exists except in the imagination. I have chosen to resurrect the history and memory of Slave Square to recover a story that predates the existing physical evidence in the cemetery landscape.

Prior to 1853, Atlanta's city cemetery apparently kept no records of any burials, but the first interment probably occurred in the latter part of 1850, the year the cemetery was established. At that time, approximately 20 percent of Atlanta's total population of about 2,500 was African American; of this number, more than 450 were enslaved and eighteen were free persons of color.[2] Later renamed Oakland, the cemetery today still reflects the racially segregated burial practices of the city's past. Research and interpretation strategies that examine cemeteries as microcosms of society—as cultural repositories containing the social, historic, and oftentimes architectural and archaeological artifacts of a community—can reveal what lies beneath the cultural landscape, even though the physical landscape no longer exists in the same fashion that it once did. Over seventy thousand people have been buried at

Oakland since 1850, most of them in the nineteenth century, thus making the city cemetery an ideal site for studying the social history and development of early Atlanta.

Because physical evidence of Slave Square has been destroyed, clues to its location were derived by analyzing a variety of sources. I began with existing cemetery research. The Historic Oakland Foundation, a nonprofit friends group, has conducted public walking tours of the cemetery for many years, and the overview tour includes African Americans who made significant contributions to the city's history. Also, the City of Atlanta has developed an African American history brochure for the cemetery. Based upon these resources and additional research on nineteenth-century Atlanta history, I developed a guided walking tour on the African American history of Oakland. For information that might lead to specific details regarding Slave Square, I consulted additional resources—Atlanta City Council minutes and cemetery ordinances, the Works Progress Administration (WPA) map and indexes from 1936–1938, nineteenth- and twentieth-century internment records created by Oakland Cemetery's sextons, US census records, Atlanta city directories, the 1907 Oakland Cemetery guidelines and regulations, and historical newspapers containing cemetery reports and obituaries. This research resulted in a brief history of Slave Square that is now recorded on an exhibit panel marking its approximate location in the cemetery:

> In 1852 the Atlanta City Council ruled that African Americans were to be buried in a segregated section at the rear of Oakland cemetery, at the eastern boundary of the original 6 acres. As more acres were purchased, the cemetery expanded around Slave Square to its current size of 48 acres. In 1866 the Atlanta City Council established a segregated burial ground at the rear of the 48 acres for African Americans. By the 1870s most of the burial plots in Oakland had been sold, and more were needed. In 1877 the City Council ordered that the bodies and bones of the African Americans buried in Slave Square were to be removed and reburied in Oakland's "colored pauper grounds." The old grave spaces in slave square were replotted and resold to whites. Legal segregation at Oakland Cemetery ended in 1963 when the City of Atlanta banned the segregation of public facilities.[3]

The Slave Square exhibit panel was developed as part of Oakland's African American interpretative initiative, *African American Voices*. Funded in part by the National Trust for Historic Preservation and the Ford Foundation, the program expanded the cemetery's African American interpretation materials to include the exhibit panel in Slave Square, a cell phone tour, and two exhibit panels placed in the extant historic African American burial ground.

No nineteenth-century cemetery maps exist to define the boundaries of Slave Square, but Atlanta City Council minutes from 1852 and 1877 describe the establishment and disinterment of the area—including geographical references that help to narrow down its probable location.[4] The earliest surviving map of Oakland, produced in the late 1930s by the WPA, also provides clues to the historical location of Slave Square. The WPA map depicts a group of plots in the northeast corner of the oldest part of the cemetery that are arranged with the same block and lot pattern used in the newer portions of the cemetery (see figure 10.1).[5] This pattern is distinctly different from the arrangement of other graves in the old section and suggests a unique, significant impact to this particular area. Furthermore, a survey of cemetery records reveals that the lots in this sector have purchase dates after the city

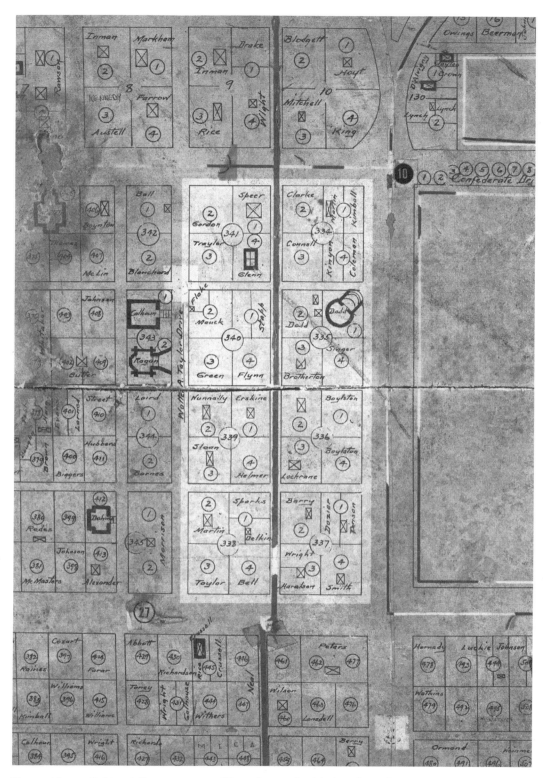

Figure 10.1. Oakland Cemetery map (Slave Square highlighted), Works Progress Administration, 1937. Courtesy of Oakland Archives.

council's disinterment order for Slave Square in 1877.[6] Taken together, these details provided evidence for mapping the general location of Slave Square in today's cemetery.

As in John's case, the interment records for Slave Square typically list the name of the slaveholder or slave broker followed by the given name of the deceased. In some instances there is no given name, but only a question mark indicating the name is unknown, or only the term "negro" is used. The interment record for three-week-old "James Teate" includes the notation "free negro." The infant may have been a member of the Tate family, a free family of color listed in the 1860 Fulton County, Georgia, census.[7] More than half of those buried in Slave Square were children under sixteen like John and James. Many of them were stillborn or died in infancy from childhood ailments such as croup, measles, or whooping cough. The high mortality rate among African Americans, especially children, is illustrated in the cemetery records of winter 1862–1863, which list numerous deaths caused by a small pox epidemic.

I have found no details concerning interment, burial services, or other information regarding the care and appearance of the graves in Slave Square, but according to the 1877 Atlanta City Council minutes, the remains of African Americans removed from Slave Square were to be reinterred in the "colored pauper grounds without any distinction of graves, except those who may have headboards, who may be interred by themselves."[8] In other words, many of the people originally interred in Slave Square in individual graves were reburied in a mass grave in potters field. The reference to headboards may be a literal description of the use of wooden markers in Slave Square, but it also provides evidence that this area of the cemetery received some level of care and attention, if not by the slaveholder, perhaps by family or friends of the deceased. While fieldstones or plants were commonly used as grave markers in early African American cemeteries, and may have also been used to mark graves in Slave Square, only those graves with headboards met the city's standard for individual reinterment. The practice of using graves goods—decorating graves with items that belonged to the deceased—was documented in Oakland's African American pauper grounds in the late nineteenth century, thus I believe this tradition also might have been practiced in earlier years in Slave Square.[9]

Historical interpretation takes many forms at Oakland. In 2012, the cast of characters for the annual Halloween celebration featured Catherine Holmes, the only identified African American currently buried in Slave Square (see figure 10.2). During the Halloween event, costumed docents portraying historic figures entertain cemetery visitors with first-person accounts of their lives and deaths. Catherine Holmes was a free woman of color born in Charleston, South Carolina, about 1823.[10] After the Civil War, she came to Atlanta with the white family for whom she worked as nurse and cook. By permission of the mayor and surrounding plot owners, in 1896 she was buried in their family plot. Holmes was a storytelling "genius" according to the memoir of one of her young charges, so I was eager to have her speak for the dead of Slave Square to tell their story to Oakland's visitors.[11] This excerpt from the Halloween performance illustrates another approach to the historical interpretation of Slave Square:

> Do any of you folks here tonight believe in the afterlife? I mean, do you believe that the spirit remains after the physical body is dead and buried? Whether you do—or you don't—most folks would say that disturbing the resting places of the dead is a violation of natural

law. By the 1870s, most of the burial plots in Oakland had already been sold. So when they started looking around for more places to bury white folks, they started looking at Slave Square—right here in a nice spot, on high ground, where all those Black people, where all of the Old Ones, were buried. Well, there's no decent way to put it, so I'll just tell you. In 1877, they dug up the bodies and the bones of the Black people buried in Slave Square and moved them to the colored pauper grounds. Back at that time, taking up a body might mean just getting up the long bones—arms and legs—and maybe the skull. The other smaller bones, like finger and toe joints, might get missed because they're hard to find in the ground after all those years. Then, they divided up the empty graves and set them up as family plots, and they resold all those old grave spaces to white people for no less than $50 apiece. That's who's buried here now—all white—except for me. But some of the remains of those Black people are still here. This is still Slave Square.[12]

While the bones of the story remain the same, the performance of Catherine Holmes, the Charleston storyteller, brings Slave Square to life in a way not possible on an exhibit panel or in a brochure—without sacrificing historical accuracy.

There are still many unanswered questions regarding Slave Square—how long the burial ground remained in use after the Civil War and the total number interred, how or if families

Figure 10.2. Catherine Holmes as portrayed by Deborah Strahorn. Photo by Moondance Photography, courtesy of Oakland Archives.

conducted services and decorated the graves, and how they may have reacted to the disinterment of their loved ones. Over the years, I have met and interviewed descendants of African American families buried at Oakland, but I have not been able to confirm any descendants of the persons originally buried in Slave Square. Additional research may yet uncover more information. In early 2014, Slave Square was added to the cemetery's self-guided walking tour map. This recognition marked another step in the continuing effort to resurrect and integrate neglected parts of the cemetery's history not only as specialized African American programming but also as an integral part of the cemetery's interpretive programs for all audiences.

Through the efforts of the Historic Oakland Foundation's multi-million-dollar restoration project to restore the historic fabric and Victorian garden landscape of Oakland, visitors to Oakland experience a beautiful, peaceful, park-like setting, representing an idyllic or heavenly garden on earth that some Victorian Atlantans envisioned. This rejuvenation of the landscape attracts heritage tourists who seek an authentic experience of history. However, as the story of Slave Square illustrates, if we are not vigilant in preserving the facts of the past, they will eventually be lost to us. The history related to the physical development of Oakland must be preserved through research and interpretation for the public. Otherwise, cemetery visitors will enjoy a beautiful setting but fail to appreciate the complex historical influences which shaped the cemetery landscape as well as the broader cultural landscape of the City of Atlanta.

Notes

1. Oakland Cemetery Interment Records, 1853–1875, Atlanta History Center Archives.
2. National Park Service, *Atlanta, Georgia: African American Experience*, accessed May 27, 2014. http://www.nps.gov/nr/travel/atlanta/africanamerican.htm.
3. *Slave Square* exhibit panel on the grounds of Oakland Cemetery.
4. Atlanta City Council Minutes, March 5, 1852, and April 2, 1877, Atlanta History Center Archives.
5. Works Progress Administration, *Key Map of Oakland Cemetery, Atlanta, Georgia*, October 1937, Oakland Archives.
6. Oakland Cemetery Plot Abstracts, Section 7: Blocks 334–345, Oakland Archives.
7. *1860 U.S. Census, Fulton County, Georgia*, population schedule, p. 929, dwelling 1552, family 1656, Charity Tate; digital images, Ancestry.com (http://www.ancestry.com: accessed May 27, 2014); citing National Archives microfilm publication M653_123.
8. Atlanta City Council Minutes, April 2, 1877, Atlanta History Center Archives.
9. Lollie Belle Wiley, "In a Meditative Mood," *Society* (April 25, 1891): 10.
10. *1870 U.S. Census, Charleston Ward 4, Charleston, South Carolina*, population schedule, p. 216A, dwelling 261, family 389, Henry Bolyston; digital images, Ancestry.com (http://www.ancestry .com: accessed May 27, 2014); citing National Archives microfilm publication M593_1486.
11. Elise Reid Boylston, *Atlanta: Its Lore, Legends, and Laughter* (Doraville, GA: Foote & Davies, 1968).
12. *Catherine Holmes*, Capturing the Spirit of Oakland Halloween Tour, October 2012.

CHAPTER 11

Furnishing Slave Quarters and Free Black Homes

Adding a Powerful Tool to Interpreting African American Life

MARTHA B. KATZ-HYMAN

IT IS THE rare historic house that can be interpreted without furnishings.[1] Most often the interpretation of such houses focuses on their architecture and construction, avoiding the issues and questions that arise when furnishing such spaces. But slave quarters and the houses in which free African Americans lived before 1860 are usually not such buildings, and it is not enough just to include these buildings on a historic house tour, or refer to them in explanatory panels, or show them on a map of a historic site. Rather, it is through a combination of furnishings plus the building that visitors come to understand the lives and circumstances of people in the past.

At many historic sites and historic house museums, attempts to furnish spaces that reflect the enslaved or free black individuals who lived there often meet with resistance from staff, who maintain that there is no documentation for how and with what such an individual or family might have furnished a particular space. After all, the argument goes, if there is no evidence for how a particular person or group of people—whether enslaved or free—furnished a particular site, how can that space be accurately furnished to reflect their occupancy? On the contrary, with sufficient planning and research, it is possible to have such furnished spaces and then use them as the foundation upon which to tell the stories of the individuals who lived there and give visitors a concrete idea of the surroundings in which these people lived.

The process of preparing a furnishing plan for a slave quarter or for a building occupied by free African Americans is not any different from the process of preparing a furnishing plan for any historic house. It involves looking at the documentary record, the visual record, and the archaeological record. It requires looking at whatever objects survive with a connection to the location being furnished and then putting all of this information into one document that lays out the evidence and comes to well-supported conclusions about the furnishings and how they fit into the house interpretation.[2]

However, an observation from a late eighteenth-century visitor to Mount Vernon demonstrates how difficult this can be:

> We entered one of the huts of the Blacks, for one can not call them by the name of houses. They are more miserable than the most miserable of the cottages of our peasants. The husband and wife sleep on a mean pallet, the children on the ground; a very bad fireplace, some utensils for cooking, but in the middle of this poverty some cups and a teapot. . . . A very small garden planted with vegetables was close by, with 5 or 6 hens, each one leading ten to fifteen chickens. It is the only comfort that is permitted them; for they may not keep ducks, geese, or pigs. They sell the poultry in Alexandria and procure for themselves a few amenities.[3]

These are the words of Julian Niemcewicz, a visitor from Poland and a close friend of Revolutionary War hero General Tadeusz Kosciuszko, who visited George Washington at Mount Vernon in June 1798. During the course of his ten-day visit, Niemcewicz took several rides around the property, for there was much for him to see, including the recently completed sixteen-sided barn at Dogue Run Farm. And, like many European visitors to the newly independent United States, he was especially interested in the institution of slavery. During the course of one of his rides, he visited a slave quarter on one of Washington's outlying quarters and described what he saw in his journal.

At first glance, this seems to be a description that answers a host of questions for a curator concerned with interpreting the material culture of slavery: Niemcewicz described the house, its furnishings, exterior details, and even included some observations about the lives of its inhabitants and the way in which Washington treated his slaves. But a closer examination of this one paragraph from a traveler's diary neatly sums up the difficulties historic sites and living history museums face today in turning descriptions such as these into solid sources for the interpretation of the material culture of eighteenth-century Chesapeake slavery and, by extension, the material culture of enslaved and free African Americans in the nearly 250 years between the arrival of the first Africans in Virginia and the outbreak of the Civil War in 1861.

Niemcewicz wrote his diary in both Polish and French; this particular entry was written primarily in French. He used the French word for "hut" to describe the house that he visited, but was what he considered a "hut" in 1798 the same thing that is considered a hut in 2014? Because this was his own journal, Niemcewicz had no need to describe either what he meant by a "hut" or the houses of Polish peasants, because he knew what he meant. Therefore the question becomes what kind of houses Polish peasants slept in that he thought slave quarter houses were worse. What did he mean by "a mean pallet," and because he described the children sleeping on the ground, was the pallet used by the adults—whom he assumed were husband and wife—on some sort of a raised bedstead? And what were the children sleeping on, anyway? Was it blankets thrown over straw, or was it a pallet as well? What did he mean by a bad fireplace, or, more to the point, what was the good fireplace to which he was comparing it? A curator who regularly works with eighteenth-century Southern kitchens might be presumed to have an idea about the cooking utensils, but what kind of cups and teapot could Niemcewicz have been describing, with what seems to be a very surprised tone of voice? And what was an amenity to Niemcewicz? What was it to the slaves? What does it mean to us?

Here, in these few sentences, written by someone observing an institution almost totally foreign to him, lies the challenge of interpreting the material culture of both enslaved and free African Americans in the years before the Civil War. Our visitors, black and white alike, come to our sites with many preconceived ideas about slaves, slavery, and the nature of slave life, as did Julian Niemcewicz to Mount Vernon. Many of our visitors know something about slavery, but they don't know how to reconcile the knowledge that they have with the stories we try to teach. They come with all kinds of information—some correct, some incorrect—about the American system of slavery. Some of what they know they learned in school, and that information, depending on when they learned it, is as up-to-date as the latest research, or as old as high school textbooks from the 1930s and 1940s. Some of what our visitors know they saw on television, in movies, in prints and paintings, or via the Internet or social media. Some of what our visitors know was told to them as family stories because they are descendants of slaves or descendants of slaveholders. Some of what our visitors know is shaped by racial differences. They have seen images of antebellum slave quarters, they may have read slave narratives of that period, and they expect to see poverty, dirt, misery, and want. They also have ideas on how slaves lived: the houses they inhabited, the objects they used, the clothing they wore. Many, if not most, equate slavery with a lack of material goods and the inability to acquire anything independently of one's owner. They are not prepared for the contradictions that are inherent in a slave society nor for the complex story that they are told. And for all but a very small number of visitors, most of what they know is a reflection of a time and place very different from the time and place in which they live.

So this is the first step in teaching historic house visitors about slave material culture: that what they see at these sites reflects its own time and place, whether that is the eighteenth century in the Chesapeake, South Carolina, or Massachusetts, or nineteenth-century Alabama or Tennessee. Those who work in any way with interpreting American slavery and slave material culture know that this institution was different in every place and every time that it existed, and it is part of the interpretive goal to make sure visitors understand that slavery was different from time to time and from place to place and master to master—that what they see at a particular site reflects that location and not any other place, and that particular time period and not anything much earlier or later, except in the most general way. In places where there was both urban and rural slavery, part of the task is explaining that even in the same general location, there were real differences in the lives of rural slaves and urban slaves. For example, although people living in both locations were slaves according to the law, there were some advantages that rural slaves had over urban slaves. Most slaves who lived on rural plantations were often housed at a distance from the main house, and that meant

Figure 11.1. Detail of a table in the home of newly freed slaves about 1804 at Freedom Park, Williamsburg, Virginia. Photo by Martha Katz-Hyman.

that, after their work was completed for the slave owner, they could occupy themselves with tending their own gardens, making baskets or furniture to sell, fishing or hunting, or visiting friends and relatives on neighboring plantations. And, because of that distance, they were under less direct scrutiny of their owners. Conversely, although urban slaves lived in very close proximity to their owners, they had access to more goods, were able to share news with slaves from rural areas who traveled to the city, and had a greater ability to earn money. This differentiation is actually a fairly easy concept to teach, because most people understand that, despite the ever-increasing homogenization of American culture, there are, in fact, still differences in culture, traditions—even language—that persist between different regions of this country. It is also fairly easy for visitors to understand that the laws that regulated slavery changed, too, and that because of those changes and the behavior that they reflected, the lives of slaves in the early eighteenth century was quite different from the lives of slaves in 1800 or, more starkly, in 1860.

A more difficult concept for most visitors to understand, but one that is crucial to the understanding of the American slave system, is that, for the most part, the legal status of slavery and the amount and quality of goods owned by enslaved people were independent of each other for most of the time period that legal slavery existed in this country. This should not be surprising to those who interpret African American material culture of the eighteenth-century Chesapeake, nor to those who interpret antebellum African American culture anywhere where slavery flourished. But to visitors, the notion that enslaved people slept in beds, lived in houses with wood floors, cooked with a variety of equipment, wore clothing that spanned the range from coarse fieldwork shirts and trousers to dresses of printed cottons or suits of fine livery seems to mock their very status as slaves. After all, being a slave implies that someone owns not only your physical body but also anything else that you might have, from the clothing you wear to the food you put into your mouth to the bed you sleep in—whatever that bed might be—to the utensils you cook with. It implies a material status so low that there is only the most basic of food, shelter, and clothing. Yet the available evidence, both archaeological and documentary, shows time and time again that enslaved African Americans lived within a fairly wide range of material levels, from those who truly did have only the most basic of the necessities of life to those who managed to acquire goods that were equal to or better than those poor-to-middling whites could obtain. And it is precisely this range of material situations that makes the legal status of slavery seem so strange to visitors' understanding. How, they will ask, did slaves accumulate all of these goods? Why didn't their owners make them give up most of their possessions if slaves didn't have any legal right to own them? And if slavery was not denoted by having few, if any, possessions of one's own, then how *was* it denoted?

The last question is probably the easiest to answer: simply, that these people of African descent were slaves by virtue of the laws that delineated their status, not because these laws dictated levels of material goods. The law said they were slaves, and the law provided the ways in which they could cease being slaves. These laws were modified, repealed, and reenacted. Sometimes they specified what slaves could and could not possess but, by and large, these laws were enacted to regulate behavior and legal status, not consumption.

How slaves acquired items is also relatively easy to answer, because there is a wealth of primary sources—letters, diaries, business records, legal records, runaway slave advertisements—that provide the information.[4] Others will ask how the material culture of enslaved men and women can be interpreted when it is not clear what that material culture included. It is true that, by and large, the materials recovered archaeologically from known slave quarter sites are the only objects that can legitimately be labeled "slave material culture," if by that term we mean only those objects—or fragments of objects—that enslaved people used in their own living spaces, in their own ways, and for their own purposes. But one must look at the question in a much more expansive way: everything used by the enslaved, whether these were goods found in their own slave quarter houses, or their work tools, or the ceramics, furniture, textiles, and other goods used by them in the course of their work, or the houses they lived and worked in as well as the landscapes in which they were situated, the clothing they wore and how they wore it, their food and how they prepared it, even their hairstyles and oral traditions, was a part of their culture.

An example of how the stories and objects of enslaved African Americans can be incorporated into an existing historic house can be found at the 1719 William Trent House in Trenton, New Jersey. In 2005, the management of the house, with the support of its friends group, the Trent House Association, embarked on a project to make sure that the enslaved people in the Trent household were included in its interpretation. When William Trent died unexpectedly on December 24, 1724, in Trenton, he was not only one of the best known and most respected residents of his area of New Jersey (at that time called West Jersey), he was also one of its wealthiest. The value of his possessions, as listed in his 1726 probate inventory, totaled £1100.18.1/2, and in the decade of his death, 1720–1730, only two other estates in West Jersey exceeded Trent's in value. But where much of the value of those inventories consisted of financial instruments or store inventory, over one-third of the value of Trent's inventory was in the form of human capital: eleven enslaved men, women, and children of African descent. This total was by far the most of any West Jersey resident who died between 1720 and 1730 and whose inventory included either Negroes and/or slaves.[5]

Beyond their names and inventory values, no information survives about these individuals. Like virtually all eighteenth-century probate inventories that included slaves, nothing in the inventory, aside from the slaves themselves, reflects the clothing, food, and personal possessions of these people. Because few of Trent's personal papers and account books survive, their roles within the Trent household, where they might have lived on the property, and what kinds of clothing, bedding, and food he provided for his slaves is unknown.

Therefore, it was necessary to use information from more generalized sources, as well as the simple list in the inventory itself, to give administrators and staff insight into the lives of enslaved people in West Jersey during the first quarter of the eighteenth. For early eighteenth-century West Jersey, runaway slave advertisements published in the newspapers of nearby Philadelphia constitute one of the best sources for information about slaves and the clothing they wore. It is apparent from a close reading of these advertisements that slaves wore a variety of clothing, from a basic "uniform" for field hands, to the much more elaborate wardrobe worn by household and personal servants. The more elaborate clothes listed in the advertisements ("a dark close bodied fashionable coat"; "a fine red-striped Vest and Breeches"; "a new Bonnett Lined with red Silk") corresponded very well to clothing shown in period paintings. The most valuable published source for this period is *The Infortunate: The Voyage and Adventures of William Moraley, An Indentured Servant.*[6] Moraley arrived in Philadelphia as an indentured servant in 1729, five years after Trent's death, and served most of his time in Burlington, New Jersey. His observations of the lives of the slaves with whom he came in contact were very helpful in understanding how some slaves were able to acquire goods for themselves.

Few business or personal account books survive from this period that shed light on items bought for slaves. Although one of Trent's own ledgers survives, it is concerned primarily with his import/export business, documenting his trade with the West Indies, Madeira, Barbados, Surinam, and England. There is also evidence of his involvement with the slave trade, but there is little, if any, record of the objects he bought for his personal use or that of his wife, children, or slaves. After studying all of these sources, as limited as they were, it became apparent that Trent's slaves lived in a varied and complex material world. They had access to many types of goods, both imported and domestic, and were able to acquire many items for themselves in a variety of ways. Based on how these individuals were listed in the inventory, it was decided that five—three men, two women, and a child—would be interpreted as living in the house; three men would be interpreted as living at some distance from the house, working at Trent's fulling mill, grist mill, or saw mill; and two men, described as "Indien Men,"[7] would be interpreted as coachmen, since Trent's inventory included several wheeled vehicles. Designated spaces within the house were furnished with clothing and a few personal possessions, as well as a rolled-up pallet (if appropriate), so that docents could talk about these people and visitors to the house could see examples of the types of clothing and goods enslaved men and women wore and used for themselves.

A very different kind of furnishing project was undertaken in 2007–2008 by James City [Virginia] Parks and Recreation, near Williamsburg. In 1995 and 1996 the county purchased over six hundred acres of land originally owned by William Ludwell Lee, a member of the famous Lee family of Stratford Hall, Westmoreland County, Virginia.[8] Lee was raised in England, and upon his death in 1802, his will directed that the slaves who lived on this property, called the "Hot Waters," were to be freed and his executor was to build them "comfortable homes." The interpretive plan for the park was developed by an advisory committee that included representatives of Colonial Williamsburg, the Jamestown-Yorktown Foundation, the College of William and Mary, local historians and descendants of the original residents of the "Hot Waters." In addition to hiking and mountain-biking trails and a botanical garden, the decision was made to construct three houses that reflected the types of buildings that these now-free African Americans could have lived in between 1804 and 1860. They decided to select families for each house who could be documented as having lived there as recorded in census and tax records.[9]

The first house, interpreting the years just after William Ludwell Lee died, reflects the typical log and timber construction used for slave quarters and for houses of poor whites in the eighteenth and early nineteenth centuries. The second house is also log and timber, but it has glass windows and a brick chimney, suggesting more permanence for the family who might have lived there around 1820-1825 (see figure 11.2). The third house, indicating the economic success that came with the marketable skills of a tradesman or artisan in the two decades before the Civil War, is a frame structure with a clapboard exterior, wooden floors, plastered walls, and an attic. Based on that information, the residents of the first house are interpreted as newly freed former slaves; the residents of the second house as a farmer and his family; and the residents of the third house as a bricklayer/plasterer, his wife, and their children.

Ironically, because they were free, less is known about their material lives than we do about the material lives of the enslaved, because these free black families left little written evidence and, archaeologically, what remains in the ground is often no different than what remains from free whites of the same economic status. Therefore, furnishings for each house were chosen based on similar furnishings in both free African American and white households of comparable economic status, as well as on archaeological evidence from both Freedom Park and the adjacent privately owned property that was under development at the time the furnishing project was in progress. The furnishings for each house reflect these very different families, and visitors to the park can look into each house, read a short description of each family and the building, and see the types of furnishings—from clothing to eating utensils to trade tools—and easily compare them. And because a conscious effort was made to show differences in family occupations and income, the furnishings vary, too, as the visitor goes from house to house, with the bricklayer's house having the "best" furnishings. Unfortunately, budgetary constraints and staffing levels prevent active interpretation of the houses except on special occasions, but the park's interpretive center includes an exhibit that explains the history of the site and incorporates some of the archaeologically recovered materials from the area around the recreated buildings as well as from the site of the

Figure 11.2. Some furnishings of a subsistence farmer and his family about 1813–1820 at Freedom Park, Williamsburg, Virginia. Photo by Martha Katz-Hyman.

Revolutionary War's Battle of Spencer's Ordinary and a seventeenth-century home, all of which are within the park's boundaries.

The furnishing projects for the 1719 William Trent House and for the three recreated houses at Freedom Park show that such projects can be done successfully for other slave- and free African American–related historic sites, even without a great deal of specific information about the men, women, and children who lived there. The challenge comes in interpreting the sources that are available. Letters and diaries written over two hundred years ago take for granted cultural norms that have long since vanished. Business records incorporate record-keeping practices that disappeared long ago, and legal records assume a system of chattel slavery that is as foreign to us as Internet law would be to eighteenth-century lawyers. Archaeological finds are conceivably easier to understand because they are usually associated with a specific time and place, but sometimes what is uncovered is completely unexpected, and great efforts are made to understand just what it is that was found and how it fit into the lives of the people who used those artifacts.

The fact that these are spaces that are meant to reflect the lives of enslaved and free African Americans, people at the lowest level of eighteenth- and nineteenth-century society, does not absolve historic sites of the obligation to do exactly what would be done if the spaces were those lived in by the wealthiest or highest-status resident of the site. For, in fact, whether the project is furnishing the Governor's Palace at Colonial Williamsburg, an enslaved man's space within a larger house, or the house of a free African American on his own land, the goal is the same: doing the best that can be done with the available evidence to present to visitors one vision of what these buildings and rooms looked like. The furnishing of a gentry residence like the Governor's Palace is not "better" than the furnishing of the others; neither is it more "true" than any of the others. There is indeed more concrete information about gentry residences and their furnishings than there is about an enslaved man's space or a free African American's because vastly more is known about the governors, their lives, the lives of their white middle- and upper-middle-class subjects, the kinds of goods they bought and lived with, what English upper-class interiors looked like, and there is some notion of what was important to them about the material goods they owned. Compared with that, knowledge of slaves' personal lives—the kinds of goods they lived with, and the choices of what they did with the goods they had—is much less, let alone an understanding of the material lives of free African Americans, for whom even less documentation survives. But for all of these scenarios there is only fragmentary knowledge of what they thought about the things they did live with, the meanings they attached to these objects, what they valued and what they didn't, what was expendable, and what wasn't. The details of object placement are unknown, as are how dirty or clean their surroundings were, how room arrangements changed as the household expanded or contracted, or even what happened to older goods when new goods were purchased. What visitors see represents the "best guesses" made about people whose lives are very different from those people who lived more than two centuries ago, and whose perspectives are not those of the people whom they seek to interpret. The Governor's Palace cannot be said to be "the way it really was" and the slave quarter or free black house to be "just speculation" solely on the basis that the former is a representation of gentry life and the latter is a representation of slave life. They both are really approximations of what may have been there, and they must be explained and interpreted in that way.

In furnishing slave quarters and free black homes, we can only guess how those items were arranged in these spaces by the people who lived and worked there. Unknown are the alternative uses and meanings that these individuals found in iron pots, mirrors, pins, buttons, spoons, bowls, and cups, or the meanings assigned to these objects: whether as talisman or adornment, utilitarian or decorative, treasure or trash, for there is no one correct answer. There is no "one-size-fits-all" history: What may be true in one place and at one time is not necessarily the case in other places and at other times. It is undeniably true that there was a material culture of slavery, no matter in what location it was found. From the very beginning it overlapped mainstream material culture and often was engulfed by it. In some cases it was hidden because of its very foreign-ness; its intimations of protest; its hint of rebellion. In other cases, it was in plain view but, because different people impart different meanings to objects, white observers saw one thing, the enslaved people who used them saw another, and the free African Americans another. But, in general, it is only the white view that survives in a coherent form more than two centuries later. The people who owned these objects used them as an expression of their individuality and independence, and as a way to help them make sense of their difficult lives. Although it is true that the meanings and uses of these objects will never truly be known, it is incumbent on historic sites to struggle with the questions, tell these stories, explore the paradoxes, and educate themselves and their visitors.

Notes

1. My thanks to Max van Balgooy for his hard work on this important project; to the late Jay Gaynor, with whom I worked on furnishing the slave quarters at Carter's Grove Plantation at Colonial Williamsburg and, over the years, discussed many of the ideas in this chapter; to Kym Rice, for our many conversations while we were working on *World of a Slave*; and to Rex Ellis, Christy Coleman, and all of the many African American interpreters not only at Colonial Williamsburg but at historic sites across the country who do the hard work of interpreting the lives of the enslaved. I am in your debt.

2. For a more detailed explanation of the process of writing furnishing plans, see Martha B. Katz-Hyman and Mick Woodcock, "The Basics of Writing Furnishing Plans," *ALHFAM: Proceedings of the 2000 Conference and Annual Meeting* 23 (2001): 158–62. For a description of the process of getting good reproductions for historic house use (e.g., furnishing, hands-on programming), see Martha B. Katz-Hyman and Mick Woodcock, "The Right Stuff: How to Get It," *ALHFAM Bulletin* 30, no. 4 (Winter 2001): 8–10.

3. Julian Ursyn Niemcewicz, "Under Their Vine and Fig Tree: Travels through America in 1797–1799, 1805 with some further account of life in New Jersey," in *Collections of The New Jersey Historical Society at Newark*, trans. and ed. Metchie J. E. Budka, 14 (1965): 100–101.

4. Martha B. Katz-Hyman, "'In the Middle of This Poverty Some Cups and a Teapot': The Furnishing of Slave Quarters at Colonial Williamsburg," in *The American Home: Material Culture, Domestic Space, and Family Life* (Winterthur, DE: Henry Francis du Pont Winterthur Museum, 1998), 197–216. The complete Carter's Grove Slave Quarter furnishing report can be found at http://research.history.org/DigitalLibrary/View/index.cfm?doc=ResearchReports\RR0350.xml.

5. The study was done using *Calendar of New Jersey Wills, Vol. I, 1670–1730. Documents Relating to the Colonial History of New Jersey: Vol. 23*, ed. William Nelson (Newark: New Jersey Historical Society, 1901), which lists the decedents in each county and includes a brief description of the will and its contents. Described in this way, it is unclear if the "Negroes" included are slaves or perhaps indentured servants.

6. William Moraley, *The Infortunate: The Voyage and Adventures of William Moraley, an Indentured Servant*, ed. Susan E. Klepp and Billy G. Smith (University Park: Pennsylvania State University Press, 2005).

7. Because Trent traded with the West Indies, the decision was made to interpret them as West Indians, rather than as Native Americans.

8. For more information about Freedom Park, see http://www.jamescitycountyva.gov/recreation/parks/freedom-park.html.

9. Historical background on the property can be found in Martha W. McCartney, "Freedom Park Interpretive Plan: Likely Housing Types, Land Use Patterns, and Material Culture on the Hot Water Tract during the Early-to-Mid 19th Century" (December 12, 2006), and "Freedom Park Interpretive Plan: The Hot Water Tract's History and Its Inhabitants during the 19th Century—James City County's Free Black Citizens" (August 1, 2007). Both reports include detailed information on the history of the property and details on its likely inhabitants. These reports, along with the archaeological reports, are on file at the James City County Parks and Recreation office.

CHAPTER 12

Six Degrees of Separation

Using Social Media and Digital Platforms to Enhance African American History Projects

LYNN RAINVILLE

WHEN FACEBOOK first landed in the mainstream of American Internet users, I couldn't imagine why anyone would want to post personal information online. When Pinterest first caught on, I predicted, in my infinite tech wisdom, that it would last a month because after all, when did corkboards resurface in popularity? And I still can't wrap my head around Twitter and its 140-character limit (this sentence is almost over that limit!). But each of these online platforms, and many more, are becoming increasingly valuable in scholarly research. I have had to eat my words.

Contemporary online tools may appear to be far removed from the collection of slave narratives compiled by the Works Progress Administration (WPA) in the 1930s. In fact, similarities abound. Both tools prioritize personal remembrances; both provide a platform for disseminating this information. Despite the biases inherent in the collection of the first-hand experiences of formerly enslaved individuals more than half a century after the end of slavery, WPA narratives remain an invaluable source of information.[1] Similarly, modern social media platforms let individuals share personal information with a wide audience. The title of this article highlights the well-known power of social media: you may only have fifty Facebook "friends," but if each of those friends has an additional twenty-five friends, your posts might reach up to 1,250 people (this does not count the friends of the twenty-five friends who might also see the post). For example, I have four friends in common with Professor Annette Gordon-Reed. In Facebook parlance, this means I am only two degrees of separation from a world expert on slavery at Thomas Jefferson's Monticello.

Social media has opened up new leads in my ongoing research into African American cemeteries, enslaved communities, and segregated schools. For example, early on in my multidecade research into African American cemeteries I began a study of the graveyard at Sweet Briar College (a former plantation), where I was a faculty member. I diligently scoured archives and local sites, but no traditional approach led to new research leads. But now, Facebook posts, blog entries, and online photograph sharing has opened up new avenues.

Why Turn to Social Media for Research?

In 2003, to share some results with community members who would be unlikely to pick up a specialized archaeology publication, I created a website that contained information about my cemetery research. The site's first iteration was static, lacking any mechanism for comments. My site didn't encourage feedback, so I received none. A site reconstruction two years later not only included a "contact us" button on the bottom of every page but also, and even more productively, a link labeled "Contribute Biographical Information" located on the left-hand side of the searchable cemetery database. I've received hundreds of emails via this link. The information has ranged from links to online obituaries (with valuable biographical information and kinship networks) to photographs of the deceased—and from personal remembrances of the dead to directions to hard-to-find family graveyards in rural areas. A decade after I first published the site, I still receive emails from descendants and other interested members of the public. For example, at the end of January 2013 a descendant alerted me to the location of three African American cemeteries in Amherst County, Virginia, that were not yet in my database.

My website contains leads sourced from community members, but Facebook is a better venue for an ongoing dialogue. Yes, the word "Facebook" conjures up college kids sharing embarrassing photos! But the research potential of reaching hundreds or even thousands of online contacts through pithy posts is extraordinary. To mine these possible leads, I created a "business" page for my African American Cemeteries in Virginia research where information on this important topic could be collected and shared. Here, I regularly accept friend requests from people I've assisted with family research, or who have seen my name in a conference program or a local newspaper article.

The value of this page is fourfold. First, it enables me to reach a more diverse audience than I can reach through scholarly publications or even my public talks (when was the last time a middle-schooler attended one of your lectures?). Second, it's quick and easy to post succinct descriptions of my current research interests or to pose questions for feedback. Third, I can share puzzling images encountered in my cemetery research and ask descendants to interpret them. And fourth, I can leverage my initial contact with one family member to make connections with an entire Facebook "family," literally and figuratively. This, in turn, nets new leads: people to interview, sites to visit, and even online obituaries. These are excellent sources.

After Facebook, one of the most powerful social networks is LinkedIn. Launched in 2003, this site allows users to post a detailed career history and then "connect" with other professionals. Unlike Facebook's personal focus, LinkedIn is geared toward professional relationships. So, although it may feel a little awkward, reach out and "connect" to your colleagues and the renowned scholars in your field. LinkedIn will update you when your connections publish new articles and books, and many scholars use LinkedIn to list their upcoming public talks and/or online courses.

One drawback to Facebook and LinkedIn is that page owners do not have full control of their page's physical layout. This sometimes changes the chronological and topical layout of your site. For this reason, a blog platform is more suitable for the display and collation of historic data. In 2007, I created a local history blog at www.LoCoHistory.org (an acronym for local county history). Active between 2007 and 2012, this site enabled me to post short, 250-word entries about local sites, artifacts, and historic events. More than one hundred posts covered aspects of local history; fifteen of them were focused on African American history. This blog was an ideal venue for many lively topics: discussing unpublished research such as an undergraduate's thesis on slavery at the University of Virginia (UVA); promoting a UVA student-based competition to design a memorial to slavery at the university; and highlighting some of Charlottesville's lesser-known historic black homes—homes that may not have been architecturally noteworthy but that had a compelling backstory.

One productive blog post came about when my husband and I were house-hunting. We found a late nineteenth-century farmhouse in rural Albemarle County. Intrigued by its craftsmanship and lack of modern amenities (e.g., plumbing, electricity), I delved into its history. The resultant blog post for Breezy Oaks revealed that a black man named Albert Johnson, who was born enslaved, built the house by hand in 1882 and that some of the logs used in its construction came from either Shadwell (Thomas Jefferson's birthplace) or Monticello (Jefferson's home).[2] A local historian saw my post and added a valuable guess, supported by archival documents, that Albert's mother was "Elizabeth"; she was enslaved by a farm manager at Monticello in the decades after Thomas Jefferson's death.

Another of my research projects demonstrates that a strong online presence boosts credibility and the impression of expertise, even for researchers new to a field. Some years ago I was a visiting scholar at the now defunct Virginia Center for Digital History (VCDH) at the University of Virginia. I decided to help some community members publicize information about the historically significant Rosenwald schools through a new website. Cofinanced by Chicago entrepreneur Julius Rosenwald and local communities, these eponymous schools were built between 1917 and 1932 (Rosenwald's death) to provide school buildings for black children during the failed "separate but equal" era of American education. What made me uniquely suitable for this project wasn't my in-depth historic background, but rather my specific combination of skills: designing online databases; organizing historic information into spreadsheets that could later be loaded online; and conducting oral histories with descendant communities. The website allows visitors to search for any of the 382 Rosenwald Schools in Virginia, organizes the schools by county, and provides links to a timeline, interviews conducted with former alumni at an Albemarle County Rosenwald School, and related resources.[3] Now, if you type "Rosenwald schools" in a Google search, my website is the sixth entry, just below sites like the National Trust for Historic Preservation and Wikipedia. Rosenwald schools are a side interest for me, but my online presence in this field has resulted in many invitations to conferences and requests to help local communities locate and preserve their historic black schools. I worked with the Scrabble School to design an exhibition (http://www.scrabbleschool.org/Precis); interviewed alumni at the St. John's Baptist Rosenwald School; and I presented a paper at the inaugural Rosenwald Schools Conference in Tuskegee hosted by the National Trust for Historic Preservation in 2012. While I am still no expert on the subject, I am a gatekeeper for those who contact me, and regularly refer other scholars and alumni groups to the most appropriate individuals or institutions to assist them with their queries.

Perhaps the most surprising historic research aide in the social media universe is Pinterest. The site's premise is misleading, "a tool for collecting and organizing things you love," producing mental images of crocheted koalas and decorated cupcakes. Returning to first principles, though, if we recast this site as one of the simplest ways to collect and organize online images, it begins to sound more useful. For example, despite having published several papers about slave cemeteries, I am still flummoxed by the motifs used on some slave gravestones. These cryptic designs are often amalgams of Christian and African symbols (see figure 12.1). Because few of these stones contain textual inscriptions, their chronological and thematic context is often hard to decipher. By posting a couple of dozen examples of these opaque symbols on a Pinterest board titled "Symbols on Slave Graveyards," I have made the images visible to informed eyes everywhere (see figure 12.1).[4] This visually appealing display of image-rich data has enabled me to share my thoughts-in-progress with colleagues all over the country and to integrate the site into my recent online course, "American Gravestones and Cemeteries." Every one of these uses emerged from a site created by me in less than five minutes and populated with photographs in less than an hour. With the click of a button, you can upload photos from your computer or other online sources. That is the power of Pinterest.

Other digital formats encourage even more direct links with colleagues. For example, online sources have enabled and later, strengthened my partnerships with local "amateur" historians, pairing my technology background with their local history expertise. The first group I teamed up with was the Central Virginia History Researchers (CVHR) of Charlottesville, Virginia. Coming from many different professional backgrounds, this group (with an average age somewhere north of fifty-five) has met once a month for over a decade. Most members research African American history, either their own ancestors or the history of African Americans in Albemarle County. This professional partnering culminated in a website I designed for the group to disseminate their remarkable research into local black communities at CentralVirginiaHistory.org. Working with CVHR members, I added a blog to publicize the topic of our monthly meetings; an explanation of one of our primary research projects (tracing descendants of enslaved men, women, and children); a sophisticated mapping project spearheaded by a GIS specialist in the group; and a searchable database.

The first phase of this African American Families Database was supported by a digital startup grant from the National Endowment for the Humanities.[5] This grant enabled me to hire database experts from the University of Virginia to create a framework for storing some of the archival information CVHR members had collected over the years. We entered information from antebellum vital records, slave lists (most often found in the wills of owners), federal census records, and church and marriage lists. This is the first step in enabling descendants to locate their enslaved ancestors. On the site I posted two examples from CVHR member research of how these records can be used to learn more about enslaved

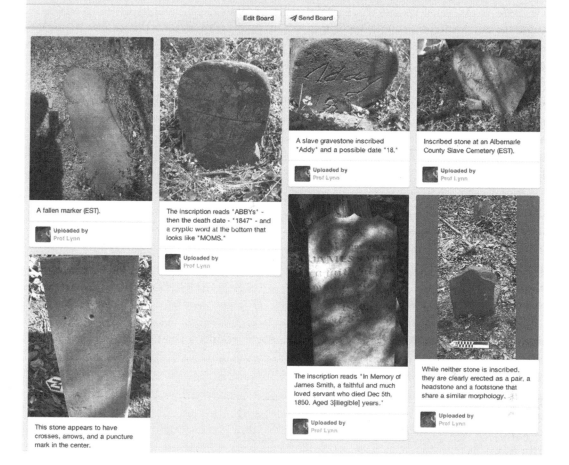

Pinterest

Symbols on Slave Graveyards

Enslaved families had limited options for designing and erecting gravestones. And yet, some individuals managed to carve beautiful examples of gravemarkers.

Edit Board   Send Board

A slave gravestone inscribed "Addy" and a possible date "18."

Uploaded by
Prof Lynn

Inscribed stone at an Albemarle County Slave Cemetery (EST).

Uploaded by
Prof Lynn

A fallen marker (EST).

Uploaded by
Prof Lynn

The inscription reads "ABBYs" - then the death date - "1847" - and a cryptic word at the bottom that looks like "MOMS."

Uploaded by
Prof Lynn

This stone appears to have crosses, arrows, and a puncture mark in the center.

The inscription reads "In Memory of James Smith, a faithful and much loved servant who died Dec 5th, 1850. Aged 3[illegible] years."

Uploaded by
Prof Lynn

While neither stone is inscribed, they are clearly erected as a pair, a headstone and a footstone that share a similar morphology.

Uploaded by
Prof Lynn

Figure 12.1. Symbols on slave graveyards, Pinterest. Courtesy of Lynn Rainville.

individuals on the Bleak House Plantation[6] and about a postbellum community of African Americans in the Hydraulic Mills neighborhood.[7]

Another group I work with is the Burke-Brown-Steppe Chapter of African American Genealogy in Charlottesville. In the early 1990s, chapter members collected information from over five thousand Albemarle County death records stored in Richmond (the capital of Virginia). This was an important resource, but their preliminary website lacked a robust search engine. In 2004 I worked with a database designer to make the records searchable by name, place of burial, or death year.[8] This is now an invaluable resource, not just for genealogists but for historians who want to use the raw data to estimate things such as black infant mortality rates or the patterning of naming within the African American community. With any of the databases that I designed the user can focus on broad patterns (such as the number of Johnson family members buried in Albemarle County) or drill down to individual biographies (learning that "George Johnson" died in 1924 at age twenty-six, having married Sadie, and worked as a coal miner).

My last suggestion is perhaps the most obvious, yet most frequently overlooked, option: build your own website, preferably with a URL using all or part of your name. Some scholars may wonder why they should bother, when their university or museum already provides a page about them. A personal website is valuable for a variety of reasons. First, those lackluster institutional pages are usually controlled by your institution. If you have an upcoming talk or publication to promote, you will have to submit an update request in the hope that the update won't be littered with typos or posted too late. Second, many scholars have multiple professional affiliations. Your online bread crumbs will be distributed across numerous institutional pages and rarely, if ever, cross-referenced or linked. If, instead, you purchase (for a nominal annual fee of about $75) a named URL (e.g., www.cartergwoodson.org), colleagues and any online searcher will find all your research in one place. Years ago I claimed the site www.lynnrainville.org and now use it for a frequently updated career history, links to my current research projects, and an archive of past projects (see figure 12.2). Access to your own page also gives you the freedom to use decade-old photos of yourself for promotional purposes!

My website is coded in simple HTML ("hypertext markup language"), and I make changes to it via Dreamweaver. An even easier option would be to select a Wordpress template. For ideas about what to include, search online for other scholars in your field to see what menu options and links they have included. Be aware: it's not wise to combine a personal website with a professional one. Inevitably your cat meme posts will annoy your professional colleagues, while your academic jargon will bore your friends. The same applies to Facebook. Plan to use a "business page" on Facebook for your research (in my case it's an African American Cemetery page) so that it is always separate from the page where you post adorable photographs of your dachshund.

Designing a Multifaceted Research Plan

In each of my historic research projects I have looked for "informants," individuals who have lived through the era that I was studying. When I decided to create the Rosenwald School database, I gathered together a group of skilled volunteers and took advantage of a nearby school's reunion to arrange for about twenty-five oral interviews. These firsthand accounts breathed life into the more prosaic records than I had read through initially when designing the website. Entries in old record books—grades or absence records—became much more compelling: for instance, an elderly former student remembered being called into the fields at harvest time to help support her family. This was the reason for the many absences recorded against her name.

I value these first-person accounts. Even with more distantly historic events such as slavery or emancipation, I use stories passed down through families. Because I incorporate my social media presence and digital platforms into my research design from the beginning,

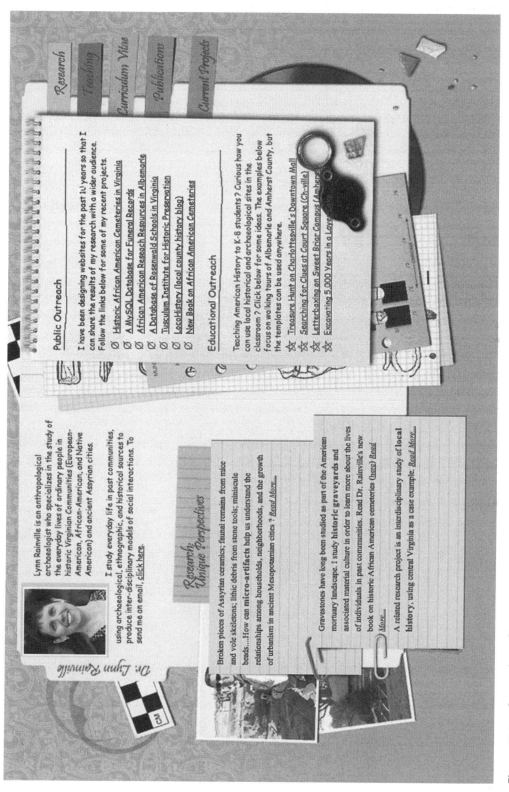

Figure 12.2. Screenshot of Lynn Rainville's website. Courtesy of Lynn Rainville.

the entire project can be informed by these citizen collaborators and I can modify my own theories and methods accordingly.

A good example of the interplay between technology and a research design is my thirteen-year project to investigate the lives of African Americans on the Sweet Briar College and its predecessor, Sweet Briar Plantation. When I moved to Virginia from New Hampshire, I had already researched other types of historic cemeteries, but I knew very little about cemeteries on antebellum plantations. In a lucky twist of fate, my second teaching job in Virginia was at Sweet Briar College. The college was founded in 1900 by the daughter of a large slaveholder who gifted the plantation's three thousand acres to become the college campus. Most of that former farmland remains free of buildings and retains the remnants of nineteenth-century orchards and fields, old fence lines, and ruined farm buildings. Perhaps most remarkably, a slave cabin still stands behind the former "big house" that today is the residence of the college's president.

Of course, with my background in historic cemeteries, my first impulse was to locate the enslaved population's burial ground. Luckily, a riding instructor who roamed the land on horseback had recently found their cemetery atop a hill about half a mile from the big house, almost completely overgrown. My first step was to map the cemetery and research the few documents and photographs attesting to its long-forgotten presence. Later, I began studying the lives of individuals who labored on the plantation before and after emancipation. I discovered that, to this day, many of the hourly workers at Sweet Briar are descended from the enslaved community. With enthusiasm I documented this fascinating research in a website, "African American Heritage at Sweet Briar."[9] Little did I know that this website, which has since grown from only two pages to more than twenty-five, would be the key to reaching many more descendants of the Sweet Briar slave community.

The website worked for two main reasons: First some descendants were simply casting a wide genealogical net and googling their surname; these individuals would come across my website and send me an email or call. Second, I was able to share the URL widely at professional conferences and via social media.

The website features short biographies of some of the African Americans who worked at Sweet Briar Plantation. One of the most compelling of these tells the story of a woman, Martha Penn Taylor, who asked a slaveholder to purchase her so that she would not be separated from her sister, who was enslaved on that plantation.[10] Martha was purchased and became the nursemaid for the slaveholder's granddaughter. In the end she outlived both the slaveholder and the granddaughter, having worked for the same family for fifty years. Mrs. Taylor's relatives contacted me via my website and then came to Sweet Briar College to visit for the first time; during their visit they were surprised to see, alongside the formal portraits of the slave owners in the President's Parlor, a photograph of their ancestor. As my research progressed, I made a conscious effort to post on the website the names of any individuals I was actively researching so that other families might encounter their ancestors online and then share their information.

Another emotional resolution came after I posted a 1920s photograph of an African American man and his family standing in front of the former slave cabin at Sweet Briar College. This man's great-granddaughter, Crystal, came across the image online and sent me an email. The family did not own a copy of the photo, which had been filed in the college archive. This email contact began a multiyear friendship and collaboration. Crystal shared information about her family tree and family lore with me, and I helped her compile documents and photographs about her relatives. Later, she invited me to view and use her family tree in Ancestry.com, saving me from dozens of hours of unnecessary research.

Perhaps the most emotional moment, for me, was when one of the descendant families, the Fletchers, contacted me in 2007 to learn more about their family history at Sweet Briar Plantation. Various family members knew parts of this history, but no one in the family had figured out the document trail to their enslaved ancestors. This is a common hurdle for African American genealogists: how can the genealogist establish the connection of individuals listed with first and last names on the 1870 Federal Census to enslaved individuals who were often only referred to by first name? With help from a local historian in the CVHR group, we found the names of Lavinia and her son Nelson on a slave list from 1860. Subsequent research revealed that Lavinia married James Fletcher. After much discussion, the modern-day Fletcher descendants agreed to host their biannual family reunion at Sweet Briar College in 2008. It was difficult for many of the family members to return to the plantation where their ancestors had been enslaved, but their visit went smoothly and I was honored to tell them what my research had revealed about their enslaved ancestors.

I discovered yet another underutilized social media platform—underused by historians for professional purposes, that is—by lucky accident. Before the reunion itself, I had taken one of the Fletcher descendants and her family for a tour of the on-campus slave cemetery, and that tour was videoed. Although I did not realize it at the time, they posted the video to YouTube.[11] These videos were seen by a couple of dozen people, possibly other family members. I have since created my own YouTube channel (http://www.youtube.com/user/ProfRainville) so that I can control and organize the videos that show up under my name.[12]

My Sweet Briar slave cemetery project, spanning more than a decade of rapid technological change, especially in social media, has taught me that it's important to monitor what I have posted. Some formats age quickly and soon appear outdated. Often there is no need to change the content, but simply its delivery format or platform. For example, podcasts were popular only a few years ago; it seemed as if everyone was downloading them to their iPods for listening while commuting or working out at the gym. I was interviewed for a couple of podcasts and they still exist, but more recently, YouTube has become a much more popular venue for distributing content, so I have added some extra cemetery research content to my YouTube channel.

Now That You're Online, Who Is Paying Attention?

At the most basic level, your research project should have an online presence. If someone googles your research topic, your website, blog, or database should come up on the first page of results. This online presence should stick to the basic principles of online effectiveness: a simple yet engaging design (without distracting sounds or animations), carefully considered keywords in the site description (to increase Google's chances of finding the site), and frequent updates.

If you want to take your genealogical research a step further and engage in a conversation with your audience, you should consider creating a more dynamic web presence. Although early social media was associated with young people, that is no longer the case: today's social media universe fosters dialogues, conversations, and engagement between individuals, organizations, and larger communities—among them, the descendants of enslaved communities. This chapter cannot cover all of the social media technologies, which range from photo-sharing applications (such as Flickr) to video sites (such as Vimeo) or from blogs (such as Tumblr) to collaborative projects (such as Wikipedia). Regardless of which program you select, the philosophy is the same: engage in a dialogue with your audience; enable them to contribute (whether photos, comments, or videos); and then measure the success of your communications.

Harnessing the power of word-of-mouth is invaluable in today's world of online connections. You may only have five hundred visitors to your site each year, but any of those visitors may have commented about your research on their blog, Twitter, or Facebook accounts, thereby reaching out to dozens of their friends. Unlike static websites, social media allows your audience to interact with you and your content. Visitors can post questions, ask for new research leads, and share their personal backgrounds as it relates to your research topic.

To take one popular example: why might it be worth your while to create a Facebook page? For starters, more than 70 percent of all Internet users in the United States are on Facebook; this translates into about 116 million active Facebook users in this country. Just over 62 percent of these users are under thirty-five years old.[13] For many historians and museum curators, this represents an age group that traditionally has been harder to attract.

What are the steps to create a Facebook page for a research project? First, you must create a "personal" account on Facebook before you can create a "business page." Second, decide on your goals for the site: is it to attract a more diverse audience? To promote your recent book? To raise money for future research? All of these? Your answers will determine the type of information that you provide and also the tone you use in writing the entries. For example, some research projects have had success using icons and the "voice" of a mascot to promote their project. In 2012, the Science Museum of Minnesota used an iguana named Iggy to personalize the answers to weekly questions (www.facebook.com/sciencemuseum).

When you have decided on your marketing goals, visit Facebook to create a new business page. A business page is set up with different features and analytical capabilities from your personal page: make certain to create a "fan"-based business page. You will be asked to select a "classification" for your project. Classifications cannot be changed later, so think through your answer carefully: your choice will impact your rankings in searches. Next, a blank page will be created. Select visually appealing photographs to upload as headers and describe your organization.

Once you are ready, invite your "friends" to "like" the page. The average Facebook user has 130 friends, so the platform's networking potential is huge. Have a plan for regular updates, whether once a week or bimonthly, so that your fans don't lose interest. On the other hand, don't post too frequently, otherwise your fans will opt to hide your updates to decrease clutter in their own newsfeeds. After you collect several dozen fans you will automatically get access to Facebook's analytical measurements. This will give you access to the "Admin Panel," which will track the number of people who visited your site and what they shared with other Facebook users.

If you decide to create a social media option other than Facebook, research their analytical tools. By definition, social media products provide you with measures of your success in terms of the number of readers or visitors.

For a variety of reasons, you may prefer to retain a traditional website, alongside the social media options. There is no reason to select only one, but make certain to cross-reference and link the two so that you reach the widest audience possible. If you build a website, be sure to track the number of visitors and their interests. There are many ways to do this, but a widely used option is Google Analytics. Once you cut and paste html code from their website (http://www.google.com/analytics), Google will track the number of visitors to your site, the time that they spend on your site, and which pages catch their interest. This will give you a great deal of data, too much to review here.

Now that you have established an online presence, you can use the analytical measures that each program provides to allocate the time and money you spend on social media. For example, most programs allow you to buy ads to promote your site. Even if you are using a "free" application, you should calculate the cost to create and update content. Using the analytical tools can help you measure your monthly success rates so that you can make informed decisions.

The standard joke about the readership numbers for any article in a scholarly journal has the punch line: "twice—once by the author and once by one of the three required reviewers." While Henry Louis Gates's 2010 article on slavery in the *New York Times* might have attracted hundreds of thousands of readers, most of us write for scholarly publications with a total readership of about two thousand.[14] Moreover, much of our audience is made up of members of the academy and other socioeconomically privileged readers. Integrating social media outlets into your publication plans will increase the audience for your work and will lead to new information that would otherwise have been lost in the midst of family history.

Notes

1. Paul D. Escott, *Slavery Remembered: A Record of Twentieth-Century Slave Narratives*. Chapel Hill: University of North Carolina Press Books, 1979.
2. The post, http://www.locohistory.org/blog/albemarle/2008/03/13/breezy-oaks-a-keswick-farmhouse/.
3. The Rosenwald Schools in Virginia database: http://www2.vcdh.virginia.edu/schools/. I gathered the core historic documentation from a Multiple Properties Nomination Form for "Virginia Rosenwald Schools," submitted by Bryan Clark Green in 2007 to the Virginia Landmarks Register and the National Register of Historic Places.
4. The Pinterest board, http://www.pinterest.com/proflynn/symbols-on-slave-graveyards/.
5. http://www.centralvirginiahistory.org/database1.shtml.
6. Bleak House: http://www.centralvirginiahistory.org/bleakhouse.shtml.
7. http://www.centralvirginiahistory.org/hydraulic.shtml.
8. http://www2.vcdh.virginia.edu/jfbell/.

9. http://www.tusculum.sbc.edu/africanamericans/default.shtml.

10. http://www.tusculum.sbc.edu/africanamericans/bio_MPTaylor.shtml.

11. There are a series of videos, one is http://www.youtube.com/watch?v=DZiXXnwsfSo, and from there you can click on "Damon Pace's videos" and see the other two in the series.

12. I am fortunate to have a somewhat rare name, so usually I can stick with "Lynn Rainville" in URLs, but on YouTube another "Lynn Rainville" beat me to it so I went with Prof Rainville. Depending on the uniqueness of your name you may have to experiment with an appropriate online *nom de plume*.

13. http://istrategylabs.com/2014/01/3-million-teens-leave-facebook-in-3-years-the-2014 -facebook-demographic-report/.

14. Henry Louis Gates, "How to End the Slavery Blame-Game," *New York Times*, April 23, 2010.

PART III

CASE STUDIES

CHAPTER 13

Asking Big Questions of a Small Place

GEORGE W. McDANIEL

I ONCE VISITED a historic site and was told by a well-meaning interpreter, "I wish we could do more to interpret African American history here, but we just don't have a place to do it." The assumption was that African American history needed a separate place, but in fact, African American history at many historic sites, especially those in the South, may be interpreted everywhere because African Americans were integral to the creation and sustaining of the site.

In thinking about African Americans at many southern historic sites, Deborah Mack, Associate Director for Community and Constituent Services with the National Museum of African American History and Culture, declared, "I'm interested in majority history," and by that, she meant not just interpreting African American history as "minority" history, but rather as the story of the majority of the residents.[1] Its interpretation therefore should not be limited to a special facility or program, but instead, be interwoven into the entire fabric of the site—into its interpretive plan, into the tours of the houses, outbuildings, landscape, and workplaces, into the school programs and public programs, and into the museum shop. This is essential because as Pultizer Prize–winning historian C. Vann Woodward explained about white Southerners and African Americans in his book, *American Counterpoint*, they "have shaped each other's destiny, determined each other's isolation, shared and molded a common culture. It is, in fact, impossible to imagine the one without the other and quite futile to try."[2]

Museums also need to develop such programs in order to meet the interests of visitors in the future. Writing in *History News*, independent curator Rainey Tisdale noted that demographic trends show that by the 2040s, America will be a "majority minority" nation, which according to the Center for the Future of Museums, will shape museum visitation. "Non-Hispanic whites who have traditionally constituted the core museum-going audience will become a smaller and smaller percentage of the population, and museums run the risk of becoming less and less relevant to American society as a whole."[3]

Keeping all of this in mind, let's still pause and reflect on the interpreter's comment about the lack of physical facilities because that is a reality many sites face, and they are looking for remedies. What to do? Drayton Hall may serve as a case in point. As at many sites, the house tour remains our principal offering and can only be about an hour in length, so how to give sufficient depth to African American history? Simply lengthening the tour is not an answer because as any good interpreter knows, the attention of visitors, no matter how strong initially, begins to fade, especially after about an hour. What follows is a description of our attempts to solve this problem with the conclusion being that the main plan is to try. Progress may not follow a straight line, but the goal is to get moving and to learn along the way, adjusting as necessary.

In the early 1990s, Drayton Hall offered visitors only the house tour, which accented the history of this remarkable icon in colonial American architecture, the Drayton family, and the site's unique story of historic preservation. Those were strong topics to be sure, but Drayton Hall's mission of preservation and education was broader than those topics. Staff realized they did not go deeply enough into the interpretation of the African American story. To fill the gap in the short term, staff turned to a source close at hand, an African American descendant, who knew the history from a deeply personal perspective and who enjoyed sharing it with others, as he had in special walking tours of the site.

The man was Richmond Bowens, who was born at Drayton Hall in 1908, the grandson of emancipated slaves. He had grown up there, learning and respecting traditional ways of life and willing to share their strategies of "making do," of finding a way when there was seemingly no way. Upon retiring from work in Chicago in the 1970s, he had returned to Drayton Hall to work as the gatekeeper in the 1980s. In the early 1990s, we asked him to work as an interpreter. To ensure visitor access, he stationed himself on the front porch of the museum shop, where all visitors arrive after buying their tickets at the gatehouse. Near his chair were table and chairs for visitors, and he used family trees and historical photographs of Drayton Hall and his family to connect with visitors. Since many visitors could not visualize the pre-industrial and rural world that Bowens had known, we furnished him with historical photographs of African American farmhouses, yards, workplaces, churches, river baptisms, schools, and cemeteries. To provide even more specificity about material culture, we gave him a reprint of a Sears and Roebuck catalog of 1908, enabling him to identify everything from farm equipment to shoes from his youth. Visitors would sit and talk with him personally about history as he knew it, sometimes staying an extra hour or two.

Being a man of deep religious faith and strong family values, he sometimes talked candidly about religion or family problems in today's society, which concerned some staff who perceived this as "unprofessional." Of course, that is a genuine concern in working with descendants at any site. But those concerns were overridden, because those beliefs came with the man. Unlike any of us on staff, he was authentic and of the place and of his time. To try to "professionalize" him would take away the heart of what he was saying, and we reasoned that visitors could separate his personal views from his wider knowledge of history.

When Bowens became ill in 1997 and unable to work, Drayton Hall was faced again with the problem of interpreting African American history in the absence of physical facilities. To respond, we did what I hope other museums do. We learned and borrowed from others, in this case, Monticello. They offered a walking tour of the garden at an appointed time. At another time, they offered a walking tour of African American history, following a somewhat similar route but with a different focus. So we devised an African American walking tour of the landscape, focusing on African American history and interpreting landscape features, the exterior of the house, archaeological sites, and workplaces, and we used copies of historical documents and photographs of people, places, and artifacts to help interpret what visitors were seeing. The tour lasted about an hour. A number of sites, such as Middleton Place and James Madison's Montpelier, now employ this method. Such a tour gets visitors to walk the landscape with a trained interpreter so they can experience real places and visualize the history of the landscape in new ways.

While the content of the tour was well received, logistically, it was difficult to produce. Interpreters found it too cumbersome to carry the photographs and photocopies with them, and visitors were of different walking abilities, making it hard to keep the group together. Today, thanks to mobile devices, walking tours work more efficiently. They enable visitors to see the landscape from different perspectives and engage the visitors' imagination by helping them to "people" the landscape in their mind's eye.

At that time, however, mobile devices were not available to us, so we experimented by stationing the program at a table near the museum shop to ensure visitor access. An interpreter gave the program at specific hours, three times a day, using photographs, artifacts, maps, and photocopies of historical documents along with interactive activities. The guide encouraged discussion. At first, it was simply called an "African American Focus Program," and visitors responded favorably. But staff realized we needed to conceptualize the program more clearly. After considerable discussion, staff realized that the purpose was to educate visitors, who come from across the nation and even overseas, often with little knowledge about African American history, or even history in general. By using Drayton Hall as a touchstone, we wanted to connect visitors today to time past, to the people of the past, and to places of the past. We wanted to connect Drayton Hall's African American history to the broader history of America and the transatlantic world. We also wanted to explain how African Americans lived and worked during slavery and how they responded to it, and also what happened when freedom came, and how key attributes of African American culture that visitors see today in the Carolina Lowcountry and elsewhere have their roots in past traditions. For more effective learning, we wanted to engage different learning styles and therefore made the program more interactive by using kinetic, visual, and auditory learning devices, and accenting questions and answers. With all this in mind, we named the program "Connections," and after considerable experimentation, discussion, and evaluation, we launched it in the late 1990s.

The Connections program is low cost and low tech, but high impact on a personal level. Visitors meet around tables under a tent by the shop (see figure 13.1). Interpreters receive in-depth training in both content and delivery, reading from an extensive bibliography and, as with the house tour, they must be approved by the senior interpreter. Just as Drayton Hall is not period specific in its interpretation of the site, so too is this program. Since the African heritage was fundamental to colonial life at Drayton Hall and the Carolina coast, it usually begins in Africa, follows the Middle Passage to the sale of slaves in Charleston, describes the work and culture of Africans and African Americans at Drayton Hall during slavery, and concludes with emancipation and the life of African Americans at Drayton Hall in the twentieth century. To give the program focus, it accents those attributes from Africa that were carried over and seen at Drayton Hall and in the Lowcountry, such as material culture, housing, rice cultivation, foodways, and language. The recollections of Richmond Bowens proved to be integral to explaining Drayton Hall in the twentieth century. Photocopies of archival documents or illustrations from books are used as visual evidence and are passed around and discussed with visitors. They include illustrations of the African slave trade and material culture, scenes from the Middle Passage, steps in rice cultivation, and the "task system" or the "rules" of plantation management, and a set of letters that describe the breakup of enslaved families among Drayton's heirs. In other words, the program does not shy away from difficult subjects and shows how slavery affected real people at Drayton Hall. To the extent possible, real individuals are named and photographs distributed to give them character.

Since the program is about forty-five minutes in length, each interpreter is charged with covering these time periods in general, but is given leeway as to how to allocate more time and discussion. No guide follows a script. To incorporate kinetic learning, especially for children, visitors may use a reproduction of a mortar and pestle to pound and polish rice or a fanner basket to toss the rice in the air and separate the chaff from the kernels. To emphasize the ongoing connection to Africa, a grass basket woven recently in Senegal is compared to

Figure 13.1. *Connections* program at Drayton Hall, Charleston, South Carolina. Courtesy of Drayton Hall.

a sweetgrass basket recently woven in Charleston, and visitors marvel at the similarities. To foster continued learning, the guides also recommend books for purchase in our museum shop that have shaped this program.

Evaluations are positive. Interpreters report that while some visitors may be hesitant at first, most are appreciative by the end. Visitors say that the program answers questions they wanted to ask and gives them new insights into African American history. Many were unfamiliar with the African background and thought it important that we begin in Africa and conclude in the recent past, because "that completes the circle." A white lady from Kansas said, "Just walking the grounds, I felt the presence of the ancestors. I just wanted to learn more and came to this program." Seeking to empathize with the Draytons and with the slaves, visitors often ask, "What were the Draytons like as slave-owners?", "What was it like being a slave?", and "What did they do when freedom came?" To answer, the interpreters seek to draw from the secondary sources to give context to Drayton Hall and use primary documents from the Drayton diaries or other sources to give site-specific examples as best they can. Postings by visitors on diverse travel websites have been favorable: "The talk on slave life was refreshingly direct"; "The interactive presentation on the enslaved labor force was riveting . . . a tremendous history lesson"; "Make sure you take time to participate in the Connections program as it helps to give a more full picture of true plantation life."

In addition to enriching the interpretation of the site for our regular visitors, Connections has also been recycled and revised for use in our school programs. Further, we have modified it for African American family reunions on site, since not only does it impart a deeper sense of history but it can also be used for intergenerational activities and hands-on learning.

Drayton Hall is seeking to ask big questions of a small place, but by no means do we have all the answers. As a work in progress, we are still learning from and exchanging ideas with other museums and are seeking to develop answers through consistent research, training, experimentation, and evaluation. Further, we are striving toward the development of physical facilities, including a new interpretive center, so we can offer such programs whatever the weather. We are also looking to develop mobile apps and an enhanced access to our website so that visitors can tour the landscape, experience this place, and connect with its people via new uses of personal technology.

To develop African American interpretive programs for visitors in the absence of major physical facilities, the main point is to be creative to find a way. The Connections program started with a table. For an increasing number of sites, striving for a holistic history is at the core of the mission, and as a result, African American history is not a subsidiary topic but rather one that is central both to the story and to making the site pertinent to today's society. They agree with Lonnie Bunch, founding director of the National Museum of African American History and Culture, who explained in his award-winning book, *Call the Lost Dream Back*,

> One of the key challenges that cultural institutions face is how to wrestle effectively with, and cross, the color line. If museums are truly to be institutions that the public admires and trusts, then more museums should expend the political and cultural capital and take the risks, (in order) to help their visitors find a useful, usable, inclusive, and meaningful history that engages us all.[4]

For us at history museums and sites, it is our responsibility to "expend" that capital and connect with our visitors so that they leave with a deeper understanding of American and African American history and feel themselves connected to that story. Lonnie Bunch makes this point well: "African American culture has the power and the complexity needed to illuminate all the dark corners of American life, and the power to illuminate all the possibility and ambiguities of American life. . . . It is a mirror that makes those who are often invisible more visible, and it gives voice to many who are often overlooked. But it is also a mirror that allows us to see our commonalities."[5] It connects.

Notes

1. Deborah L. Mack, interview with George W. McDaniel, March 18, 2014.
2. Woodward quoted in Eugene Genovese, *Roll, Jordan, Roll: The World the Slaves Made* (New York: Vintage, 1976), xv.
3. Rainey Tisdale, "Do History Museums Still Need Objects?" *History News* 66, no. 3 (2011): 21.
4. Lonnie Bunch, *Call the Lost Dream Back: Essays on History, Race and Museums* (Washington, D.C.: AAM Press, 2010), 65.
5. Bunch, *Call the Lost Dream Back*, 65.

CHAPTER 14

Power in Limits

Narrow Frames Open Up African American Public History

BENJAMIN FILENE

GENERALIZATIONS (to start with one) have real limits. Historians seek patterns and trends, but we should also recognize what gets effaced when we speak of "the African American experience," "black culture," or "life during slavery." The richness of people's lived experience recedes when we reduce individuals to a single label or category. How can we understand the multiplicity of people's identities if we define them by just one attribute? Crosscut threads get lost in the big weave of history. The issue is particularly acute for public historians. When we speak in broad terms, we can compromise one of our main assets: the ability for our audiences to identify personally with our historical subjects, to connect with history's humanity. Moreover, the pressure to seek out generalities and sweeping conclusions can steer us away from the idiosyncratic and the atypical. Lacking the source materials to make decisive, overarching assertions, we may hesitate to embrace local history, with its rich and revealing exceptions to the rule.

For all of these reasons, in doing public projects about African American history I have come to appreciate the power of the closely observed story—the individual, humanized, and exceptional subject. This approach, which one might call "micro-public history," can lead to new ways of understanding the past, handling source limitations, building partnerships, and reaching audiences. These attributes are evident in three collaborative, community-based projects that I completed with my graduate students at the University of North Carolina at Greensboro, where I run a public history program (our students complete a two-year master's program in history with concentration in museum studies). I initiated and directed these projects as centerpieces for courses I teach, but they depended on the creative and devoted work of the students, classes of eight-to-ten members each year, who shaped and executed them.

Each of these projects focused on an African American history that had been largely overlooked; each depended on a strong sense of place, concentrating on particular communities within North Carolina; each drew heavily on oral history; and, importantly, each worked within real interpretive limits, self-imposed boundaries that tightened our story.

Three Case Studies

The first project, *The Class of '63* (completed in 2007), focused on alumni of the Rosetta C. Baldwin school, an African American private school in High Point, North Carolina, affiliated with the Seventh-Day Adventist church. Founded in 1942 by Baldwin in her living room, the school went on to educate four generations of African Americans in High Point, a city where the schools remained segregated until 1969. When Baldwin died in 2000, she left her house to a favorite former student, Julius Clark, who had spent his career as a postal worker. With no experience and few funds, Chambers opened a museum to honor her legacy. The museum is a heartfelt and winning place that teaches one much about Baldwin and local African American history. When I saw it, I was eager to help, but wanted to do so without undermining what Julius had already achieved. Could my students and I bring a new set of stories or perspectives into the museum? As I toured Julius's exhibit, I was struck by a photograph showing the full student body in 1963—forty-six students and their teachers, kindergarten through eighth grade (see figure 14.1). All dressed up and neatly posed, the students look at the camera earnestly. The image struck me as emblematic of the school's determination and its hope for these young people. It also raised a question: What happened to these students? A photo like this is a moment in a time, a point in a life arc. How did that arc play out?

With that simple question, my nine students began a detective hunt to track down the people in the photo. Starting with a few initial names from Julius Clark, the students tracked down addresses and descendants through birth, death, and marriage certificates and then gathered more names by word of mouth, and in response to a newspaper article that featured our quest. In the end, we identified thirty-five faces in the photograph, and recorded oral interviews with eighteen of them and their descendants. These first-person voices became the basis for an exhibition about the Baldwin school: *The Class of '63* was featured at the High Point Museum May–August 2007 and then moved to the Rosetta C. Baldwin Museum for long-term display.

The second project, *Community Threads: Remembering the Cone Mill Villages*, centered on the company towns that the Cone Mills Corporation built in the early 1900s to house its textile factory workers. Thousands of workers and their families made their lives in these "towns within a town" until the company began selling the houses (sometimes to workers) in the late 1940s. The villages were segregated—one built for each of the Cones' four factories, with a separate village, East White Oak, for African American workers. (Until the 1960s, African Americans could hold only the most menial jobs in the factories, often custodial.) While the Cone name is prominent in Greensboro—adorning the hospital, an elementary school, and art collections—the former factory workers are largely invisible in the city. We decided to focus on understanding what it was like to live in the villages, which included

Figure 14.1. Rosetta C. Baldwin School, 1963. Collection of Julius Clark.

churches, schools, ball fields, community centers, and company stores, and we made a special effort to learn about the African American village, whose story had been almost completely overlooked.

The mill villages don't look like tourist destinations today. The company added aluminum siding to the houses in the white villages before selling them, and the entire African American village, except for the school building, was torn down. We sought to animate the area with stories. Although the neighborhood looks plain to outsiders, we knew it was fertile with memories for those who had lived and worked there. Across two years, from 2008 to 2010, students recorded over forty oral interviews with mill villagers. We also created a community "Memory Map"—a seven-foot-by-six-foot blow-up of contemporary northeast Greensboro, detailed enough to show individual houses. We took the map to a dozen locations across the city, such as the VFW hall, branch libraries, retiree group meetings, the community center, and the Greensboro Historical Museum. At each stop, we invited people to write directly onto the map what happened to them in this place: where they lived, the site of their first kiss, their exploits on the ball field (see figure 14.2). The map became a glorious mess of memories, layers of stories, with cross-outs reflecting change over time and disputes about the details. The map also was wonderfully effective as a convening tool, a focal point across which mill villagers from different eras could swap recollections.

Harvesting stories from the interviews and from the map, in 2009 we created a public van tour of the neighborhood, narrated by students with mill villagers chiming in along the way. In one memorable trip, the former African American residents excitedly shared recollections of East White Oak from the front seat while descendants of the Cone family listened attentively from the back. The van tour was just a one-day affair, but we created a

Figure 14.2. Constructing a memory map, 2012. Photo by Benjamin Filene.

self-guided, printed tour that lives on. The next year, a new cohort of students extended the project online, through a website designed both to share memories and to gather them.[1] The scrawls of the Memory Map became legible through Google Maps, and we linked audio excerpts to specific map points; we invited people to contribute and tag photos through Flickr; we set up a chat forum for informal conversation (activity quickly gravitated instead to our Facebook site: lesson learned); and we adopted a "choose your adventure" format to trace daily life in the villages across the season.

Finally, a third project focused on a different local segregated community. In the 1880s, the Quaker owners of the Pomona Terra Cotta Manufacturing Company built a small company town to house the families of the African American workers who made clay sewer pipes in their factory. In the early 1960s, the rental housing was torn down as the plant began to shut down operations. Only one square block of the neighborhood remains, with houses that workers built themselves in the 1920s–1940s (often with pieces of clay in the foundations and chimneys) on land sold to them by the company. In the early 2000s, a former resident who had grown up in Terra Cotta, Dennis Waddell, returned to the neighborhood and launched the Terra Cotta Day Festival, an annual reunion for current and former residents. With response strong, he opened a museum in one of the houses.

One of Dennis's goals is to document the individual histories of over two hundred families that lived in the neighborhood over time.[2] In talking with him, I realized that this might be one way in which I could help. As a first step, I assigned each student one Terra Cotta family to research, including conducting oral interviews. Students created handmade mini-exhibits about each family, which we then presented to the community in a public program. From there, Dennis and I agreed to expand the project into a full-fledged exhibition at his museum. To make more connections and gather materials, students joined in on the Terra

Cotta Day Festival as participants, recording additional interviews on the spot, working with a local photo collector to link names to unidentified images on a "photo find" wall, and creating a Terra Cotta–focused version of the Memory Map. With so much of the neighborhood literally vanished (displaced by car dealerships and new road patterns), the map was a great way to reconstruct the lost landscape and populate it with stories. From there, students wrote label text, selected images, edited audio excerpts, designed interactives, repainted the walls of the gallery, and installed an exhibition, *Past the Pipes: Stories of the Terra Cotta Community*, which opened with a public celebration in December 2012.

New Views of History

Most simply, these three projects documented a set of African American stories that were largely absent from the historical record. All of the interviews that we conducted were archived in University of North Carolina at Greensboro's (UNCG) library, in the Greensboro Historical Museum, and with our partner institutions such as the Baldwin Museum and the Terra Cotta Heritage Center. More broadly, though, these projects led to fresh ways of understanding the past. We found, counterintuitively perhaps, that narrowing the frame of our focus—a single photograph, a few square blocks—enabled us to talk about bigger topics and to do so in a richer way.

For instance, focusing on individual families and communities surfaced a surprising degree of nostalgia for life during segregation. Without disputing the heroism and power of the civil rights movement, our interviews demonstrated a clear sense that integration came at a cost: many feel that the close-knit communities that had sustained African Americans for a century in the face of poverty, legal restrictions, and everyday discrimination began to crumble in the late 1960s. Terra Cotta residents, for example, lived in undeniably difficult circumstances. In a segregated village on what was then the outskirts of town, they worked long shifts in the heat of the factory and lived in crowded houses that often lacked running water; the neighborhood's electricity was connected to the factory, so when operations shut down for the weekend, the lights went out. Nonetheless, Terra Cotta residents have overwhelmingly positive recollections of this life and feel a sense of loss that this life has disappeared in recent decades.

Indeed, the overriding theme in the Terra Cotta interviews was of interconnection and mutual dependence. Jacqueline Lyles, who had nearly thirty family members sharing a house as she grew up, recalled simply: "It was wild. But it was the best life." Wilhelmina Waddell echoed, "Everybody took care of anybody in the community. Anytime you did something [wrong], by the time you got home your mom knew about it." "Everyone helped raise everyone's kids," Sam Fogle added. "There weren't any extremely bad kids as far as robbing people, going to jail, or killing each other. I could spend the night with my friends. They called my mother, 'Mama.' I called their mother, 'Mother _____'—whatever their last name might be." "We had freedom before we really got freedom," summarized Marion Staples. "You hear of people down in South Carolina and Mississippi; they couldn't do nothing without the man that owned them. . . .[In Terra Cotta] it wasn't like that."[3] The boundaries and opportunities for Terra Cotta's residents have certainly expanded in recent decades, yet most of the interviewees see decline. "It's changed a whole lot," Paul Hughes reflected. "I can remember when we used to sleep on the porch, but you better not do it now, you know. I mean everybody was friendly, and like if you need something, they chip in together to help, neighbor-like—someone needs something, they help him out. But these days ain't like that. Seems like everybody's for theyself these days." Says Jacqueline Williams Perkins, "Even though we were considered poor in this area we didn't really realize that we were poor until we moved into the city part of town, because we had everything we needed. . . .[W]hen you got love, you have more than anything."[4]

That lack of focus on the community's poverty was likewise a refrain among the East White Oak mill villagers we interviewed. Sarah Murray stated, "We didn't know that we were poor and I guess because everyone around us was in the same fix." Franklin Richmond (whose brother David became one of the "Greensboro Four" sit-ins leaders in 1960) said, "[W]e was so well protected, we didn't know about the . . . problems in society outside of the community here. We was shielded, protected. We had everything we needed right here inside this community except for a few things."[5]

Similarly, interviewees in *The Class of '63* project spoke passionately about their community bonds and the more recent fraying of them: "[It was a] strictly black community but it was good," former Baldwin student Barbara Collier recalled. "Nothing was run down— everything was perfect. . . . Nobody ever heard of welfare and food stamps. Everyone worked hard." Eleanor Wonce, a friend of Rosetta Baldwin, reflected that today "the community is not tight, and I think this is everywhere. A whole lot of drugs have come in and took over our community."[6]

One might well dismiss these fond memories as the nostalgia of aging people propping up visions of the good old days. But a key element in the phrase "We didn't know we were poor" is that the speakers don't dispute the fact now. They see the constrictions in their old life, but they take pride in the community they built within them. That sense of community is just as real as the limits within which it was crafted.

To take another example, the narrow geographic focus of these projects also revealed a richer sense of how segregation operated in the Jim Crow South. While the traditional images of "colored "and "white" water fountains carry a powerful message in their stark simplicity, listening to how segregation operated in these small communities revealed a more complex reality. One of the residents of the white mill villages, Buddy Owens, recalled that in the early 1950s, he and his teenage buddies would get in a car on some Sundays, drive over to East White Oak, and find an African American baseball team to play. "They'd beat us every time, but we went over. We loved to play with them."[7] Many Terra Cotta men recalled working as caddies for whites at nearby country clubs to earn extra money. When the white men would throw their old golf clubs into the woods in frustration, the Terra Cotta youth would pick up the clubs for their own use. And instead of playing on formal courses, Terra Cotta residents made their own golf courses in fields throughout the neighborhood. Such recollections don't overturn our understanding of segregation, but in their day-to-day specificity they illustrate how these boundaries were continually, and often in unspoken ways, blurred, reinforced, and renegotiated.

Nuanced historical insights of these sorts tend to get lost in tracing the broader story of the push for civil rights in the century. Moreover, the sense of loss behind "we didn't know we were poor" is difficult for a museum to discuss in its "institutional voice." Does the museum dare risk romanticizing segregation? This uneasiness is particularly challenging when, as so often is the case, the museum's staff is overwhelmingly white. (Ninety percent of my students have been white, middle class, and female.) When a museum showcases specific, locally rooted stories told by willing partners, though, the institution gains the freedom to depict the fuller complexity of African American history. Stories gain validity from being told in the voices of the individuals who lived them. Instead of struggling to generalize, the museum is illustrating lived experience, allowing room for contradictions, surprises, and challenges to received opinions.

New Kinds of Sources

Beyond enriching our historical understanding, the closely observed story can also enable public historians to overcome the paucity of historical sources available about local African American history. "There is no information" is the most common excuse for omitting the African American experience from our museums and historic sites. But how can this be acceptable? Museums simply must push harder to show their commitment to represent their communities.

A starting point is to admit that not every story needs to be sourced in the same way or told with the same narrative approach. In some respects, the tight frames I put around the topics for my projects heightened our research challenge, but they also freed us up to dig deeply into untapped sources and to think creatively about what constitutes a story.

Outside of the well-documented civil rights struggle of the 1960s, there is almost no published scholarship about the African American experience in Greensboro. Archival materials are hard to come by, too: as in most communities, the rich and literate are disproportionately documented in our museums and libraries. There are no collections on Rosetta Baldwin, East White Oak, or Terra Cotta, but our goal for these projects didn't depend on vast amounts of material.[8] Instead of setting out to "cover" African American history in our region, these projects were fired by a question: Can we reclaim these individual lives from the anonymity of the past? We were driven by an urgency to document and share the stories of communities that draw such passion from their members but are absent from the usual accounts of our city.

That mission opened us up to consider sources sometimes overlooked by traditional historians. Public records, for instance, yield just shards of information about individual people, but when those fragments are all that you have, they become worthy of a second look that can become illuminating. In *The Class of '63* exhibition, for instance, we included biographical sketches of every person in the 1963 photograph, even if we had only tidbits of information about them from public records. Through city directories and birth records, for instance, we were able to give at least a glimpse of the working-class life of the Parker family in our biography:

Juliuse Parker, often known as "Red," was born in High Point in 1957.[9] He was six years old when he attended the Baldwin Chapel School. His father, Johnny Edward Parker, worked at American Bakeries, at 920 West Broad Street, where he was a shop worker and machine operator, making breads for Merita.

When we truly hit a dead end, we acknowledged that in the biographical sketches:

> Sammie Steele, Jr., was born in High Point on February 15, 1951. City death records show that he died on February 28, 2007 at the age of 56. So far no additional information has surfaced in public documents.

In its own way, this lack of information is telling. In just over half a century since his birth, Sammie Steele Jr. seems to have vanished. What does that convey to our visitors about the possibilities and limits of doing African American history? If we resist glossing over gaps in our knowledge, these needle-in-a-haystack projects can offer museum audiences a useful illustration of how history works—the uncertainties and erraticness of historical documentation and the challenges in trying to represent ordinary African Americans in ways that reflect their individual humanity. Instead of trying to offer the last word on history, museums have the opportunity to instruct audiences about historical silences.[10]

This lesson invites us also to embrace the power of oral history, whether gathered through recorded interviews or through more informal programs such as our Memory Map. Memory is fallible, of course, and usually not the best source for factual precision, but where dispassionate written records seem thin and frail, oral history can robustly animate experience. Consider just one recollection from longtime Terra Cotta resident Paul Simpson:

> We made kites. There was more land then; there's so many buildings and stuff now. We'd put tails on the kites of rags and stuff. Sometimes, that kite on a string, we'd almost let them out of sight. The wind would get so high sometimes they'd break loose. Some of them would fall in the trees.[11]

Simpson's seemingly simple reflection evokes the geography of the neighborhood, the changes brought by urbanization, the community's resourcefulness within limited means, and, **perhaps, a metaphorical vision of freedom.**

We needn't claim ground-breaking historical significance for such recollections to have value. Without further comment, they illustrate a fundamental lesson: history happened, and it was lived by—and sometimes shaped by—ordinary people who made a host of everyday choices across the span of their lives.

New Partnerships

Foregrounding individual voices in African American history also conveys a powerful message about historical expertise. When we acknowledge the limits of traditional historical sources, we allow room for other people to be recognized as experts. No one knows more about life in East White Oak than those who lived it. To pretend otherwise is not only interpretively arrogant but logistically impractical. Each of these projects fundamentally depended upon community partners: Dennis Waddell from Terra Cotta; Julius Clark from the Rosetta C. Baldwin School; Marthella Richmond who grew up in East White Oak and welcomed us as the director of the East White Oak Community Center in the village's former schoolhouse. These community leaders provided us with both information and access. For an elderly person to share her life story with a stranger is an incredible act of trust. Having introductions from these well-known and historically minded neighborhood figures made it easier for people to let us into their lives.

Working with community partners can raise fears among historians of losing interpretive control, but I've had few such issues, in part, I believe, because of how I framed the projects and the partnerships. I did not represent us as outside authorities coming in to evaluate these communities' histories. On the contrary, we were hoping to learn from these communities and then to help them share their experiences and reflections with wider audiences. In that sense, we constructed these projects in ways that were in sync with our partners' missions.

That close relationship did not mean that we could only do "happy history." These projects directly addressed such issues as segregation, class and poverty, religion, urban redevelopment, and intergenerational conflict. They did so, though, in ways that allowed the communities we were working with to reflect on these issues in their own voices: our goal was to raise questions and open dialogue, not pronounce judgment. Early in the Terra Cotta project, for instance, the students wondered if Dennis Waddell's palpable pride in the neighborhood would push us to downplay the extent to which the community lived in poverty while the factory owners profited. It soon became clear, though, that Dennis is well aware of that dynamic; he just wants people to recognize the resilience that Terra Cotta residents showed while living in those circumstances. "Community within constraints" became an explicit and overarching theme for the exhibition, one that all the community members involved in the project quickly recognized and accepted.

This process of navigating and negotiating interpretive authority is partly why I find these micro-community projects to be such powerful teaching tools. So much of attending graduate school is about building authority, learning how to take on the expert voice. But for my young students, working with these elderly African American partners and learning really to listen to them decentered their sense of expertise in useful ways. They learned important lessons about the limits of their training that ultimately will make them open and engaged public historians. As well, they realized that relationships—with partners and with each other as collaborators—take work, that the interpersonal dynamics of public history both demand and reward attention. Finally, the students learned about the power of local history and how to make the case for it. Only a very few museums in America (mostly Smithsonian-affiliated) can argue that their work focuses on historical issues with as broad a scope as those that preoccupy academic historians. Most museums, perpetually, have to make the case to funders and constituents for why their state, city, town, or site *matters*. The answer lies not just through dogged research but also through relationship-building, making one's institution visible and present in the lives of its constituents.

New Audiences

The immediate communities on which we focused responded very positively to these projects. The alumni of the Rosetta C. Baldwin School and residents of Terra Cotta were thrilled to literally see themselves in a museum. Former East White Oak neighbors on our van tour were excited to revisit the neighborhood and to hear and share stories. For the institutions involved, the projects opened up new possibilities. The Class of '63 drew scores of African American visitors to the High Point Museum who had never before set foot in the building; Julius Clark and the Rosetta C. Baldwin Museum received not only the exhibit itself but connections to the professional staff of the High Point Museum down the road. The Terra Cotta exhibition's opening gave a boost to Dennis Waddell's ongoing plans for the museum. The success of the mill village tours ensured that any permanent exhibition at the redeveloped factory site, a subject of ongoing discussion, would certainly need to—and be able to—include the East White Oak experience.

The power of the microhistory approach, though, resonates far beyond those immediately depicted and involved. Tell people that you are searching for mystery people in a photograph or puzzling over mute names on a census list, and right away you hear about unidentified photos that they have in their own dresser drawers and the silent names on their own family trees. People instinctually are drawn to the challenge of bringing the past to life; they understand and want to share in that process of historical recovery. Micro-public history, then, becomes not only an opportunity to connect with overlooked African American audiences but also a way to build bridges between African American stories and wider audiences. Indeed, public response to these projects far outstripped their modest budgets and their relatively simple final products.[12] Strength of story trumps the razzle-dazzle of design. With little prompting, all of these projects drew newspaper, radio, online, and, sometimes, television coverage. We had 100 percent success in the grant applications we submitted for the projects (primarily from the North Carolina Humanities Council, as well as UNCG's Office for Leadership and Service-Learning). Drawn by the story and the coverage, hundreds of people attended who had no immediate connections to these communities.

People respond to the idea of history as a human endeavor. Creating narrative boundaries—of time, place, and characters—helps audiences recognize African American history as a story, a search, a collaboration, and a cause. The approach invites us to turn the challenges of doing African American history into opportunities, ones that can lead us to become better stewards, better historians, and better advocates for the past.

Notes

1. *Community Threads: Remembering the Cone Mill Villages*, accessed May 21, 2014, http://conemillvillages.weebly.com/index.html.
2. Terra Cotta Heritage Foundation, accessed May 21, 2014, http://www.terracottaheritage foundation.org.
3. All interviews cited are in the author's possession and can be accessed in the Martha Blakeney Hodges Special Collections and University Archives, University Libraries, University of

North Carolina at Greensboro. Jacquelyn Lyles and Christina Lyles Melvin, interview by Erick Noble, October 10, 2014, p. 6 of transcript; Wilhemina Hughes Waddell, interview by Elizabeth Baker, September 1, 2012, p. 5; Samuel Fogle, interview by Shawna Prather, September 1, 2012, p. 4; Marion Staples, interview by Ashley Wyatt, October 17, 2011, p. 19.

4. Paul and Betty Hughes, interview by Elizabeth Baker, October 10, 2011, p. 10; Jacqueline Williams Perkins and Edwina Williams Monroe, interview by Amber Williams, September 1, 2012, p. 7.

5. Sarah Andrews Murray, interview by Emmanuel Dabney, April 6, 2009, p. 6; Franklin Richmond, interview by Emmanuel Dabney, April 9, 2009, pp. 4–5.

6. The Collier and Wonce quotations appeared on the exhibition panel "Community: Then and Now" in *The Class of '63* exhibition, High Point Museum.

7. Jerry "Buddy" Owens, interview by Ashley N. Boycher, March 18, 2009, p. 14.

8. The Southern Historical Collection at UNC-Chapel Hill holds the Cone Mills Corporation Records, but it is stronger on the institutional history of the mills than on daily life in the villages, and information is thinner on East White Oak.

9. Records suggest that Parker spelled "Juliuse" with an "e."

10. Michel-Rolph Trouillot, *Silencing the Past: Power and the Production of History* (Boston: Beacon Press, 1995), 26; Robert R. Weyeneth has called for historians to "lift the veil" on doing history. See "What I've Learned along the Way: A Public Historian's Intellectual Odyssey," *Public Historian* 36, no. 2 (May 2014): 9–25.

11. Paul Simpson, interview by Shawna Prather, October 25, 2011, p. 15.

12. The mill village projects were completed for less than $1,500; *The Class of '63* totaled less than $2,000; we worked with a freelance designer for Terra Cotta, a permanent exhibition, but even so it cost less than $7,000.

CHAPTER 15

Connecting Students with Community History

STACIA KUCEYESKI

A S PROFESSIONALS in the history field, we often take for granted that neighborhoods and buildings have stories to tell. Driving in our cars or walking down the street, we have a sense of the historic significance of our environment, but it can be hard to imagine the impact a neighborhood once had on the experiences of thousands of people. This is especially true for those communities that time, as well as prosperity, has forgotten.

The Near East Side of Columbus, Ohio, specifically the Mount Vernon Avenue area, is such a place. While neighborhood pride centers and local business groups try to restore the community's sense of place and economic viability, the Mount Vernon Avenue of today is still a far cry from the bustling African American commercial and social hub of the first half of the twentieth century.

The Ohio History Connection (formerly the Ohio Historical Society), in collaboration with the Columbus City School's East Pilgrim Elementary and Monroe Middle Schools, developed and implemented a local history initiative during the 2006–2007 school year focusing on the Near East Side of Columbus. The project centered on the Mount Vernon Avenue neighborhood, which was a gateway for African Americans migrating to the North in the late nineteenth and early twentieth centuries. Mount Vernon Avenue was the center of life for much of central Ohio's black community in the mid-twentieth century until highways severed the community from the downtown area.

Funded by an $11,000 grant from the Ingram-White Castle Foundation, the project trained sixty third-grade and twenty-six eighth-grade students to conduct historical research on the Near East Side of Columbus. Students conducted new research and identified significant people, places, and/or events in the community's history. The students then applied for five Ohio Historical Markers in the community and developed a walking tour of the neighborhood based on the markers.

The Near East Side Community History Project consisted of three phases: research, interviews, and markers. The research phase enabled students to gain a background on the historic content about which they would be writing and interviewing. Students learned about the Great Migration in class and attended a research workshop at the Martin Luther King Branch of the Columbus Metropolitan Library. Ohio History Connection and library staff created research stations with primary sources from the branch's collection and reproductions of primary sources from the Ohio History Connection collections. These stations consisted of items relating to themes such as artists, churches, schools, and businesses in the Mount Vernon Avenue area.

Ohio History Connection staff visited the classroom to discuss primary sources with the students and engage them in activities where they interpreted primary sources. Staff also utilized the Aminah Robinson book, *A Street Called Home*, to talk to the students about the role of memory and art in history and historical research. The students also learned more about the Great Migration with their teachers in the classroom.

The second phase of the project consisted of a series of oral history interviews. The video production staff at the Ohio History Connection instructed the eighth-grade students in formulating interview questions, operating the video camera, and conducting oral history interviews. The eighth-graders conducted interviews in pairs. They interviewed longtime community residents whose names we culled from local organizations. After the

Figure 15.1.   Mount Vernon Avenue Historical Marker, Columbus, Ohio. Photo by Stacia Kuceyeski.

eighth-graders finished all their interviews, they participated in a video conference to share their experiences with the third-graders. This peer-mentoring piece helped the third-graders prepare for their oral history interview, which they conducted as a group. It also empowered the eighth-graders and made them the experts in the process.

The final phase of the project was the Ohio Historic Markers. The funding allowed for the placement of five historic markers. The Ohio Historic Markers program identifies people, places, and events that have contributed to Ohio's history and places a permanent marker commemorating this history on the landscape. Students selected each marker's topic, and their content reflected student research and oral histories.[1]

Even for the most seasoned history professional, writing text for historic markers is a challenging art form. How does one detail decades' worth of history in only eighty or so words? Knowing that the students would find this somewhat frustrating, Nancy Clendenen, Middle School Gifted/Talented Specialist Coordinator for Columbus City Schools, enlisted help from two graduate students in history from The Ohio State University to assist. The third-graders completed an assignment on the importance of their school based on their interview, and Antoinette Wolfe, Gifted/Talented Specialist at East Pilgrim Elementary School, distilled their ideas to create the text for the Mount Vernon Community School marker. After the markers were accepted, students created a walking tour anchored by new markers and the two historic markers that were currently in the area.

After a year of hard work, the day finally arrived when the students could proudly display their efforts and see what their research meant to the Near East Side Community. Community members, parents, and administrators from both the Ohio History Connection and the Columbus City Schools were all in attendance at the dedication of the markers on June 4, 2007, in an event held at the East Pilgrim Elementary gymnasium.

As part of the project, the eighth-grade students wrote reflections on their work. The comments in these reflections were what every educator and historian would hope to read. Many focused on writing the historic marker texts, which was a highlight for many students. One reported it made her "feel like I was a special part in history and I guess I am." One of the main reasons for the project's success was that it gave the students ownership over *their* work. They saw these markers as their markers, the product of their hard work. And not only did the students think the project was both fun and educational, many also saw the greater

---

Mount Vernon Avenue

The commercial area of Mount Vernon Avenue originated in the early 1900s as a safe haven for African American people segregated from the primarily white community of the time. Not permitted to enter many businesses in downtown Columbus during the 1940s, a distinct economy was created, building on establishments already developed in the area. The construction of Interstate 71 through Columbus and the social upheaval and riots of 1967 injured the community to the point where many moved away. Today, Mount Vernon Avenue survives and is being targeted for economic and historic revitalization. *Ohio Historical Marker #102-25 in Columbus, Ohio.*

use for their newly acquired knowledge and skills. One student used the knowledge she gained during the project to assist in creating her church's Black History Program.

The Near East Side History Project was one of those special projects that emerge from solid partnerships and enthusiastic participants, and we're delighted that the American Association for State and Local History recognized it with an Award of Merit and WOW Award in 2008. The students may have been wary at first of a history project, but by seeing the significance to their own lives and their own community they were able to find relevance in the project.

Note

1. To read the marker text, visit the Ohio Historic Markers website at www.remarkableohio.org.

CHAPTER 16

Do You Have What It Takes to Be a Freedom Fighter?

ANDREA K. JONES

I N 1963 Howard Zinn wrote, "The most vicious thing about segregation—more deadly than its immediate denial of certain goods and services—is its perpetuation of the mystery of racial difference. Because there is a magical omnipotent dispeller of the mystery; it is *contact*."[1] During the Jim Crow era, the disconnections between people of different races, living across town from one another and going to separate schools, perpetuated stereotypes and created images of two-dimensional racial characters instead of human beings.

In many ways, today's youth is segregated from those who lived this history. As students sit in classrooms with textbooks full of bold words, names, and dates, they are disconnected from the real lives of the people who struggled for justice, as well as from the people who fell through the cracks as our nation's foundation shifted over time. Using experiential learning, my work has focused on dispelling the mystery of the differences between "us" (who live in the present) and "them" (who lived in the past) by providing a forum for "contact." *Fight for Your Rights* (FFYR) is a school program geared toward students in grades three to eight that I designed for the Atlanta History Center. FFYR contains a series of three simulations— three experiences—that immerse students in the civil rights movement as firsthand participants. Although a simulation cannot achieve the kind of contact that Zinn described, it is the closest thing to a time machine that a history museum can create. If designed with care, a simulation is not only engaging; it is a powerful tool to build authentic empathy and provoke powerful conversations that are hard to spark within the confines of a typical point-and-tell tour. As an added bonus, within two years, this new tour paradigm boosted attendance at the Atlanta History Center by 47 percent as compared with the previous black history tour.

Using a powerful teaching tool was only part of the key to making the civil rights movement relevant and engaging to students. Making history real is an immense responsibility.

Knowing that, it is my practice to first immerse myself in research. Before starting to design FFYR, I devoured everything I could get my hands on about the civil rights movement: books, films, audio recordings, and obscure YouTube videos. I also interviewed several participants in the movement, including Lonnie King (a leader of the Atlanta Student Movement). What are those magical "nuggets" that provoke deep, lingering thoughts? To discover these, I found it necessary to walk away and to let my mind digest the information. I talked to friends and my spouse about what they found compelling in these stories. I looked for echoes of the same human narratives in popular culture. One night, I dreamt vividly about the marches, the dogs, and the white faces filled with hate. The feeling of this era was starting to come to life in my head.

Through this process I realized that living through the civil rights movement was at once a very individual journey and an experience of being part of something greater than one's self. Most school curricula emphasize the heroes: Martin Luther King Jr., Rosa Parks, and a few others. But for the movement to be successful, civil rights had to be an everyday activity for legions of average citizens. I wanted to give students a historically accurate sensation—the power of being average. And yet this kind of monumental social change was not average. Participants were of a generation that could no longer tolerate the injustices their parents endured. Consequently, freedom fighters put themselves in harm's way and sacrificed their futures to force the government to recognize equality. My partner and I sat on the couch one night after watching the documentary series, *Eyes on the Prize*, and imagined living in 1965. Would we have had the fortitude to join the march from Selma to Montgomery as police attacked with billy clubs and tear gas? Would our commitment have changed depending on our race? On our age? On our wealth? This became the guiding theme of the program. Each of the three experiences within FFYR operates to allow students to investigate one essential question: "Do you have what it takes to be a Freedom Fighter?"

During the first experience, students file into a small room that looks like a church, much like those that became the incubators of the movement. (During the rest of the day, this church room was part of an exhibit on folk art.) An interpreter playing an Atlanta mail clerk and activist, John Wesley Dobbs, takes to the pulpit and delivers a speech that starts calmly and then builds to an emotional crescendo. The year is 1946 and Dobbs is rallying African Americans around the goal of registering ten thousand Negro voters. "Voting is about power!" he says. "The power to bargain with the white men who run this city . . . and this power will not be obtained with violence and bloodshed. No! It will be obtained by rising UP from that seat of fear and complacency, picking up a pen, and registering to vote!" Students are usually moved to answer the call with claps and cheers and often rise to their feet—swept up in the spirit of the movement. After they leave to register, they return back to the church. But the interpreter has taken off his hat and changed roles. He is now a narrator, informing the students that the power of their numbers as a voting block has convinced the mayor to hire eight black police officers—the first ones the city has ever had. A discussion ensues around the voting issues today: photo identification requirements, age minimums, and the disenfranchisement of those in prison.

In the second station, participants play the role of black college students who are trained in nonviolence and then taken to the Pickrick, a segregated restaurant (actually a

1950s-themed diner in the museum) to conduct a sit-in. Four students play bit parts: a white waitress who dislikes the protesters, an affluent white customer who is slightly sympathetic to the cause, a black busboy who resents the protesters for disrupting his wages, and a journalist. The Pickrick was a restaurant owned by a staunch segregationist named Lester Maddox whose principles gained him enough favor in the state of Georgia that he later became governor. The students enter the restaurant with trepidation and bit of fear. An interpreter playing Maddox bursts out of the kitchen and discovers the students, who attempt to order from the waitress as he taunts them to leave his property (see figure 16.1). The student playing the waitress, whose character has a family to feed, is coached beforehand that it is her choice whether to serve the protesters, but that she will likely be fired for doing so. In about half the tours, the students who play this part decide to take the order. It's important to note that if a simulation is designed with choices built in, those choices should have real consequences. The script must be written to allow for improvisation and alternate paths so that participants feel the gravity of their decisions. Sometimes the sit-in waitress talks back to Lester Maddox or even quits her job, so the Maddox character must be prepared to improvise. As the protesters continue the sit-in, Maddox's rhetoric intensifies. He raises his voice and gets uncomfortably close to several protesters. Much of the script was adapted from Maddox's own words. "I believe in separation. For my good AND for your good. If the Lord had meant the races to mix, He wouldn't have made us all different. I don't want to live in a world where my race and your race are mixed together!" After a police siren sound is activated by remote control, the scene ends and the interpreter playing Lester Maddox introduces himself. The mood lightens and the debriefing discussion allows students to express how Maddox's tirade made them feel and how they would have reacted if this were real. This is usually the most powerful experience of the three stations for the students, as well as their teachers, because of the emotions they feel. That is why it would be irresponsible to exclude dialogue as a key component of a simulation like this. Participants need help making sense of what just happened and connecting it to the history. It is during the dialogue that many of the "aha" moments occur. One eighth-grade student described "that powerful moment when you realized that others really went through this."

In a final station, students join CORE (Congress of Racial Equality) and set out to desegregate interstate bus travel by participating in the Freedom Rides. The Freedom Ride takes place in a classroom with a painted bus façade and audiovisual equipment run by a simple PowerPoint file. Students are assigned a race randomly: black or white. As the bus roars through several states, students practice civil disobedience by sitting in the "wrong" section of the bus and waiting rooms. When they reach Anniston, Alabama, the bus is attacked (mob sounds are heard and the actor playing the leader reacts with anxious energy) (see figure 16.2). When a gas bomb is thrown through the window (crash!), the Freedom Riders crawl out of the bus to safety, coughing and wheezing from the nonexistent smoke, only to realize that the ambulance will only take the white riders. Students playing white riders must decide whether to help themselves or stay with the group. This is often a tough decision, even when the injuries aren't real. The simulation ends with a vote. Should they continue on to Birmingham despite the dangers? The interpreter, coming out of role, shows students photos of the burned bus and a video of a real Freedom Rider in a hospital bed. Again, a debriefing

Figure 16.1. "If the Lord had meant the races to mix, He wouldn't have made us all different" warns a museum interpreter playing former governor Lester Maddox. Photo by Andrea Jones, courtesy of Atlanta History Center.

discussion allows the students the necessary forum to sit with the gravity of what the real protesters faced.

What is the right mix of theater and education for a program like this? As a high school social studies teacher, I regularly experimented with classroom simulations and role playing. These strategies help students to reach higher levels of thinking and engage many types of learners. But it was at the Atlanta History Center that I teamed up with museum theater guru Dr. Catherine Hughes and began to rigorously test the potential of experiential learning. We arrived at a name for our brand of programming: the Peak Experience. In a museum setting, the Peak Experience is one that offers visitors an opportunity for transformation, of thought, and perspective. Along a spectrum of possible experiences one could have, it is the most meaningful and inspires long-lasting memories. The Peak Experience borrows from many excellent thinkers and ideas, including:

- Abraham Maslow's Hierarchy of Needs
- Mihalyi Csikszentmihalyi's Theory of Flow
- Nina Simon's *The Participatory Museum*
- Constructivist learning theory
- Concept of cognitive dissonance

Although scholarship gave us the foundation, it was also personal experience in the classroom and on the stage that led us to formulate four simple tenets for all peak experiences:

1. Peak experiences must be *thought-provoking*. Designing a program around what educators call an "essential question" gives learners a way to organize their thoughts. These questions, by nature, are ones that have no correct answer and are compelling on a personal level. When students are asked "Do you have what it takes to be a Freedom Fighter?" they examine their own deeply held beliefs and values. They learn about themselves while they're learning about history. Being thought-provoking means that a

Figure 16.2.
Students react to sounds of explosions and shouting while participating in a simulated Freedom Ride. Photo by Andrea Jones, courtesy of Atlanta History Center.

learner is exploring the difference between previous assumptions about the world and new information, and reconciling the two. To a constructivist, that's authentic learning.

2. Peak experiences must be *inclusive* of different perspectives. History is complex and there are inherently many version of the same event. This richness is often left out of the history class and the point-and-tell tour and replaced with one correct narrative. Real life isn't that simple. Sorting through different perspectives builds life skills that are increasingly needed in the twenty-first century. When students who are playing white Freedom Riders have to decide whether or not to seek medical attention and leave in the white-only ambulance, that choice allows them to see that commitment to the cause was different for whites. In the sit-in station, the student who plays the part of the unsympathetic black busboy who is afraid of losing wages becomes a lens that allows the group to discover that the movement's success may have been dependent on the rise of the African American middle class. History is messy. Peak experiences honor the mess while helping learners to make sense of it.

3. Peak experiences must enlist visitors to *participate* in their own learning. Becoming part of the story helps learners to use their own experience to build new connections and imagine historic circumstances with more depth. "We stood up for what was right, but he [Lester Maddox] didn't care what we said. That was as real as it gets. Now, I know how the African Americans got treated back then," wrote one sit-in student. Comments like these are a result of students learning by doing.

4. Peak experiences must *connect to visitors' emotions*. There is ample research that shows connections between memory and emotion. This is certainly a benefit, but perhaps not as important as engendering empathy through emotional content. If students can learn to hone the skill of empathizing they'll be more equipped to build relationships, have a global perspective, and communicate with others.[2] To walk in another person's shoes as she catches a bus is not the same as playing the role of someone who was threatened as she stood up for justice. Emotional content draws a line from one person's experience to another's. "I actually felt how my ancestors felt," another student wrote.

The four tenets of peak experiences can also be used in "backwards design" to determine what topics to explore. It would be difficult, for example, to create a peak experience about tax fraud or photosynthesis. Simulations are often effective at breaking down complex concepts or helping people to visualize processes, but to be a peak experience visitors have to achieve more than understanding—they have to care deeply. The civil rights movement was an excellent subject for this formula because of the almost spiritual nature inherent in becoming a part of social change. Watching students become empowered each day was part of the reward of creating a program like this. About a month after we began FFYR, a group of energetic fifth-graders participated in the sit-in. One very serious boy led the group in a chant. "The 14th Amendment gives us the right to be served!" During the debriefing, the boy came forward to announce that his grandfather was Julian Bond, organizer of the movement that the boy just participated in. It was obvious that until that day, this young man had never truly realized what his grandfather had accomplished. Providing a space and a vehicle for this type of connection illustrates the impact that museums can have when they embrace the goal of creating peak experiences for learners.

Notes

1. Howard Zinn, *Howard Zinn on Race* (New York: Seven Stories Press, 2011), 18.
2. Homa Tavanger, "Empathy: The Most Important Back to School Supply," *Edutopia*. Accessed March 20, 2014. http://www.edutopia.org/blog/empathy-back-to-school-supply -homa-tavangar.

CHAPTER 17

Preserving Los Angeles's African American Historic Places

JENNY SCANLIN AND TERESA GRIMES

I N JANUARY 2010, the State of California honored the Community Redevelopment Agency of the City of Los Angeles (CRA/LA) for producing the first historic, thematic study of African American properties in the state—one of only a handful of such studies nationwide. Thanks to CRA/LA's work, more than one hundred buildings of historical significance relating to Los Angeles's black community are now protected with a National Register of Historic Places listing.

For its extraordinary work documenting Los Angeles's African American history, CRA/LA received the Governor's Award for Excellence in Historic Preservation, its second such honor; the California Historical Resources Commission lauded the project as well. The awards underscore the key role redevelopment agencies can play in historic preservation. How CRA/LA secured the National Register (NR) listing is an example and a case study for other cities on how redevelopment agencies can help recognize and protect local, historic places. It also provides an overview of a methodology for the listing that could become increasingly useful as the nation's diverse population increases.

The Redevelopment Agency Role

The Los Angeles project started with the redevelopment agency itself. When redevelopment agencies began in the 1960s, they were often blunt instruments, scraping sites clean of old structures to erect brand new shopping malls and apartments. CRA/LA, however, took the opposite tack. Los Angeles's redevelopment agency has an extensive record of historical preservation and rehabilitation. Nearly fifty historically related projects are underway now, including restoration of historic gateways in Chinatown, conversion of the 1926 Westlake Theatre from a swap meet back to a performing arts center, and façade renovation of the famed Hollywood Palladium nightclub on Sunset Boulevard.

The city's Community Redevelopment Agency fulfills its mission to revitalize older neighborhoods by adding not only new developments but also by rehabilitating historical commercial districts and neighborhoods. Consultants, developers, and staff members are often knowledgeable of local, state, and federal standards and guidelines for historical preservation. The agency long ago realized that historic preservation generates neighborhood goodwill, creates historic attractions, and opens access to national and state historic preservation grants, valuable alternative funding in an economic downturn. The agency is not alone. Increasingly, redevelopment agencies nationwide are embracing historic preservation. Older neighborhoods in which historic buildings exist often sit within redevelopment project areas. Thus, a key first stop in any group's historic preservation efforts is a check with the local redevelopment agency.

Unique Approach

Los Angeles also used a unique approach to obtain its NR listings, namely, surveying structures associated with the history of its African American communities and neighborhoods. Surveys of African American structures (indeed any racial or ethnic group surveys) are rare. That's because structures on the NR usually exemplify dazzling architecture. The focus is often on style, design, workmanship, and structural details. Yet historically significant buildings are not always architectural gems. Such was the case in South Los Angeles, many of whose attractive historical buildings had been demolished or modernized. Only a few older buildings remained along Central Avenue, the historic jazz and commercial street, not enough to form a historical district.

So CRA/LA hit upon using a Multiple Property Documentation form (MPD). Typically, MPD's are written for entire small towns or neighborhoods. As previously noted, they typically highlighted architecture or historical periods. The Community Redevelopment Agency focused instead on the function the neighborhood buildings performed in the history of the city's African American community. The MPD provided a way to identify and document buildings collectively and comprehensively. It also served as a cover document, providing themes and a context around which to organize the buildings surveyed. The form also streamlined the application process as it provided historical background for the seven structures and two neighborhoods later added to the NR. Further, any other Los Angeles building within the survey area can use the MPD for historical context to more easily be added to the NR.

Creating and Completing the Project

Once CRA/LA decided upon an approach, the agency began the tasks outlined next, though not necessarily in sequence. The process involved ongoing work on a number of fronts.

Recognizing the Need to Protect Buildings

South Los Angeles's Central Avenue is well known as a past entertainment center in the development of West Coast jazz and the history of L.A.'s black community. During its heyday—the 1910s through the 1940s—Central Avenue and neighboring streets were the locales of a vibrant community, including African American newspapers, churches, and businesses. The vibrant street life supported a thriving, neighborhood-based community with homes radiating from the avenue. In the late 1920s, it was the heart of black L.A. In 1948, *Negro Digest* magazine called Los Angeles one of "America's Ten Best Cities for Negroes," largely because of Central Avenue.

Change began in the 1950s as city and county governments removed race restrictive covenants from previously all-white neighborhoods. Once housing loans became available to nonwhites and white prejudices lessened, middle-class blacks began moving out of Central Avenue. Mexican and Central American immigrants replaced blacks as homeowners and renters there, while African Americans dwindled to 13 percent of the population. Buildings associated with the African American city history soon began to suffer from neglect and decay.

Deterioration characterized the majority of Central Avenue buildings and those in surrounding streets when, in late 1995, CRA/LA created the Recovery Redevelopment Plan for the Council District Nine Corridors South of the Santa Monica Freeway (CD9 Corridors). The 2,817-acre CD9 Corridors project area contained rundown and poorly maintained buildings, driveways, and walkways with few businesses, scarce parking, and broken public sidewalks, curbs, and gutters. Project staff set about refurbishing the area, realizing the value its history held for Los Angeles, particularly its African American community, for West Coast jazz, and for the Latino community whose struggles paralleled those of its former black residents. Staff also realized that many historical buildings had been demolished or significantly altered. Others lacked historic designation or recognition and were vulnerable to destruction by slow decay. Staff was concerned that the physical remnants of Central Avenue's African American history would soon be lost forever.

Obtaining Funding

To start the preservation work, CRA/LA staff members contacted the city's Office of Historic Resources, a central point for L.A.'s historic preservation efforts. Janet Hansen, Deputy Director of the city's Office of Historic Resources, conducted an initial reconnaissance survey. From this, Hansen determined that the dispersed historical buildings, unsuitable for a historic district, lent themselves to the MPD. She suggested outside expertise to help prepare it. Because the full City Council must approve all Community Redevelopment Agency projects and expenditures, support from the district council offices was key to funding the survey, estimated initially at $100,000 and later expanded to $130,000. The prime mover in this endeavor was L.A. City Council member Jan Perry, whose district includes Central Avenue.

In July 2007, CRA/LA issued a public bid for work that would include a forty-five block survey along Central Avenue, surveys of adjacent residential neighborhoods, research into the historic context of Central Avenue for the MPD, and NR applications for individual buildings and neighborhoods. With government funding secured, staff was able to undertake the broad survey and historic research needed to prepare the MPD and NR applications, extensive tasks that otherwise would have been out of reach for most nonprofit, historical societies. Wayne Donaldson, executive secretary of the California Historical Resources Commission and the state historic preservation officer, called CRA/LA's approach truly unique: "[Thematic surveys are] very expensive and it's normally not what a small nonprofit could do."

Assembling a Team

Teresa Grimes, Senior Architectural Historian at Christopher A. Joseph and Associates, coordinated the survey. With seventeen years of experience in historic preservation, Grimes had run her own consulting firm, specializing in identification and documentation of historic resources. Plus, she had served as Los Angeles Conservancy's Preservation Officer and had been a research assistant at the Getty Conservation Institute.

Grimes quickly assembled a qualified team of assistants and advisors for the project. It included Becky Nicolaides, an adjunct history professor at UCLA and author of *My Blue Heaven: Life in the Working Class Suburbs of Los Angeles, 1920–1965*. Nicolaides conducted major research and wrote much of the historical context for the applications. Joseph Fantone worked as a research assistant, helped perform the fieldwork, and contributed to the analysis of property types. Josh Sides, Whitsett Chair of California History at California State University at Northridge and author of *Los Angeles City Limits: African American Los Angeles from the Great Depression to the Present*, served as a project advisor. Hansen, of the Office of Historic Resources, helped prepare the MPD and individual NR applications. The Los Angeles Conservancy and West Adams Heritage Association also provided support.

Understanding the NR Process

Most buildings make the NR list because of the historical quality of their architecture, as excellent examples of a period style or construction type. However, the criteria for historical significance are much broader. As explained in detail online, significance in military history, the early settlement of an area, literary and ethnic history, and other factors also qualify. Further, buildings need not be of national significance for listing. Structures can qualify based on their significance to city, region, or state history—the case with the Los Angeles buildings. Accordingly, the Los Angeles properties were documented, not for architectural significance, but for their function as churches, residences, schools, fire stations, theaters, club buildings, and commercial buildings within the history of the African American community.

Touring the Area

Walking the streets had been a key step for CRA/LA's team. It led them to choose the MPD approach to begin with. Further, because most of the commercial buildings from the targeted time period had been demolished and many of the churches altered, the team again adapted, making a special effort to identify key historic individuals and their homes. This work led to defining two historical neighborhoods, also slated for NR listing.

Reviewing the Area's History

Once survey boundaries were established, the team researched an overall history of the area. They consulted a number of well-researched and scholarly books on the history of African Americans in Los Angeles and also examined unpublished master's theses and PhD dissertations. The Los Angeles Public Library's newspaper archives, in particular the *California Eagle* and the *Los Angeles Sentinel*, provided a wealth of historical information. These two local African American newspapers had run stories on notable events, people, businesses, and places in the community. Los Angeles city phone books and directories contained occupations of those listed and, in parentheses, specified colored or black, Chinese, Japanese, and other ethnicities.

Researchers also reviewed existing listings of African American historical properties in the California Register of Historical Resources and the local landmarks registry. The study included three African American historical properties already listed in the NR: the Dunbar/Sommerville Hotel, the Golden State Mutual Life Insurance Building, and the Ralph Bunche Home.

Obtaining Data on Specific Buildings

This research resulted in a study list of 150 properties. For details on these specific addresses, the team visited the county tax assessor's office for subdivision and tract maps and the city building departments for building permit information. Sanborn Maps provided additional details. The team sought basic information required by the NR, including date of construction, history of the building, major alterations, names of the original owners, brief biographies of them, and similar information on the architect and builders.

As required, staff located historical and current black-and-white photographs from the City of Los Angeles's online photo collection, the Automobile Club of Southern California's extensive collection, and the Los Angeles Public Library photo collection of the city's former daily newspaper, the *Los Angeles Herald Examiner* (1903–1989). Researchers also obtained a US Geological Survey map and consent from building owners for listing in the NR—both required for placement on the list.

Writing the Application

Every building has a history, but not every building is historically significant. For the NR application, the team wrote not a history of each building, but how the buildings met the criteria for a listing. It is persuasive writing. Key to the effort was preparation of the sixty-three-page cover MPD document, "Historic Resources Associated with African Americans in Los Angeles." It provided the foundation and historical context for all the other submittals. It listed eighty-seven bibliographical references, including sixty-two books and dissertations and twenty-five articles.

In the MPD, surveyed properties were grouped in five historic contexts, all spanning roughly the same time period but focusing on different historical trends and forces affecting Los Angeles's black community:

- Settlement patterns and the mechanisms of residential segregation (1890–1958)
- Employment and labor conditions (1900–1958)
- Key institutions in the development of the community including churches, race papers, and businesses (1872–1958)
- Civil rights and political activism (1870–1958)
- The role of blacks in the entertainment industry (1915–1958)

Submitting the Application

NR applications first go to a state historical preservation office. L.A. sent its documents to the California Historical Resources Commission in July 2008 for review and recommendation for approval from the state board. Once approved at the state level, the documents then go to the National Park Service (NPS), which posts them in the Federal Register, the federal government's daily publication for public notices. The process can take some time. NPS announced final approval for L.A.'s listings of its seven sites in March 2009 and June 2009 for the two neighborhoods.

Results

Thanks to CRA/LA and the team's work, seven structures were listed on the NR of Historic Places. They include:

- 28th Street YMCA—Designed by noted African American architect Paul Williams and built in 1926, the YMCA pool provided swimming for blacks, excluded at the time from public pools.
- Second Baptist Church—At its 1926 opening, the building was named the most elaborate Baptist church on the West Coast.
- Angelus Funeral Home—Built in 1934, this family-run funeral home was one of the most successful African American–owned businesses in the nation at that time.
- Fire Station No. 14—Built in 1949, this was one of two all-black firefighter stations in Los Angeles (see figure 17.1).
- Fire Station No. 30—This building is now home to the African American Firefighter Museum.
- Lincoln Theater—This 1926 theater hosted so many acts from Harlem's Apollo Theater that it was dubbed the West Coast Apollo.
- Prince Hall Masonic Temple—Built in 1926, it is one of two remaining club buildings founded by and for Los Angeles's African Americans.

The two neighborhoods also on the NR list include the 52nd Place Historic District with fifty-six residences built in 1895–1922, most in the Victorian Queen Anne style, and the 27th Street Historic District with forty-four residences, all wood-framed, one-story Craftsman-style houses built in 1911–1914.

Figure 17.1. Fire Station No. 14, 3401 S. Central Avenue, Los Angeles, California, one of two all-black segregated fire stations in Los Angeles. Listed on the National Register of Historic Places in 2009. Photo by Teresa Grimes.

The listing dramatically boosted the number of Los Angeles African American structures on the NR and helps incentivize historic rehabilitation. The listing qualifies building owners for a 20 percent investment tax credit for rehabilitation work, plus tax depreciation. The homes may also qualify for federal historic preservation grants. These help make rehabilitation more attractive, a goal the CRA/LA sought. The listing also helps meet another CRA/LA goal, raising awareness of heritage as a draw to bring residents and visitors back to older neighborhoods.

The project also garnered media attention. *Preservation Magazine* ran an online story on the designation. Stories also ran in the *Los Angeles Times* and *The Wave*, a newspaper specifically aimed at today's Los Angeles black neighborhoods. Recognition from both the governor's office and the state historical resources commission underscored the contribution made by CRA/LA. It was called a "landmark achievement in recording the ethnic history of California."

CRA/LA's commitment to historic preservation continues. In February 2010, the agency received a $10,000 grant from the National Trust for Historic Preservation to restore two historic Chinatown gateways. The agency is compiling a database of all its past and present historic preservation activities. Those number in the hundreds and include Los Angeles

Central Library, Grand Central Market, the famed Bradbury Building used in the movie *Blade Runner*, the historic Egyptian and El Capitan theaters in Hollywood, and Victorian residences near downtown. Meanwhile, staff in CRA/LA's seven regions are engaged in historic preservation work, including prototype projects that will provide design solutions that can be used when historic structures need security, façade lighting, recreation of original architectural features, or signage.

"CRA/LA's commitment to preservation is part of our culture because it contributes to the stabilization and revitalization of our communities," said Glenn F. Wasserman, CRA/LA's chief operating office. "We hope these efforts set an example for others to follow."

CHAPTER 18

More Than Just a Building

Interpreting the Legacy of Frederick Douglass Elementary School

WENDI MANUEL-SCOTT AND
SARA HOWARD-O'BRIEN

LOUDOUN COUNTY, located in the northwestern region of Virginia about thirty miles outside of Washington, D.C., is one of the fastest growing counties in the nation. Loudoun's population is nearly 350,000, and its exponential growth over the last twenty years necessitates the constant construction of new schools to meet the needs of growing communities. The demand for the construction of new schools is especially difficult because identifying land for new schools presents unique challenges. This plight came to the fore in 2010 when the Loudoun County School Board (LCSB) determined that a new school was needed in Leesburg, the county seat. With few options available, officials identified LCSB-owned support services facility as a potential site. Originally the building had served as a segregated school for African American students. While it was determined by the Virginia Department of Historic Resources in 2008 that the 1950s building was ineligible for the National Register of Historic Places, a study commissioned by LCSB examining desegregation in Loudoun County found that the events surrounding the construction of this former school and what took place in the local African American community were quite significant.

In June 2010, the LCSB on its own initiative visited the local Black History Committee (BHC) during a monthly meeting at the Thomas Balch Library to share information about the former Frederick Douglass Elementary School (Douglass), alert committee members of the impending plans to construct a new school, and invite conversation about how to honor the prior school's history. The LCSB gave the BHC copies of the research conducted on the property, including an archaeological investigation and a history of desegregation in Loudoun County Public Schools.[1]

The BHC members, many who had deep community roots, were aggrieved that the old school would be demolished. Nonetheless, the BHC agreed to take the matter under review and in late August offered a list of recommendations they wanted to see implemented as a part of the new school project:

- A permanent plaque of the history of Douglass Elementary
- A take-home package at the opening of the new school
- A summary of the struggles of building the original school
- Videos, interviews, and photos of former students
- Records of years of development and struggle deposited at the Thomas Balch Library
- Walkway of bricks from the old school
- An icon in the garden built from parts of the old school
- A small room and display case dedicated to the old students and their history

The LCSB designated a staff member to work with the BHC and to be the liaison between the BHC and the LCSB for implementation.

Over the next few months, a series of difficult conversations followed, as the LCSB and BHC members discussed the need to recognize the rich history of the school, the students, and teachers. Toward this end, many ideas were proposed and explored. Pursuing the idea of an icon in the garden, the concept of a sculpture, or celebratory mural was considered along with applications for grant monies. Neither the LCSB nor the BHC had readily available funding for such an undertaking. Dismantling the old school and salvaging materials for reuse also proved infeasible. Eventually the BHC and LCSB decided that a permanent exhibit housed in the new school would be the best way to honor the legacy of Douglass School.[2]

The BHC had already compiled extensive research and documentation on the struggles of the African American community. This research became the foundation for a timeline telling the story of the local community's struggle for equal education and the creation of Fredrick Douglass Elementary School. The BHC research was supplemented by an examination of LCSB and County Board of Supervisors records, review of local authors' publications, newspaper and magazine articles, the History Matters Desegregation report, community roundtable discussions, and oral history interviews. A dozen interviews were conducted and videoed with a variety of individuals affiliated with the school, including the former principal, a PTA representative, and students.

Educators identified the need to provide historical context, and the project was expanded to add timelines for both the Virginia state and national civil rights periods. As the timeline developed, the architect of the new school building provided a series of timeline sketches, pro bono, for consideration. Touchscreens were also suggested as an addition to the wall timeline because they would allow for expansion of the exhibit. Over the course of two years, the exhibit design and content continued to be refined with review and input by the BHC and the LCSB.

The collaboration was not without difficulty because the opening of old wounds was unavoidable and past disappointments, frustrations, and injustices had to be recognized. The June 2010 meeting was the first hurdle. For many, the impending destruction of the school served as another example of LCSB ignoring the needs of the African American community. Thus, building trust was difficult but imperative. Addressing recent history with living participants required sensitivity, empathy, and a measure of humility. This was a delicate task, especially because Leesburg is a very small community and for many the impact of racial segregation remains a painful and not-so-distant past. Through honest listening, admitting mistakes, and valuing the voices from the community, the BHC and LCSB evolved into a dedicated team.

Details were paramount. From confirming dates in records that contain conflicting information to agreement on what events are most important, every aspect was carefully examined. For the Douglass project, there were two aspects in particular that involved extended discussion. The first was terminology. The timeline began in the mid-1930s extending to the late 1960s. During this period the records contained the terms *colored*, *Negro*, and *black*. Some of the committee members preferred *black* rather than *African American*, but the BHC and LCSB decided that the exhibit would only use the current vernacular: *African American*. The second, more problematic, discussion focused on the timeline. The question was whether the local, state, or national timeline should be on the main exhibit wall. Some suggested that the national civil rights events are most familiar and thus this timeline would provide an important historical context for students. Conversely, some suggested that the history being preserved was local and precisely because it was less known it should be at the forefront. The BHC was split, and in the end the LCSB made the decision to place the local timeline on the main wall and the remaining two on the touchscreens.

While the terminology and timeline presented two challenges, a third was how to address why Douglass opened as a segregated school in 1958 and remained segregated until 1968. Answering these questions was challenging because some wanted the exhibit to be inspirational and forward-looking and not dwell on the difficult historical past. Here, the timeline served as an invaluable tool. For the 1930s, it shows that white students benefitted from tax-supported school bus transportation while African American students in Loudoun endured long walks to school. By revealing that discontented parents and teachers from all over the county came together and formed the County-wide League to better organize their efforts to improve the educational conditions of African American children, it poignantly shows the LCSB efforts to stave off integration after 1954, and it focuses on the indefatigable and brave efforts of African American parents who pushed for integrated schools.

The timeline also presents the August 1956 decision by the Loudoun County Board of Supervisors to cease funding for any public school ordered by the federal government to integrate, rather than desegregate.[3] In the end, Loudoun public schools did not close. Unlike other Virginia counties, Loudoun pursued a different path and built a new school for African American children in hopes of avoiding integration. The timeline notes that in 1956, the School Board purchased land for a new segregated elementary school and that two years later, Frederick Douglass Elementary School opened as a segregated facility. Douglass was the last segregated school built in Loudoun County, and it was not until September

1968, nearly fifteen years after the *Brown* decision, that Douglass was integrated and racial segregation in Loudoun County Public Schools came to an end.[4]

The exhibit figures prominently in the new Frederick Douglass Elementary School: located in the middle of the main hallway, across from the library and adjacent to the assembly room (see figure 18.1). It consists of four colorful panels depicting a local timeline plus two panels that honor the school's namesake, Frederick Douglass. The local, state, and national timelines support contextual discussion and are an integral part of Virginia's Standards of Learning for the civil rights period.

The design intentionally incorporates three touchscreen stations to allow teachers to provide instruction. Digital presentations include state and national timelines, short biographies of the local leaders, a slideshow providing additional history of the segregated school, and a twelve-minute video created from the oral histories of former students and faculty and historic films of the old school to help connect the past to the present. The inaugural students received a take-home copy of the video. These are complemented by two display cases containing artifacts and donations from former students. The history documented in this exhibit is available to all Loudoun County Public Schools via the school's intranet and to the public at the Black History Committee's website. The exhibit is both a memorial to the local African American struggle for equal education and a powerful teaching tool.[5]

This exhibit could only have succeeded through the partnership between the LCSB and the BHC of the Thomas Balch Library. The accomplishments are visible at many

Figure 18.1. History exhibit at Frederick Douglass Elementary School, Leesburg, Virginia. Photo by Javier Pierrend, courtesy of Loudon County Public Schools.

levels: the reflections preserved in the oral histories testify to the perseverance of a small African American community, the awards bestowed on the project from local, state, and national organizations, the ownership taken by the children at the new Frederick Douglass Elementary School, and, most importantly, it brought to light a little-known history that will be taught for generations to come.

Notes

1. Evelyn D. Causey and Julia Claypool, "Desegregation in Loudoun County Public Schools, 1954–1970," History Matters, LLC, April 30, 2010, and Kimberly A. Snyder, "Phase I Archeological Investigations of the +/– 9.28 acre Douglass Support Center Property, Leesburg Virginia," Thunderbird Archeology, Wetlands Studies and Solutions, Inc., June 2010.
2. We are grateful for the support of community members and all those that shared their memories of Douglass Elementary School and life in Loudoun County.
3. "Loudoun Board Drops Desegregation Fight," *Washington Post*, August 7, 1962, 21; "Vote 'for' the Amendment," *Loudoun Times-Mirror*, January 5, 1956, 1.
4. "Voluntary Segregation Part of Building Program," *Loudoun Times-Mirror*, January 12, 1956, 1; "Board Hears Bid for New Negro School," *Loudoun Times-Mirror*, May 17, 1956, 1; "Negroes Sue for Entry into School at Leesburg," *Washington Post*, September 21, 1962, 2; "Schools Now Integrated in Loudoun," *Washington Post*, September 13, 1968, 23.
5. *Frederick Douglass Elementary School Dedication Video: Then and Now*, Loudoun County Public Schools Department of Planning and Legislative Services and LCPS Department of Support Services, October 2012, http://vimeo.com/54796947. Javier Pierrend, a talented videographer, merits recognition for his dedication, unwavering support, and attention to detail.

CHAPTER 19

Soul Soldiers
Giving Voice to Vietnam's Veterans

ROBBIE DAVIS

I N THE LATE 1950s, brewing conflicts in Southeast Asia were little more than articles in the newspaper to most Americans. But in the constant battle to contain communism's sphere of influence during the Cold War, the US government grew increasingly concerned about establishing a foothold in the region. After the French abandoned Vietnam in 1954 and the country was partitioned in a peace agreement, the United States worked to bolster the creation of a new democracy in South Vietnam. The American military role in Vietnam was limited at first, with fewer than one thousand military advisors present in 1960. During President John F. Kennedy's administration, the number of military advisors grew, but Americans saw little military action.

An increase in the American presence and military engagement in Vietnam began in earnest after the Gulf of Tonkin incident in 1964 led President Lyndon B. Johnson to ask for greater authority for a military response. By the end of 1965, more than 180,000 American troops were in Vietnam. The number of American personnel in Vietnam peaked at more than 540,000 early in 1969.

The mix of politics, diplomacy, military action, and public opinion over Vietnam ultimately grew toxic for the United States. Public dissatisfaction with the Vietnam War bubbled up across the country and grew more fevered as casualties mounted and a draft began in 1967. Protests against the war moved off college campuses and into the streets. Clashes between protestors, police, and the National Guard led to thousands of arrests and often turned violent. President Richard Nixon's efforts to shift greater responsibilities onto South Vietnamese troops through his Vietnamization effort further eroded US military endeavors and did little to turn around public antiwar sentiments.

Soldiers in Vietnam were inextricably linked to the growing dissatisfaction with the status quo at home. With millions of African Americans fighting for racial equality, millions of women clamoring for equal opportunity, and millions rallying against the war in

Vietnam, the United States seemed to be fighting with itself as much as it was fighting abroad. Military personnel in Vietnam did not live and fight in a vacuum. Everything happening at home affected them too. And thousands—whether they wanted racial equality or wanted an end to a war they did not support—actively engaged in and embraced the movements and changes in American society.

More than fifty-eight thousand US personnel died in Vietnam. For many soldiers returning home, the unpopular nature of the war meant a tarnished homecoming. Many felt unappreciated or ashamed to reveal their role in the war. Like past conflicts, veterans found the stresses of war difficult to overcome. For years to come, reliving the traumatic events of the war was a constant element in the lives of thousands of veterans. In the 1970s and 1980s, many veterans simply chose to conceal their emotions about the war, the horrors they had witnessed, and lingering fears. For years, Vietnam remained a polarizing moment in American history, and veterans, in particular, seemed to carry a certain reticence about exploring its history in public.

In recent years, historical organizations sought to chip away at the silence that long enveloped so many involved in the Vietnam War. Their efforts to bring forward the stories of Vietnam veterans resulted in highly successful exhibits, oral history collections, and public programs. But even more powerfully, these efforts opened a door to a new level of discourse and civic engagement for many Vietnam veterans, providing an environment where it was safe and even therapeutic to reveal their personal experiences and their own thoughts. Involving veterans and veterans' groups in the development of the exhibits can result in museum exhibits that are not only rich in historical content, but also bring the voices of veterans forward to provide an enlightening experience for visitors. Exhibits can successfully enable people with differing viewpoints to engage in honest, yet respectful, discussions about a divisive period.

The effort to develop *Soul Soldiers: African Americans and the Vietnam Era* at the Senator John Heinz History Center in Pittsburgh, Pennsylvania, began with Samuel W. Black, curator of African American collections at the History Center. Black proposed the exhibit as an opportunity to develop a significant national exhibit that explored the experiences of African American Vietnam veterans and tied them to the civil rights movement and the breadth of experiences for African Americans during the Vietnam era. The exhibit development team

Introductory Label for *Soul Soldiers*

Soul Soldiers: African Americans and the Vietnam War explores the events of civil rights and the Vietnam War as they impacted African American life and culture. The mid-1950s to the 1970s was an era of great change in America as new social, political, and cultural perspectives began to reshape the American landscape. In Vietnam and at home, African Americans were impacted by these events, resulting in a greater expression of political and cultural identity. This was the era of street demonstrations and court battles; of protest and musical expression; of black arts and Black Power. African American men and women, Soul Soldiers, battled on two fronts, for equality at home and democracy abroad. Their service in war was valor and their activism in civil rights was historic.

Figure 19.1. *Soul Soldiers* exhibit at the Heinz History Center, Pittsburgh, Pennsylvania. Courtesy of the Senator John Heinz History Center.

desired to tell a new story about Vietnam by rooting it in the experiences and perspectives of African American soldiers told in their own words. The team also wanted to ensure that they actively involved the African American community in all aspects of the development of the exhibit, from research to design.

Black and the *Soul Soldiers* team drew on the activism of local veterans groups in Pittsburgh to create an advisory committee that grew to more than twenty members. Most were Vietnam veterans, but all had experience working with Vietnam veterans and understood how to help the History Center gain the confidence of African American veterans. Black noted that the members of the committee became true advisors. Not being a veteran himself, he wanted to ensure that he fully incorporated the veterans' voices into the exhibit. The committee provided advice, access, assistance, and feedback at nearly every turn. It helped to identify key individuals for oral history interviews and assisted with the interviews. Members offered their own experiences and personal collections for the exhibit, suggesting and locating objects and media for the exhibit. They also reviewed design elements and played a crucial role in audience development and public relations through their connections to veterans organizations.

Research for the exhibit centered on oral interviews. Several members of the advisory committee worked with counseling groups and led Black to veterans who came to view their interviews with him as part of their personal therapy. The exhibit team worked hard to help interview subjects feel comfortable and invested in the historical and educational goals of the project. "It helped that [we] weren't reporter[s]," Black noted. There were many times when an interview subject asked him to turn off the recorder and preferred to share an experience in confidence. Through building such a high level of trust with local veterans, the History Center obtained detailed interviews that became part of the center's archival collections.

Obtaining objects for the exhibit proved to be a challenge for the development team. Black, whose eldest brother served two tours in Vietnam, obtained some items from his family. After that, items slowly began to trickle in through the committee. The result was a rich collection of more than two hundred objects, letters, photographs, and art from the period.

Although the exhibit closed in Pittsburgh in November 2007, it continued to have a major impact for the Heinz History Center. A national tour of *Soul Soldiers* began in 2008, and the exhibit traveled to Chicago, Dallas, Philadelphia, Birmingham, and Memphis through 2010. The exhibit team still hears from the veterans it interviewed and from many others who recognize the History Center as a trusted partner for documenting African American history and the experiences of Vietnam veterans. It also resulted in a companion book that looks at black life through the eyes of veterans by bringing together essays, poetry, oral histories, and riveting recollections that recall the horrors of war, the complexities of race, and the duality of African American life. *Soul Soldiers: African Americans and the Vietnam Era* earned several awards, including an Award of Merit from the American Association for State and Local History and an American Advertising Federation Mosaic Award. Curator Sam Black was honored by the African American Historical and Genealogical Society of Pittsburgh in large part for his work on *Soul Soldiers*.

Soul Soldiers: African Americans and the Vietnam Era is an example of the success historical organizations can achieve when they employ individual experiences as an interpretive tool for helping visitors learn more about important national events and how they had an impact on their own communities. As author and historian Wallace Terry mentioned at the exhibit's opening ceremony, "America knows the valor of the 54th regiment in the Civil War, the Buffalo soldier, and the Tuskegee airmen. It would be a disgrace for us not to honor the black Vietnam vet. Now is the time."[1] By allowing veterans to take ownership of their own history and welcoming visitors to learn from their fellow citizens' experiences and question their own perceptions of history, the Senator John Heinz History Center created a powerful exhibit that became a model of civic engagement.

Note

1. Ervin Dyer, "Soul Soldiers: Exhibit Reveals Story of Blacks in Vietnam," *The Crisis* (January/February 2007): 43.

CHAPTER 20

Making African American History Relevant through Co-Creation and Community Service Learning

ROBERT P. CONNOLLY AND ANA MARIA REA

T THE C. H. Nash Museum (CHNM) at Chucalissa, located on the grounds of a prehistoric Mississippian culture (1000–1500 CE) earthwork complex, we employ community service learning as a bridge between the museum and the predominantly African American community surrounding the forty-acre complex. Discovered indirectly as a result of Jim Crow–era segregation policies in the 1930s, the Chucalissa archaeological site and later the CHNM were estranged from the local community throughout most of the twentieth century. To establish a sustainable archaeological research program, in 1962 the University of Memphis (UM) agreed to administer the CHNM and site complex.

In 2007, the museum expanded its mission to interpret the "traditional" cultures of the area, including the African American community, and initiated an aggressive outreach program based in community service learning.[1] The CHNM's initial attempts at community engagement produced mixed results and constructive lessons. Because the museum had no links to the surrounding community, the starting point was to simply make contacts with area residents for decades ignored by the institution. As an extension of the UM, neighbors viewed the CHNM as an organization interested in self-serving research of little relevance to the community. As one resident stated at a community meeting in the spring of 2008,

"Don't tell me what the University of Memphis is going to do for my community. The last time you all were here doing your research for two years, all we got was a map on the wall."

Beginning in 2008, the CHNM stated in words and demonstrated through actions that community engagement would not be based solely on generated grant monies or research interests. Rather, the museum intended to function as a true stakeholder and social asset in the southwest Memphis community. In so doing, the CHNM participated as a service learner in the community who "listens to the concerns of the group or person, lets the 'other' define the situation, and responds by trying to meet that need. In listening and learning, receiving and giving, the service-learning relationship is horizontal, lateral, parallel. It is not hierarchical."[2] This approach is a key component of co-creative museum experiences that Simon argues are meant "to give voice and be responsive to the needs and interests of local community members; to provide a place for community engagement and dialogue; and to help participants develop skills that will support their own individual and community goals."[3] By incorporating these perspectives, we expanded the traditional concepts of community service learning from the classroom to a museum and historic site.

Substantive results at the CHNM from this process to date include a permanent exhibit on the African American Cultural Heritage of Southwest Memphis created by area high school students; hosting of annual Black History Month celebrations; providing space for the community's urban garden; creation of a www.southwestmemphis.com that features the cultural heritage of the southwest Memphis neighborhoods; and coordinating the recruitment of AmeriCorps Teams for community projects.

The AmeriCorps Team Projects

The CHNM has hosted four eight-week AmeriCorps National Civilian Community Corps (NCCC) teams from 2011 to 2013. The teams were cosponsored by the CHNM, the adjacent T. O. Fuller State Park, and the Westwood Neighborhood Association (WNA) of southwest Memphis. The eight-week teams divide their work time as follows: 25 percent at the museum, 25 percent at the state park, and 50 percent in the community surrounding the museum. The AmeriCorps Teams are housed at the museum complex.

The AmeriCorps work in the community is determined and organized by the community residents. The community projects focus on assisting elderly and military veteran homeowners with minor house repairs along with landscaping tasks to keep their properties from facing municipal code violations. The teams also perform area cleanups, mentor youth in area Boys and Girls Clubs, and perform other forms of community service.

So how does the AmeriCorps work relate back to African American history and the CHNM? The AmeriCorps NCCC teams either by specific design or as a logical consequence of community engagement expand and form a bridge for "learning and listening" opportunities of community "needs and interests" that can be cocreated with the CHNM.

One example of this process is preserving and presenting the role of community members who are veterans of the US military. In February 2012, the WNA chose the topic "Celebrating Black History in the US Military" for the annual Black History event at the CHNM. Organized by community volunteers who were veterans, in the fall of 2012 the Delta 9 AmeriCorps NCCC Team worked on repair and refurbishment projects for the homes of several veterans in the community. For the Veterans Day celebration held at Westwood Community Center, the AmeriCorps Team presented a banner to the assembled veterans that contained their photos and years of service (see figure 20.1). For Global Youth Services Day in April 2013, the River 7 Team promoted an event at the CHNM that expanded the community garden created in large part by military veterans. In fall 2013, the River 4 AmeriCorps Team painted, repaired, and landscaped the home of an eighty-eight-year-old World War II Veteran, Mr. Ford Nelson. At the November Veterans Day event at the Community Center, the River 4 Team presented a second banner honoring black military service and featured Mr. Nelson as a special guest. In February 2014, Mr. Nelson spoke and was honored at the CHNM Annual Black History Month Celebration.

Flowing from the activities, CHNM launched a community service learning project, Hidden Histories, in the summer of 2014. Hidden Histories continued an earlier project that collected oral histories and photographs of community residents, including veterans initially contacted through the AmeriCorps service projects. The oral histories and photographs are curated on the www.southwestmemphis.com website. The 2014 Hidden Histories Project provided service learning opportunities for students from the Freedom Prep Academy, a southwest Memphis charter school whose students commit service hours to the CHNM. The museum's relationship with the school is enhanced through multiple AmeriCorps and Teach for America engagements. The CHNM and WNA proposed an expanded AmeriCorps presence in fall 2014 that will partner team members with Freedom Prep students in additional community-based cultural heritage projects.

The AmeriCorps role is summarized by River 4 Team Leader Megan Rawson, who notes that "presenting a banner to local veterans thanking them for their service on Veteran's Day—this best exemplified our roles as current service members related to the history and

Figure 20.1. Banner presentation at Veterans Day event. Photo by Robert Connolly.

heritage of the area. . . . Our team worked to further the museum's mission through a variety of projects including the rehabilitating an outdoor exhibit and running educational field trips for local elementary students; this enabled us to more effectively serve as ambassadors for the museum within the community and engaged citizens to think about the museum as a current resource for them."

Lessons Learned in Co-Creative Community Service Learning Projects

We have learned important lessons in the co-created community service learning projects. First, co-creation is not a linear process. True co-creation must be based on the needs and interests of the community. As John Cotton Dana noted nearly one century ago, "Learn what aid the community needs: fit the museum to those needs."[4] This approach is substantially different than having an institutional agenda and attempting to fit or manipulate the community needs to that agenda. In 2007, the southwest Memphis community expressed a "need and interest" in correcting environmental code violations and assisting the elderly homeowners. This need was beyond the scope of the CHNM mission. However, as a stakeholder and social asset in the community, the CHNM facilitated access to the resources that could address those needs by hosting AmeriCorps Teams. As a result, the CHNM, AmeriCorps, and the WNA discussed other community interests and needs, including documenting the historic contribution of the African American community to the US military.

A simple gauge of the success of this reciprocal relationship was demonstrated at the 2013 Veterans Day Celebration at the Westwood Community Center. After greetings by public officials and others, the AmeriCorps River 4 Team presented their banner to the assembled veterans. The meeting chair, president of the WNA, and Vietnam-era Air Force veteran, Mr. Robert Gurley, then asked each of the thirty attending veterans to state their name, years served, and military rank upon discharge. As each member spoke, Mr. Gurley noted their picture and name on the banner, or if their photograph appeared in the article "The C. H. Nash Museum at Chucalissa: Community Engagement at an Archaeological Site" published in the journal *Museums and Social Issues*.[5] Without question, the banner and article addressed the expressed community interest and need for recognition of their role and contribution in the US military. Neither the banner nor article could have been produced had the three partners not participated as equal members in the co-creation process.

A second lesson is that co-creation and community service work with AmeriCorps, the WNA, and the CHNM is truly a process and not a singular event. The first AmeriCorps projects in 2011 were limited to participation in community trash pick-ups. Because of the "listening and learning" process over the next two-year period, the three agencies were better able to address the community "interests and needs" based in the mission and expertise that each partner brought to the table. This understanding is particularly true for the CHNM's mission to interpret the traditional cultures in the Chucalissa site vicinity. For example, the Hidden Histories project in summer 2014 grew directly out of the previous two years of oral history work. Looking forward, the CHNM and the southwest Memphis community are now in a position to co-create the preservation and presentation of a diversity of cultural

Figure 20.2. Robert Gurley (neighborhood association president) and Ana Rea (AmeriCorps Team Leader). Photo by Robert Connolly.

heritage research projects. Additional subjects include documentation of abandoned cemeteries, the impact of Jim Crow–era segregation in shaping the cultural institutions of the community, the leadership in the southwest Memphis community, and more. We emphasize that without the equal and co-creative participation of the three partners—the CHNM, the WNA, and the AmeriCorps NCCC teams—the same process and results could not have occurred. As well, had the CHNM and the WNA not begun collaborating on projects in 2008, the 2011 introduction of AmeriCorps teams could not have occurred. In this way, we consider each action as a node along a process or continuum of engagement. Simply put, the events of 2014 could not have occurred without the preceding six years of engagement. In the same way, activities that we might envision for 2020 will require going through the co-creative relationship over the next five years.

Conclusion

The service learning component of the AmeriCorps program not only exposes members to the history and heritage of a community, giving their work a deeper meaning, but also provides an outlet/opportunity for community residents to share and educate team members to the essential components of their cultural heritage. These stories are carried forward by members as part of their AmeriCorps experience. For example, in addition to the culture history work in Memphis, the River 7 AmeriCorps Team also performed tasks related to Appalachian economic history and the implications of coal mines (Williamson, West Virginia), Appalachian Mountain Music (Pikeville, Kentucky), and recorded stories about Hurricane Katrina shared by community members in the greater New Orleans area. The involvement of the River 7 Team in these projects was one of working *with* and not *for* communities.

Community service learning proved integral for the CHNM to realize its role as a stakeholder and community asset in the southwest Memphis community. The AmeriCorps NCCC played a pivotal role in the "listening and learning" process. As a result, the CHNM is better able to live into the very essence of the International Council of Museums' definition of a museum as an "institution in the service of society and of its development."[6]

Notes

1. Robert P. Connolly, Samantha E. Gibbs, and Mallory L. Bader, "The C. H. Nash Museum at Chucalissa: Community Engagement at an Archaeological Site," *Museums and Social Issues* 7, no. 2 (2012): 227–34.
2. Robert F. Kronick, Robert B. Cunningham, and Michelle Gourley, *Experiencing Service Learning* (Knoxville: University of Tennessee Press, 2011), 23.
3. Nina Simon, *The Participatory Museum* (Santa Cruz: Museum 2.0, 2010), 187.
4. John Cotton Dana, *The New Museum* (Woodstock: Elm Tree Press, 1917), 38.
5. Connolly, Gibbs, and Bader, "The C. H. Nash Museum at Chucalissa."
6. International Council of Museums, *Running a Museum: A Practical Handbook* (Paris: International Council of Museums, 2004), 222.

CHAPTER 21

The Scottsboro Boys Museum

University-Community Collaboration Yields Unanticipated Results

ELLEN GRIFFITH SPEARS,
IN COLLABORATION WITH
SHELIA WASHINGTON

NOT UNTIL 2011 was the first public commemoration held in Scottsboro, Alabama, of the trials eighty years earlier that had irrevocably linked the town's name with Jim Crow. The stories of the nine young men riding through Alabama on the Depression-era rails from Chattanooga to Memphis in search of work are often obscured today, absent from many high school textbooks. But the events of March 1931 in northeast Alabama were covered in nearly every major US newspaper. The news of their successive trials reverberated globally, prompting demonstrations in cities from Cape Town to Delhi. Then, nearly as suddenly, the cause dropped from view, displaced by a war to extend democratic rights the Scottsboro nine did not enjoy.

The nine young men falsely accused of rape in 1930s America—Haywood Patterson, Clarence Norris, Charley Weems, Olen Montgomery, Willie Roberson, Ozzie Powell, Eugene Williams, and brothers Andrew and Roy Wright—collectively served more than 130 years in prison for an alleged crime that did not occur. With a defense team led by the International Labor Defense (ILD), a close affiliate of the US Communist Party, in contentious association with the National Association for the Advancement of Colored People (NAACP), the trials led to landmark Supreme Court decisions. *Powell v. Alabama* extended the right to competent counsel and *Norris v. Alabama* challenged the exclusion of African Americans from jury pools, affirming an equal right to a trial of one's peers.[1]

Knowledge among a wider public about the Scottsboro Boys, as they were called at the time of the trials, has risen and fallen from historical memory, shrouded or revealed according to place and time. Two of the defendants published autobiographies, Haywood Patterson in 1950 (*Scottsboro Boy*) and Clarence Norris in 1979 (*The Last of the Scottsboro Boys*). Beginning in 1969, with the publication of Dan Carter's definitive account of the trials, *Scottsboro: A Tragedy of the American South*, scholars wrote about the importance of the cases, but most residents of Scottsboro wanted little to do with the story.

That remained true until Shelia Washington, who grew up in Scottsboro in an African American neighborhood not far from the railroad tracks that carried the defendants to their fate, began a campaign to lift up their memory. Washington dates her interest in the cases to the day her father snatched a book she was reading out of her hand. The forbidden book: defendant Haywood Patterson's *Scottsboro Boy*. Curiosity provoked, she began learning all she could about the cases. As the first and only African American professional staffer for the City of Scottsboro beginning in 1978, she had her own encounters with discrimination to share. Early in her tenure at City Hall, she noted the separately marked drinking fountains; the "Colored" fountain was quickly dismantled. She was moved to acknowledge the Scottsboro defendants, at least in part, by her brothers' experiences with the US criminal justice system, including one who died in custody in Kilby Prison, near Montgomery, Alabama, where the Scottsboro defendants once had been held while awaiting retrial.

By the 2000s, Washington, along with others, had embarked on an effort to place a historical marker placed at the courthouse at which the nine young men were hastily convicted, all but one sentenced to death. A proposed marker was initially slated not to reference the trials at all. But Washington pressed for recognition of the historical facts, and the Alabama Historical Commission, Jackson County Historical Association, and the Alabama State Bar dedicated a marker at the courthouse in 2003.

In 2009, Washington saw an opportunity to press her campaign forward again. The oldest African American church in Jackson County—the Joyce Chapel CME Church on West Willow Street, believed to have been built by former slaves on land acquired in 1878—was about to be vacant, the congregation having dwindled to a few stalwarts. The United Methodist Church was looking to sell the building, but would rent the site to the Multicultural Foundation while the board sought to raise the $75,000 to buy the church and create the Scottsboro Boys Museum and Cultural Center to honor the nine defendants. The caveat: the funds would have to be raised by April 15, 2010. An anonymous donor pledged one-half the funds. At the last possible moment, through the support of Jackson County's state legislative delegation—Rep. John Robinson (D-Scottsboro), Sen. Lowell Barron (D-Fyffe), and Rep. Albert Hall (D-Gurley)—the board secured the additional funds to buy the church as a permanent home for the museum. Just a few blocks from the city square, the roughly two-thousand-square-foot brick sanctuary dates from the late nineteenth century. The wooden pews remain. The pastor's study has become an office, and a small annex off the nave now houses documents, memorabilia, and artifacts relating to the infamous trials.

During spring 2010, Washington began a partnership with students and faculty at the University of Alabama (UA) in Tuscaloosa, three hours distant. What began as a local

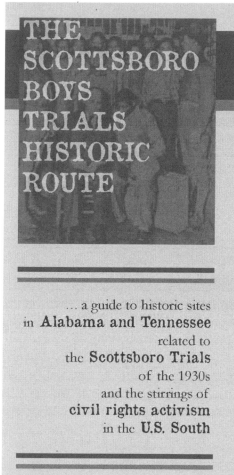

THE
SCOTTSBORO
BOYS
TRIALS
HISTORIC
ROUTE

... a guide to historic sites
in **Alabama and Tennessee**
related to
the **Scottsboro Trials**
of the 1930s
and the stirrings of
civil rights activism
in the **U.S. South**

The Scottsboro Boys
Museum and Cultural
Center

SCOTTSBORO
BOYS MUSEU&
CULTURAL
CENTER

The Scottsboro
Boys Museum and
Cultural Center
is dedicated to
commemorating the
lives and legacy of
the Scottsboro Boys.
Located adjacent
to downtown
Scottsboro, one
long block from the
railroad tracks, the
building was witness
to the infamous
events beginning in
1931 and may have hosted meetings for the defense.
Joyce Chapel, the building which houses the museum,
served as home to the Christian Methodist Episcopal
(formerly Colored Methodist Episcopal) Church of
Scottsboro congregation for more than 100 years
since the land for the church was originally gifted
in 1878. Now, the building serves the community
with a fresh set of goals: to promote knowledge,
reconciliation, and healing.
    The museum holds a collection of artifacts
from the Scottsboro trials. Acquisitions include
Defense Committee posters, trial transcripts,
scrapbooks, photographs, original newspaper articles,
and a juror's chair from the first trial courtroom
in Scottsboro, among other documents and
memorabilia. Public lectures and video resources are
among the many educational offerings at the Center.

Figure 21.1.   Students at the University of Alabama collaborated with the Scottsboro Boys Museum and Cultural Center to create "The Scottsboro Boys Trials Historic Route" brochure. Courtesy of the Scottsboro Boys Museum and Cultural Center and New College, University of Alabama.

history project ended up changing Alabama law. At the instigation of UA student Jennifer Barnett from nearby Fort Payne, who had interviewed Washington for an oral history project, and UA's New College Director James C. Hall, UA Assistant Professor Ellen Griffith Spears visited the city with Scottsboro scholars James A. Miller, author of *Remembering Scottsboro: The Legacy of an Infamous Trial* (2009), and Susan Pennybacker, who wrote *From Scottsboro to Munich: Race and Political Culture in 1930s Britain* (2009). An initial project brought together the museum and the UA faculty, students, and staff, with the support of the National Trust for Historic Preservation Partnership-in-Scholarship program, funded by the Ford Foundation. Students created a website for the museum at scottsboroboys.org and a printed guide to the Scottsboro Boys Trials Historic Route. The guide provided a map from Chattanooga, Tennessee, where several of the young men boarded the train, to Decatur, Alabama, where a courageous Judge James E. Horton famously set aside a jury's guilty verdicts because they did not comport with the evidence (see figure 21.1).

One result of the collaboration was an article for *Alabama Heritage* magazine by UA Department of History doctoral student Tom Reidy that talked about the 1976 Clarence Norris pardon and raised the question: Why had not all the defendants been pardoned, since it had been clear since the early 1930s, even before accuser Ruby Bates had recanted her testimony, that the accusations were false? That article caught the eye of some members of the Alabama Trial Lawyers Association and then of Governor Robert Bentley, who appeared willing to approve pardons but lacked the constitutional authority to do so. The Alabama Pardons and Paroles Board had the authority to issue pardons, but members of the board felt there was no mechanism for them to issue *posthumous* pardons. Washington saw no recourse but to take her campaign for pardons to the state legislature. She, Tom Reidy, Rev. Robert L. Shanklin, and others visited state legislators in Jackson County, where the initial convictions had taken place, in Huntsville, where the accusers lived, and Morgan County, in Decatur, where the retrials had taken place. She ultimately enlisted the support of five key north Alabama legislators, Rep. Robinson, Rep. Laura Hall (D-Huntsville), Sen. Arthur Orr (R-Decatur), Rep. Shadrack McGill (R-Woodville), and Rep. Wayne Johnson (R-Ryland). These state officials guided two pieces of legislation: one a resolution that exonerated all nine men, the other—The Scottsboro Boys Act—a bill that would enable the Alabama Pardons and Paroles Board to grant posthumous pardons in cases in which racial injustice had undergirded a false conviction. The bills passed unanimously in both houses, no doubt the most significant unanimous 2013 vote in the sharply divided legislature. Based on a petition expertly crafted by University of Alabama's New College Assistant Director John Miller, the Alabama Board of Pardons and Paroles granted "full and unconditional pardons" to the three defendants with standing convictions—Charles Weems, Haywood Patterson, and Andy Wright—in November 2013.

Chattanooga, Tennessee

On March 25, 1931, nine young African Americans hopped a train in a Chattanooga freight yard and headed west. Unemployed and desperate for a better life, they were not unlike millions during the Great Depression. In Memphis, perhaps, there would be work. Instead, they found themselves at the center of a life and death courtroom drama, falsely accused of rape. The Scottsboro Boys' cases became an international spectacle spotlighting Jim Crow in America.

Rail travel is central to the story of the Scottsboro Boys. In Chattanooga, the Tennessee Valley Railroad Museum (4119 Cromwell Road, Chattanooga, TN 37421, 423-894-8028) lies about one mile from the freight yards where both the defendants and their accusers boarded a westbound train. The Rail Museum displays Southern Railway gondola cars similar to those the nine teenagers rode. *Excerpt from "The Scottsboro Boys Trials Historic Route" brochure.*

"This is a history-making change," said Washington. The pardons campaign reframed the local historical memory of the cases in Scottsboro. When Alabama's Governor Bentley came to sign the historic pardon legislation in Scottsboro, many local leaders, some who had not supported the museum's presence, turned out.

Annual commemorative events have brought an unlikely collection of people to Scottsboro: a federal district judge from Detroit, a Broadway producer, a high school teacher from Chicago, the chair of the local Jackson County Commission, and the state of Alabama's tourism director—their presence often straining the capacity of the small local church. Hundreds have visited at other times of the year from across the nation and around the globe. Each person has a compelling reason for visiting. Their shared mission in Scottsboro: a commitment to remembrance, a belief that the injustice done to the nine young men should not be forgotten. Moreover, as many have expressed, remembering Scottsboro could promote racial healing today.

Punctuated by train whistles and the noise of freight cars rolling past—along the same route that carried the young men in search of work in 1931—compelling moments from these commemorations recall the cases' significance. At the Scottsboro courthouse in 2011, federal District Court judge from Detroit, the Honorable Victoria A. Roberts, spoke movingly about the continued need for adequate legal counsel from the very bench from which segregationist Judge Alfred E. Hawkins issued the first convictions.

New knowledge about the cases came to light at these commemorative events. Also in 2011, New Yorker Aggie Kapelma presented the museum with documents revealing her father's role in a little-known chapter of the Scottsboro story. Her father, David Scribner, was arrested after responding to a ruse designed to entrap the defense team. Kapelma recounted the circumstances: One of the accusers, Ruby Bates, not only recanted her original testimony, but had even spoken out at Scottsboro Boys' defense rallies. Representatives of Victoria Price who had also accused the nine of rape enticed members of the defense team working with ILD attorney Samuel Leibowitz to meet with Price in Nashville, implying that she also might recant. Upon their arrival in Nashville, however, Kapelma's father and another junior lawyer were arrested on charges of "attempted bribery," Kapelma said. Extradited to Alabama to stand trial, only later were the two men released.

Another museum supporter who has attended anniversary events in Scottsboro is Catherine Schreiber, one of the producers of the controversial Broadway musical, "The Scottsboro Boys," which opened in New York in 2010 and went on to run in London beginning in 2013. The production was simultaneously acclaimed (despite its short two-month run in New York, the musical garnered Tony nominations in a dozen categories, including Best Musical) and critiqued as racist for presenting black actors in blackface and retelling the story through the vehicle of the minstrel show. "'The actors actually deconstruct the [minstrel show] device in front of the audience,' and in the end, rebel against it," director Susan Stroman explained in response to Freedom Party protests outside New York's Lyceum Theater during the run.[2] Coproducer Schreiber and cast members have extended significant support to the new museum and deployed the musical's high visibility to focus attention on the history of the unjust prosecutions.

Local speakers have acknowledged the racial injustice done to the nine teenagers. At the first commemoration, the Benson family, white residents of Jackson County, donated the plot of land that stretches from behind the church to the railroad tracks as a park. With the land cleared, Benson Park offers a view to the route on which the young men traveled to their fate. In announcing the gift, family spokesperson John David Hall told those gathered that prominent Scottsboro citizens John Bernard and Elma Kirby Benson "shared, with these tragic young men we remember here, a common humanity and, also, a common sense that justice has not always been done!" Expressing a desire for reconciliation, Hall said, "In their later years, 'Dad and Mama' Benson shared with their family and friends their sense that wrongs done by us and others must be corrected and that lessons learned must be shared and passed on." Rep. John Robinson, who represents several north Alabama counties in the state legislature in Montgomery, expressed similar sentiments. "Rights are still being righted," he said.

Dozens of young people have taken part in these events, both in person and through video productions. In 2011, Dr. Eric Arnall brought video messages—original songs and spoken word performances—from his students at Westcott Elementary School in Chicago who shared what learning about the trials meant to them. "As an African American young man," wrote one seventh-grader, about the age of the youngest Scottsboro defendant Roy Wright, "I could be bitter or better." The nearly all-black gospel choir from Alabama A&M in Huntsville rocked the church with "I've Been Buked and I've Been Scorned"; the nearly all-white choir from Scottsboro High followed, sweetly singing another hymn. To close out, local musician Franklin McDaniel channeled the wail of the train horn through his harmonica as he played "Amazing Grace."

Historical memories remain a complicated affair. The narratives projected at civil rights heritage tourism sites can be fraught with triumphalism that fails to acknowledge either the full weight of the past or the far-from-fulfilled demands of the present.[3] Until now, the main tourism attraction in Scottsboro has been Unclaimed Baggage, a bargain mecca for a reported one million tourists each year, plugged on TV by Oprah Winfrey, which sits just a block from the new museum. Blending genuine historical interest and expressions of commitment to racial equality with heritage entrepreneurship, Alabama tourism officials are acknowledging the state's rich concentration of civil rights sites. The marking of physical space in Scottsboro makes tangible the memories. Donations of artifacts related to the cases are drifting out of closets and attics—scrapbooks of the trials, intriguing photographs, a juror's chair, a metal table that came from the old Jackson County jail, at which the defendants may have taken their meals.

The recovery of memory and of places so long obscured is both a material and emotional challenge for the fledgling museum. Physically, many of the sites touched by the multiple trials no longer stand, erased from the cultural geography of north Alabama: the Paint Rock train station where the teenagers were pulled from the train and arrested; the old jail where the young men spent their first night in fear of a lynch mob outside, protected only by Jackson County Sheriff M. L. Wann's threat to use his pistol on anyone who approached; the Decatur courthouse where Judge Horton made his crucial ruling reversing the verdict against Haywood Patterson, thus ending any hope of continuing his promising career as a judge in north Alabama.

Beyond the physical challenges facing small museums, amassing the resources to construct and display a robust collection meets local objections, from people who would just as soon forget. While resistance to remembering the trials is still palpable in Jackson County, the Scottsboro Boys Museum and Cultural Center seeks to be a place of unity and healing from long-held racial wounds. A reconciliation model requires truth-telling, and the history of local responses to the Scottsboro cases was only hinted at on this day. "[G]enuine healing requires a candid confrontation with our past," wrote historian Timothy Tyson in his 2004 book *Blood Done Sign My Name*.[4] The museum's founders aim not simply to memorialize the past, but also to embrace a broader mission promoting equity.

Dan T. Carter, who wrote *Scottsboro: A Tragedy of the American South*, the definitive account of the trials, sounded a similar theme in his 2011 keynote address, urging those present to link the struggles of the Scottsboro Boys to the high rates of incarceration of young African American men and other persons of color today. Despite the civil rights revolution, disparities in sentencing in American criminal courts have become more marked, not less. In the 1930s, black Americans were three times as likely as whites to face jail or prison; by the 1990s, the incarceration rate had more than doubled, making African Americans seven times as likely as whites to do jail time.[5]

The handling of the Scottsboro cases kept nine falsely accused young men in the grip of the courts and jails, some for long periods of their lives. In the 1930s, as mass pressure was forcing an end to public lynching, the treatment of the nine defendants foreshadowed a reworked system of social control. Eighty-plus years later, through a network of penal institutions, parole, or probation, the criminal justice system oversees one-third of African American men in their twenties.[6] The lessons the museum has to draw on are rich, highlighting formative moments in the long black freedom movement that are strongly linked with the unfinished work the movement faces today.

Notes

1. *Powell v. Alabama*, 287 U.S. 45 (1932); *Norris v. Alabama*, 294 U.S. 587 (1935).
2. Patricia Cohen, "'Scottsboro Boys' Is Focus of Protest," *New York Times*, November 7, 2010.
3. Owen J. Dwyer and Derek H. Alderman, *Civil Rights Memorials and the Geography of Memory* (Chicago: Center for American Places at Columbia College, distributed by the University of Georgia Press, 2008); Renee Christine Ramano and Leigh Raiford, *The Civil Rights Movement in American Memory* (Athens: University of Georgia Press, 2006).
4. Timothy B. Tyson, *Blood Done Sign My Name: A True Story* (New York: Crown Publishers, 2004), 10.
5. Christopher J. Lyons and Becky Pettit, "Compounded Disadvantage: Race, Incarceration and Wage Growth," *Social Problems* 58, no. 2 (May 2011): 258.
6. Dorothy E. Roberts, "The Social and Moral Cost of Mass Incarceration in African American Communities," *Stanford Law Review* 56, no. 5 (April 2004): 1272.

Selected Bibliography on the Interpretation of African American History and Culture

PREPARED BY MAX A. VAN BALGOOY

FRED WILSON'S innovative exhibits at the Maryland Historical Society in 1992 and Haas-Lilienthal House in 1993 did not dramatically transform the interpretation of African American history and culture at museums and historic sites as some had hoped (or perhaps feared), however, much has happened in the last twenty years as demonstrated by this bibliography of theses, dissertations, official reports, articles, and books that appear in major library databases, such as ProQuest and JSTOR, and other online sources, such as the National Park Service. This bibliography is not comprehensive nor definitive, yet it provides a gateway to the breadth and width of the work underway in the United States for inspiration and best practices, as well as needs and opportunities.

This bibliography primarily focuses on theories and methods (the "how") of interpreting African American history and culture at museums and historic sites, such as tours, exhibits, events, and school programs. Museums, historical societies, and historic sites often interpret history through books, exhibit catalogues, and websites, but those formats are intentionally excluded because they are extensive and deserve their own study. Related, but not part of this bibliography, are guidebooks to museums and sites such as *African American Historic Places* (Wiley, 1994) and studies on the teaching and interpretation of African American history in the classroom and in textbooks. The history and historiography of the African American experience (the "what") are collected in such works as *The Harvard Guide to African-American History* (Harvard University Press, 2001) and *The Columbia Guide to African American History Since 1939* (Columbia University Press, 2006), although they typically exclude unpublished studies such as archaeological excavations, architectural surveys, and historic structures reports. Resources on historical research and interpretation in general are available from such organizations as the American Historical Association, American Association for State and Local History, the National Association for Interpretation, National Council on Public History, and the National Park Service.

Acuff, Joni Boyd, Brent Hirak, and Mary Nangah. "Dismantling a Master Narrative: Using Culturally Responsive Pedagogy to Teach the History of Art Education." *Art Education* (September 2012): 6–10.

Agarwal, Vinod B., and Gilbert R. Yochum. "Tourist Spending and Race of Visitors." *Journal of Travel Research* 38 (1999): 173–76.

Alderman, Derek H. "Surrogation and the Politics of Remembering Slavery in Savannah, Georgia." *Journal of Historical Geography* 36 (2010): 90–101.

———. "Southern Hospitality and the Politics of African American Belonging: An Analysis of North Carolina Tourism Brochure Photographs." *Journal of Cultural Geography* 30, no. 1 (2013): 6–31.

Alderman, Derek H., and Rachel M. Campbell. "Symbolic Excavation and the Artifact Politics of Remembering Slavery in the American South: Observations from Walterboro, South Carolina." *Southeastern Geographer* 48, no. 3 (November 2008): 338–55.

Ash, Carol S. "Rehabilitating MLK's Neighborhood." *CRM* 24, no. 2 (2001): 27–29.

Ash, Carol S., and Margie Ortiz. "New Orleans Jazz National Historical Park: Evolution of the Jazz Complex." *CRM* 2 (2001): 25–27.

Baud, Lauren. "Changing Interpretations: The Homes of Tennessee's Presidents and the Issue of Slavery." MA thesis, Middle Tennessee State University, 2013.

Baumann, Timothy, et al. "Interpreting Uncomfortable History at the Scott Joplin House State Historic Site in St. Louis, Missouri." *Public Historian* 33, no. 2 (May 2011): 37–66.

———. "An Historical Perspective of Civic Engagement and Interpreting Cultural Diversity in Arrow Rock, Missouri." *Historical Archaeology* 45, no. 1 (2011): 114–34.

———. "Evidence Unearthed: Digging into Scott Joplin's St. Louis." *Gateway* (2009): 38–49.

Berlin, Ira. "American Slavery in History and Memory and the Search for Social Justice." *Journal of American History* 90, no. 4 (March 2004): 1251–68.

Biran, Avital, Yaniv Poria, and Gila Oren. "Sought Experiences at (Dark) Heritage Sites." *Annals of Tourism Research* 38, no. 3 (2011): 820–41.

Bonilla-Silva, E. "Rethinking Racism: Toward a Structural Interpretation." *American Sociological Review* 62, no. 3 (1997): 465–80.

Boutte, Gloria Swindler, and Jennifer Strickland. "Marking African American Culture and History Central to Early Childhood Teaching and Learning." *Journal of Negro Education* 77, no. 2 (Spring 2008): 131–42.

Bowers, Dwight Blocker. "And Now for Something Completely Different: Reconstructing Duke Ellington's Beggar's Holiday for Presentation in a Museum Setting," in *Exhibiting Dilemmas: Issues of Representation at the Smithsonian*, edited by Amy Henderson and Adrienne L. Kaeppler, 262–72. Washington DC: Smithsonian Institution Press, 1997.

Bowman, Amanda. "Hampton Plantation: Interpreting Slavery in South Carolina." MA thesis, University of South Carolina, 2010.

Brandon, Lavada Taylor. "W/Righting History: A Pedagogical Approach with Urban African American Learners." *Urban Education* 39 (2004): 638–57.

Brooms, Derrick R. "Lest We Forget: Exhibiting (and Remembering) Slavery in African-American Museums." *Journal of African American Studies* 15 (2011): 508–23.

Brown, Audrey L. "Amplifying the Voices of All Americans: Ethnography, Interpretation, and Inclusiveness." *CRM* 24, no. 7 (2001): 15–16.

Bulger, Teresa D. "Personalising the Past: Heritage Work at the Museum of African American History, Nantucket." *International Journal of Heritage Studies* 17, no. 2 (March 2011): 136–52.

Bunch, Lonnie G. *Call the Lost Dream Back: Essays on History, Race, and Museums.* Washington, DC: AAM Press, 2010.

———. "Embracing Ambiguity: The Challenge of Interpreting African American History in Museums," *Museums and Social Issues* 2, no. 1 (Spring 2007): 44–56.

Burg, Steven. "'From Troubled Ground to Common Ground': The Locust Grove African-American Cemetery Restoration Project: A Case Study of Service-Learning and Community History." *Public Historian* 30, no. 2 (May 2008): 51–82.

Burns, Andrea A. *From Storefront to Monument: Tracing the Public History of the Black Museum Movement.* Amherst: University of Massachusetts Press, 2013.

Butler, David, Perry Carter, and Owen Dwyer. "Imagining Plantations: Slavery, Dominant Narratives, and the Foreign Born." *Southeastern Geographer* 48, no. 3 (November 2008): 288–302.

Buzinde, Christine N. "Interpreting Slavery Tourism." *Annals of Tourism Research* 36, no. 3 (2009): 439–58.

Buzinde, Christine N., and Carla Almeida Santos. "Representations of Slavery." *Annals of Tourism Research* 35, no. 2 (2008): 469–88.

Buzinde, Christine N., and Iyunolu F. Osagie. "Slavery Heritage Representations, Cultural Citizenship, and Judicial Politics in America." *Historical Geography* 39 (2011): 41–64.

Byrne, Karen. "The Power of Place: Using Historic Structures to Teach Children about Slavery," *CRM* 3 (2000): 9–10.

———. "'We Have a Claim on This Estate': Remembering Slavery at Arlington House," *CRM* 4 (2002): 27–29.

Caniglia, Joanne. "Math in the City: Experiencing Mathematics through Visiting Black Historic Sites." *Journal of Experiential Education* 26, no. 2 (Fall 2003): 70–74.

Carter, Perry, David Butler, and Owen Dwyer. "Defetishizing the Plantation: African Americans in the Memorialized South." *Historical Geography* 39 (2011): 128–46.

Celauro, Christopher. "Representations of Slavery in Washington, DC: A Case Study on Presenting Slavery at Dumbarton House." MA thesis, American University, 2006.

Chappell, Edward A. "Museums and American Slavery." In *"I, Too, Am America": Archaeological Studies of African-American Life*, ed. Theresa Singleton, 240–58. Charlottesville: University Press of Virginia, 1999.

Chew, Elizabeth. "Institutional Evolution: How Monticello Faced and Interpreted a Legacy of Slavery." *Museum* 92, no. 5 (September/October 2013): 33–41.

Church, Lila Teresa. "Documenting Local African American Community History." Technical Leaflet #256 in *History News* 66, no. 4 (Autumn 2011).

Clark, Carol, et al. "Visitor Responses to Interpretation at Historic Kingsley Plantation." *Journal of Interpretation Research* 16, no. 2 (2011): 23–33.

Cohen, Rick. "Searching for Juneteenth: The State of Black Museums—Part II." *Nonprofit Quarterly*. June 23, 2014. https://nonprofitquarterly.org/policysocial-context/24402-the-state-of-black -museums-part-ii-searching-for-juneteenth.html.

———. "The State of Black Museums—Part I." *Nonprofit Quarterly*. June 6, 2014. https://nonprof-itquarterly.org/policysocial-context/24310-the-state-of-black-museums-part-i.html.

Connolly, Robert P., Samantha Gibbs, and Mallory Bader. "The C. H. Nash Museum at Chucalissa: Community Engagement at an Archaeological Site." *Museums and Social Issues* 7, no. 2 (Fall 2012): 227–43.

Corrin, Lisa G. *Mining the Museum: An Installation by Fred Wilson*. New York: New Press, 1994.

Crane, Susan A. "Memory, Distortion, and History in the Museum." *History and Theory* 36, no. 4 (December 1997): 44–63.

Dagbovie, Pero Gaglo. "Strategies for Teaching African American History: Musings from the Past, Ruminations for the Future." *Journal of Negro Education* 75, no. 4 (Fall 2006): 635–48.

Danker, Anita C. "African American Heritage Trails: From Boston to the Berkshires." *Historical Journal of Massachusetts* 37, no. 2 (Fall 2009): 17–32.

Danzer, Gerald A. *Teaching with Historic Places Lesson Plan: Chicago's Black Metropolis*. Washington, DC: National Park Service, n.d.

Davis, Patricia. "The Other Southern Belles: Civil War Reenactment, African American Women, and the Performance of Idealized Femininity." *Text and Performance Quarterly* 32, no. 4 (2012): 308–31.

De Levante, Sandi, and Kristi Planck Johnson. "Capturing Historical Adventure: Inside and Outside a Black Heritage Museum." *Social Studies Review* 45, no. 1 (Fall 2005): 49–51.

Denker, Ellen Paul. *Maggie L. Walker House National Historic Site: Historic Furnishings Report*. Boston: National Park Service, 2004.

Denkler, Ann. *Sustaining Identity, Recapturing Heritage: Exploring Issues of Public History, Tourism, and Race in a Southern Town*. Lanham, MD: Lexington Books, 2007.

Dennis, Samuel F. "Seeing the Lowcountry Landscape: 'Race,' Gender, and Nature in Lowcountry South Carolina and Georgia, 1750–2000." PhD dissertation, Pennsylvania State University, 2000.

Dillard, Benita R. "African American Women's Voices: Using Primary Sources to Introduce Students to the Civil War." *Black History Bulletin* 73, no. 2 (Summer 2010): 16–20.

Dimitriadis, Greg. "'Making History Go' at a Local Community Center: Popular Media and the Construction of Historical Knowledge among African American Youth." *Theory and Research in Social Education* 28, no. 1 (2000): 40–64.

Dorsey, Allison. "Black History Is American History: Teaching African American History in the Twenty-First Century." *Journal of American History* 93, no. 4 (March 2007): 1171–77.

Dubin, Steve. "Crossing 125th Street: *Harlem on My Mind* Revisited." Chapter 2 in *Displays of Power: Memory and Amnesia in the American Museum*. New York: New York University Press, 1999.

Dungey, Azie Mira. *Ask a Slave* series, directed by Jordan Black. 2012–2013. Video.

Dwyer, Owen. "Interpreting the Civil Rights Movement: Place, Memory, and Conflict." *Professional Geographer* 52, no. 4 (2000): 660–71.

Dwyer, Owen, David Butler, and Perry Carter. "Commemorative Surrogation and the American South's Changing Heritage Landscape." *Tourism Geographies* 15, no. 3 (2013): 424–43.

Edwards-Ingram, Ywone. "Before 1979: African American Coachmen, Visibility, and Representation at Colonial Williamsburg." *Public Historian* 36, no. 1 (February 2014): 9–35.

Eichstedt, Jennifer L., and Stephen Small. *Representations of Slavery: Race and Ideology in Southern Plantation Museums*. Washington, DC: Smithsonian Institution Press, 2002.

Erickson, Beth, Corey W. Johnson, and B. Dana Kivel. "Rocky Mountain National Park: History and Culture as Factors in African-American Park Visitation." *Journal of Leisure Research* 41, no. 4 (2009): 529–45.

Ferguson, Helena. "Reconnecting the Physical and Cultural Landscapes at the Hampton-Preston Mansion in Columbia, South Carolina." MA thesis, University of South Carolina, 2011.

Fleming, John E. "African-American Museums, History, and the American Ideal." *Journal of American History* 81, no. 3 (December 1994): 1020–26.

Fletcher, Patsy M. "Historic Preservation and the African-American Community." *Afro-Americans in New York Life and History* 20, no. 2 (July 31, 1996): 93.

Foner, Eric. "Changing Interpretation at Gettysburg NMP." *CRM* 21, no. 4 (1998): 17.

Forbes, Robert T. "Connecticut Connections: African American Sites in Connecticut: A Laboratory for the History of Slavery and Human Rights." *Connecticut History* 44, no. 2 (Fall 2005): 316–20.

Fordham, Monroe. "African American Historiography and Community History: A Position Paper." *Afro-Americans in New York Life and History* 33, no. 1 (January 2009): 11–12.

Fortier, Byron. *Teaching with Historic Places Lesson Plan: Vieux Carre*. Washington, DC: National Park Service, n.d.

Furer, Rebecca. Review of *Bristow: Putting the Pieces of an African-American Life Together*, by the Noah Webster House and West Hartford Historical Society. *Connecticut History* 45, no. 1 (Spring 2006): 153–56.

Gallas, Kristin L., and James DeWolf Perry. "Developing Comprehensive and Conscientious Interpretation of Slavery at Historic Sites and Museums." Technical Leaflet #266 in *History News* 69, no. 2 (Spring 2014).

Gates, Laura Soulliere. "Frankly, Scarlett, We Do Give a Damn: The Making of a New National Park." *George Wright Forum* 19, no. 4 (2002): 32–43.

Geist, Christopher. "African-American History at Colonial Williamsburg." *CRM* 20, no. 2 (1997): 47–49.

Gibbs, James G. "Necessary but Insufficient: Plantation Archaeology Reports and Community Action." *Historical Archaeology* 31, no. 3 (1997): 51–64.

Goldsmith, Jack. "Designing for Diversity." *National Parks* 68 (May 1994): 5–6.

Gotham, Kevin Fox. *Authentic New Orleans: Tourism, Culture, and Race in the Big Easy*. New York: New York University Press, 2007.

Grant, Elizabeth. "Race and Tourism in America's First City." *Journal of Urban History* 31, no. 6 (September 2005): 850–71.

Grassick, Mary, and Carol Petravage. *Historic Furnishings Report: Moton Airfield*. Harpers Ferry, WV: National Park Service, 2006.

Grover, Kathryn, and Janine V. da Silva. "Historic Resource Study: Boston African American National Historic Site." Washington, DC: National Park Service, 2002.

Handler, Richard, and Eric Gable. *The New History in an Old Museum: Creating the Past at Colonial Williamsburg*. Durham, NC: Duke University Press, 1997.

Hanna, Stephen P. "A Slavery Museum? Race, Memory, and Landscape in Fredericksburg, Virginia." *Southeastern Geographer* 48, no. 3 (November 2008): 316–37.

Harper, Rayford. "Beyond Simply Black and White." *CRM* 19, no 2 (1996): 5–6.

Harris, Leslie M. "Imperfect Archives and the Historical Imagination." *Public Historian* 36, no. 1 (February 2014): 77–80.

Hartnell, Anna. "Katrina Tourism and a Tale of Two Cities: Visualizing Race and Class in New Orleans." *American Quarterly* 61, no. 3 (September 2009): 723–747.

Hayden, Dolores. *The Power of Place: Urban Landscapes as Public History*. Cambridge, MA: MIT Press, 1997.

Hillyer, Reiko. "Relics of Reconciliation: The Confederate Museum and Civil War Memory in the New South." *Public Historian* 33, no. 4 (November 2011): 35–62.

———. *Designing Dixie: Landscape, Tourism, and Memory in the New South, 1865–1917*. PhD dissertation, Columbia University, 2007.

Holyfield, Lori, and Clifford Beacham. "Memory Brokers, Shameful Pasts, and Civil War Commemoration." *Journal of Black Studies* 42, no. 3 (2011): 436–56.

Horton, James O. "Confronting Slavery and Revealing the 'Lost Cause.'" *CRM* 21, no. 4 (1998): 14–20.

Horton, James O., and Lois Horton. *Slavery and Public History: The Tough Stuff of American Memory*. New York: New Press, 2006; paperback edition by the University of North Carolina, 2009.

Huegel, Casey. "Interpreting with Poetry: Using Verse at the Dunbar State Memorial." *Legacy* (July/August 2013): 9–11.

Hull, Elizabeth Arnold, and Melissa Prycer. *Teaching with Historic Places Lesson Plan: The Pope House of Raleigh, NC*. Washington, DC: National Park Service, n.d.

Inwood, Joshua F. J. "Constructing African American Urban Space in Atlanta, Georgia." *Geographical Review* 101, no. 2 (April 2011): 147–63.

Jackson, Antoinette T. "Shattering Slave Life Portrayals: Uncovering Subjugated Knowledge in U.S. Plantation Sites in South Carolina and Florida." *American Anthropologist* 113, no. 3 (2011): 448–62.

———. *Speaking for the Enslaved: Heritage Interpretation at Antebellum Plantation Sites*. Walnut Creek, CA: Left Coast Press, 2012.

Jay, Bethany. "The Representation of Slavery at Historic House Museums: 1835–2000." PhD dissertation, Boston College, 2009.

Johansen, Bruce Richard. "Imagined Pasts, Imagined Futures: Race, Politics, Memory, and the Revitalization of Downtown Silver Spring, Maryland." PhD dissertation, University of Maryland, 2005.

Joseph, Linda C. "African American Experiences: Window to the Past." *MultiMedia and Internet @ Schools* 12, no. 1 (January/February 2005): 16–18.

Joyner, Brian D. *African Reflections on the American Landscape: Identifying and Interpreting Africanisms*. Washington, DC: National Park Service, 2003.

Kaufman, Ned. *Place, Race, and Story: Essays on the Past and Future of Historic Preservation*. New York: Routledge, 2009.

King, Charlotte. *Teaching with Historic Places Lesson Plan: New Philadelphia*. Washington, DC: National Park Service, n.d.

King, LaGarrett J., Ryan M. Crowley, and Anthony L. Brown. "The Forgotten Legacy of Carter G. Woodson: Contributions to Multicultural Social Studies and African American History." *Social Studies* 101 (2010): 211–15.

Klugh, Elgin L. "Reclaiming Segregation-Era, African American Schoolhouses: Building on Symbols of Past Cooperation." *Journal of Negro Education* 74, no. 3 (Summer 2005): 246–59.

Kuceyeski, Stacia. "Near East Side Community History Project." *History News* 64, no. 1 (Winter 2009): 29–30.

Lawson, Anna Logan. "'The Other Half': Making African-American History at Colonial Williamsburg." PhD dissertation, University of Virginia, 1995.

Leggs, Brent, Kerri Rubman, and Byrd Wood. *Preserving African American Historic Places*. Washington, DC: National Trust for Historic Preservation, 2012.

Levin, Jed. "Activism Leads to Excavation: The Power of Place and the Power of the People at the President's House in Philadelphia." *Archaeologies: Journal of the World Archaeological Congress* 7, no. 3 (December 2011): 596–618.

Litvin, Stephen, and Joshua D. Brewer. "Charleston, South Carolina Tourism and the Presentation of Urban Slavery in an Historic Southern City." *International Journal of Hospitality and Tourism Administration* 9, no. 1 (2008): 71–84.

Loewen, James. "Using Confederate Documents to Teach about Secession, Slavery, and the Origins of the Civil War." *Magazine of History* 25, no. 2 (April 2011): 35–44.

———. *Lies across America*. New York: New Press, 1999.

Lowe, Tukiya L. "Commemorating African American History through National Historic Landmarks." *OAH Newsletter* 36, no. 1 and 2 (May 2008): 11.

Lubar, Steven. "Curator as Auteur." *Public Historian* 36, no. 1 (February 2014): 71–76.

Lucander, David. "Exhuming Hidden History: Sources for Teaching about Slavery in New England." *Historical Journal of Massachusetts* 39, no. 1 (Summer 2011): 242–58.

Marable, Manning. *Living Black History: How Reimagining the African-American Past Can Remake America's Racial Future*. New York: Basic Civitas Books, 2006.

Marrone, Jenna. "Inspiring Public Trust in Our Cultural Institutions: Archives, Public History, and the President's House in Philadelphia." MA thesis, Temple University, 2012.

Masur, Jenny. "African American History in National Parks." *CRM* 19, no. 2 (1996): 45–47.

Masur, Jenny, and Kent Lancaster. "Interpreting Slavery at Hampton NHS." *CRM* 20, no. 2 (1997): 10–12.

Matthews, Christy. "Where Do We Go from Here? Researching and Interpreting the African-American Experience." *Historical Archaeology* 31, no. 3 (1997): 107–13.

McDavid, Carol. "Archaeologies That Hurt; Descendants That Matter: A Pragmatic Approach to Collaboration in the Public Interpretation of African-American Archaeology." *World Archaeology* 34, no. 2 (2002): 303–14.

McKee, Larry, and Brian W. Thomas. "Starting a Conversation: The Public Style of Archaeology at the Hermitage." *Southeastern Archaeology* 17, no. 2 (Winter 1998): 133–39.

Mills, Elizabeth Shown. "Demythicizing History: Marie Thérèse Coincoin, Tourism, and the National Historical Landmarks Program." *Louisiana History* 53, no. 4 (Fall 2012): 402–37.

Modlin, E. Arnold, Jr. "Tales Told on the Tour: Mythic Representations of Slavery by Docents at North Carolina Plantation Museums." *Southeastern Geographer* 48, no. 3 (November 2008): 265–87.

Mooney, Barbara Burlison. "Looking for History's Huts." *Winterthur Portfolio* 39, no. 1 (Spring 2004): 43–68.

Moye, J. Todd. "The Tuskegee Airmen Oral History Project and Oral History in the National Park Service." *Journal of American History* 89, no. 2 (September 2002): 580–87.

Moyer, Teresa S., and Paul A. Shackel. *The Making of Harpers Ferry National Historical Park: A Devil, Two Rivers, and a Dream*. Lanham, MD: AltaMira Press, 2008.

Murphy, Teresa Anne, et al. "Historical Interpretation and the National Park Service at Hampton National Historic Site." Washington, DC: American Studies Department, George Washington University, 1996.

National Park Service. "*Brown v. Board of Education* National Historic Site General Management Plan, Development Concept Plan, Interpretation and Visitor Experience Plan," 1996.

———. "George Washington Carver National Monument Long-Range Interpretive Plan," 2007.

———. "Kennesaw Mountain National Battlefield Park Long-Range Interpretive Plan," 2010.

———. "Little Rock Central High School National Historic Site Long-Range Interpretive Plan," 2004.

———. "Mary McLeod Bethune Council House National Historic Site General Management Plan/Environmental Impact Statement."

———. "Nicodemus National Historic Site Long-Range Interpretive Plan," 2009.

———. *Places of Cultural Memory: African Reflections on the American Landscape.* Washington, DC: National Park Service, 2001.

Norkunas, Martha. "Teaching to Listen: Listening Exercises and Self-Reflexive Journals." *Oral History Review* 38, no. 1 (January 2011): 63–108.

O'Donovan, Susan Eva. "Teaching Slavery in Today's Classroom." *Magazine of History* 23, no. 2 (April 2009): 7–10.

Ogline, Jill. "'Creating Dissonance for the Visitor': The Heart of the Liberty Bell Controversy," *Public Historian* 26, no. 2 (Summer 2005): 49–57.

Olio, Brenda K. "Teaching with Historic Places Lesson Plan: Mary McLeod Bethune Council House." Washington, DC: National Park Service, n.d.

Petravage, Carol. *Historic Furnishings Report: The William Johnson House.* Harpers Ferry, WV: National Park Service, 2004.

Pogue, Dennis. "The Domestic Architecture of Slavery at George Washington's Mount Vernon." *Winterthur Portfolio* 37, no. 1 (Spring 2002): 3–22.

Reeves, Matthew. "Reinterpreting Manassas: The Nineteenth-Century African American Community at Manassas National Battlefield Park." *Historical Archaeology* 37, no. 3 (2003): 124–37.

———. "Asking the 'Right' Questions: Archaeologists and Descendent Communities." In *Places in Mind,* edited by Erve Chambers and Paul Shackel, 71–81. New York: Routledge Press, 2004.

Rice, Kym S., and Martha Katz-Hyman. *World of a Slave: Encyclopedia of the Material Life of Slaves in the United States.* Westport, CT: Greenwood, 2010.

Richards, Sandra L. "Space, Water, and Memory: Slavery and Beaufort, South Carolina." *Cultural Dynamics* 21 (2009): 255–82.

Richardson, Judy, and James O. Horton. *A Fragile Freedom: African American Historic Sites.* New York: History Channel, 2002. Video.

Rizzo, Mary, and Martha Swan. "Public History and Mass Incarceration: Interview with Martha Swan." *Public Historian* 36, no. 1 (February 2014): 61–70.

Rocksborough-Smith, Ian. "Margaret T. G. Burroughs and Black Public History in Cold War Chicago." *Black Scholar* 41, no. 3 (Fall 2011): 26–42.

Rose, Julia. "Interpreting Difficult Knowledge." Technical Leaflet #255 in *History News* 66, no. 3 (Summer 2011).

Rosenzweig, Roy, and David Thelen. *The Presence of the Past: Popular Uses of History in American Life.* New York: Columbia University Press, 1998.

Ruffins, Fath D. "Culture Wars Won and Lost, Part II: The National African-American Museum Project." *Radical History Review* 70 (1998): 78–101.

———. "Mythos, Memory, and History: African American Preservation Efforts, 1820–1990." In *Museums and Communities: The Politics of Public Culture,* edited by Ivan Karp, C. M. Kreamer, and S. D. Levine, 506–611. Washington, DC: Smithsonian Institutional Press, 1992.

————. "Revisiting the Old Plantation: Reparations, Reconciliation and Museumizing American Slavery." In *Museum Frictions: Public Cultures/Global Transformations*, edited by Ivan Karp et al., 395–434. Durham, NC: Duke University Press, 2006.

Saito, Leland T. "African Americans and Historic Preservation in San Diego: The Douglas and the Clermont/Coast Hotels." *Journal of San Diego History* 54, no. 1 (Winter 2008): 1–15.

Scanlin, Jenny, and Teresa Grimes. "Preserving Los Angeles' African American Historic Places." *History News* 64, no. 3 (Summer 2010): 12–15.

Schein, Richard H. "Teaching 'Race' and the Cultural Landscape." *Journal of Geography* 98, no. 4 (July/August 1999): 188–90.

Schreiber, Susan P. "Interpreting Slavery at National Trust Sites." *CRM* 23, no. 5 (2000): 49–52.

Seitz, Phillip. "When Slavery Came to Stay." *Museum* 90, no. 3 (May–June 2011): 40–47.

Shackel, Paul A. "The John Brown Fort: African-Americans' Civil War Monument." *CRM* 20, no. 2 (1997): 22–26.

Sinclair, Bruce. "Teaching about Technology and African American History." *OAH Magazine of History* 12, no. 2 (Winter 1998): 14–17.

Singleton, Theresa A. "The Archaeology of Slavery in North America." *Annual Review of Anthropology* 24 (1995): 119–40.

Small, Stephen. "Still Back of the Big House: Slave Cabins and Slavery in Southern Heritage Tourism." *Tourism Geographies* 15, no. 3 (2013): 405–23.

Smith, Laurajane. "'Man's Inhumanity to Man' and Other Platitudes of Avoidance and Misrecognition: An Analysis of Visitor Responses to Exhibitions Marking the 1807 Bicentenary." *Museum and Society* 8, no. 3 (2010): 193–214.

————, ed., et al. *Representing Enslavement and Abolition in Museums: Ambiguous Engagements.* Oxford: Routledge, 2011.

Spencer, Robyn C. "Mad at History." *Radical Teacher* 85 (Fall 2009): 67–69, 77.

Summar-Smith, Joy Theresa. "Interpretation of Slavery in Southern Historic House Museums." MA thesis, Baylor University, 2003.

Sutton, Karen E. "Confronting Slavery Face-to-Face: A Twenty-First Century Interpreter's Perspective on Eighteenth-Century Slavery." *Common Place* 1, no. 4 (July 2001).

Tagger, Barbara A. "Interpreting African American Women's History through Historic Landscapes, Structures, and Commemorative Sites." *Magazine of History* 12, no. 1 (Fall 1997): 17–19.

Taylor, Ula. "Women in the Documents: Thoughts on Uncovering the Personal, Political, and Professional." *Journal of Women's History* 20, no. 1 (2008): 187–96.

Thacker, Thom, and Michael A. Lord. "Reading Between the Lines: Imagining Runaway Slaves," *Museum News* 85 (May/June 2006): 18–20.

Tretter, Eliot M. "The Power of Naming: The Toponymic Geographies of Commemorated African-Americans." *Professional Geographer* 63, no. 1 (2011): 34–54.

Tucker, John. "Interpreting Slavery and Civil Rights at Fort Sumter National Monument." *George Wright Forum* 19, no. 4 (2002): 15–31.

Tyler-McGraw, Marie. "Becoming Americans Again: Re-envisioning and Revising Thematic Interpretation at Colonial Williamsburg." *Public Historian* 20, no. 3 (Summer 1998): 53–76.

Tyson, Amy M., and Azie Mira Dungey. "'Ask a Slave' and Interpreting Race on Public History's Front Line: Interview with Azie Mira Dungey." *Public Historian* 36, no. 1 (February 2014): 36–60.

Walker, Martha Lentz. *Teaching with Historic Places Lesson Plan: The Shields-Ethridge Farm.* Washington, DC: National Park Service, n.d.

Wallace, David H. *Martin Luther King, Jr., National Historic Site: Historic Furnishings Report.* Harpers Ferry, WV: National Park Service, 1989.

Weber, Diane James. "Teaching with Historic Places Lesson Plan: The Old Courthouse in St. Louis." Washington, DC: National Park Service, n.d.

Weber, Joe, and Selima Sultana. "The Civil Rights Movement and the Future of the National Park System in a Racially Diverse America." *Tourism Geographies* 15, no. 3 (2013): 444–69.

———. "Why Do So Few Minority People Visit National Parks? Visitation and the Accessibility of 'America's Best Idea.'" *Annals of the Association of American Geographers* 103, no. 3 (May 2013): 437–64.

Weeks, James P. "A Different View of Gettysburg: Play, Memory, and Race at the Civil War's Greatest Shrine." *Civil War History* 50, no. 2 (June 2004): 175–91.

Weinberg, Carl R. "The Discomfort Zone: Reenacting Slavery at Conner Prairie." *Magazine of History* 23, no. 2 (April 2009): 62–64.

Weyeneth, Robert R. "Historic Preservation and the Civil Rights Movement." *CRM* 18 (Fall 1995): 6–8.

———. "The Architecture of Racial Segregation: The Challenges of Preserving the Problematical Past." *Public Historian* 27, no. 4 (Fall 2005): 11–44.

Wilson, Mabel O. *Negro Building: Black Americans in the World of Fairs and Museums.* Berkeley: University of California Press, 2012.

Yeingst, William, and Lonnie G. Bunch. "Curating the Recent Past: The Woolworth Lunch Counter, Greensboro, North Carolina." In *Exhibiting Dilemmas: Issues of Representation at the Smithsonian*, edited by Amy Henderson and Adrienne Kaeppler, 143–55. Washington, DC: Smithsonian Institution Press, 1997.

Yellis, Ken. "Fred Wilson, PTSD, and Me: Reflections on the History Wars." *Curator* 52, no. 4 (October 2009): 333–48.

———. "Museums and Race." *Museum* 92, no. 6 (November/December 2013): 54–59.

National Organizations

THE FOLLOWING national organizations offer conferences, publications, work-shops, and webinars for board members, staff, and volunteers at history museums and historic sites on the preservation and interpretation of African American history. They also serve as gateways to the hundreds of local, state, and national museums, libraries, historical societies, and historic sites that preserve, collect, and interpret African American history and culture for the public, such as the Bronzeville Historical Society, Buffalo Soldiers National Museum, Georgia African American Historic Preservation Network, Southwest Michigan Black Heritage Society, Center for African American Heritage at the Delaware Historical Society, and the Middle Peninsula African American Genealogical and Historical Society of Virginia.

Afro-American Historical and Genealogical Society: *www.aahgs.org*
American Association for State and Local History: *www.aaslh.org*
American Historical Association: *www.historians.org*
Association for the Study of African American Life and History: *www.asalh.org*
Association of African American Museums: *www.blackmuseums.org*
National Association for Interpretation: *www.interpnet.com*
National Council on Public History: *www.ncph.org*
National Park Service: *www.nps.gov*
National Trust for Historic Preservation: *www.preservationnation.org*
Organization of American Historians: *www.oah.org*
Smithsonian National Museum of African American History: *www.nmaahc.si.edu*

Index

About the Contributors

ISTORIAN, author, curator and educator, **Lonnie G. Bunch III** is the founding director of the Smithsonian's National Museum of African American History and Culture and was previously the president of the Chicago Historical Society, associate director for curatorial affairs at the National Museum of American History, and curator of history for the California Afro-American Museum. The American Alliance of Museums recognized Bunch as one of the one hundred most influential museum professionals in the twentieth century, and *Ebony* named him one of its 150 most influential African Americans. He received undergraduate and graduate degrees from the American University in Washington, D.C., in African American and American history.

Lila Teresa Church is an independent archival consultant and the sole proprietor of LTC Consulting, based in Durham, North Carolina. Her research interests include the documentation of local African American community history through primary source materials. She holds a Bachelor of Arts in English from Radford College; a postbaccalaureate certificate in Information Systems from Virginia Commonwealth University; a Master of Arts in English/Creative Writing from Brown University; and a Master of Science in Library Science and a Doctor of Philosophy in Information and Library Science from the University of North Carolina at Chapel Hill.

Robert P. Connolly is an associate professor in the Department of Anthropology at the University of Memphis. He is also the director of the C. H. Nash Museum at Chucalissa. He conducted long-term research projects at the Hopewell Fort Ancient hilltop enclosure in southwest Ohio and at the Poverty Point earthwork complex in northeast Louisiana. He is the chairperson of the Public Education Committee at the Society for American Archaeology. Connolly's current research is at the intersection of Museum Studies and Applied Archaeology. In Memphis, he works collaboratively with community partners to develop cultural heritage programs. Connolly blogs at rcnnolly.wordpress.com.

Robbie Davis joined the Smithsonian Institution Traveling Exhibition Service in 2002 and currently serves as a project director for the Museum on Main Street program. Active in the museum field since 1993, he previously worked for the South Carolina State Museum; the

South Carolina Department of Parks, Recreation and Tourism; and the American Alliance of Museums.

Benjamin Filene is associate professor and director of public history at the University of North Carolina Greensboro (UNCG). Since 2006 he has worked with his students to complete a series of community-based, collaborative projects, and he consults on exhibit projects across the country. Prior to UNCG, Filene was Senior Exhibit Developer at the Minnesota Historical Society (1997–2006). He served as lead developer on *Open House: If These Walls Could Talk* (winner of a WOW Award for innovation and an Award of Merit from the American Association for State and Local History) and *Sounds Good to Me: Music in Minnesota*. Filene coedited the collection *Letting Go? Historical Authority in a User-Generated World* (2011). bpfilene@uncg.edu

Kristin L. Gallas has led the Tracing Center's public history work since its founding, facilitating workshops for public history professionals and speaking regularly at public history conferences, museums, and historic sites. She can be reached at kgallas@tracingcenter.org.

Teresa Grimes is a principal architectural historian at Galvin Preservation Associates. Ms. Grimes has over twenty-five years of experience in the field of historic preservation in the public, private, and nonprofit sectors. She is widely recognized as an expert in the identification and documentation of historic resources and has worked on the rehabilitation of major landmarks including the Masonic Temple in Vallejo, Herkimer Arms in Pasadena, and United Artists Theater in Los Angeles. Ms. Grimes has a bachelor's in political science and a master's in architecture from University of California, Los Angeles.

D L Henderson is an independent historian whose current research and writing focuses on the intersection of history, memory, and culture in African American life. She received a doctor of arts degree in humanities from Clark Atlanta University, and she researches and writes tours on the history, art, and architecture of Atlanta's Oakland and South-View cemeteries. In 2012, she was awarded the Atlanta Urban Design Commission's Jenny D. Thurston Memorial Award to an Outstanding Preservation Professional, and in 2013, she was recognized by the Atlanta City Council for her contribution to the preservation and interpretation of African American history and culture.

Sara Howard-O'Brien is an AICP land use planner with over thirty years of experience in both the public and private sector. She acquired a BS in psychology and sociology from Davis and Elkins College, Elkins, West Virginia, in 1978 and a master's in urban planning from the University of Michigan in 1980. Presently, the Land Management Supervisor for Loudoun County Public Schools (LCPS) in Loudoun County, Virginia, Howard-O'Brien was the liaison to the Black History Committee on the Frederick Douglass Elementary School exhibit, the most rewarding project of her career.

Andrea K. Jones serves as the director of programs and visitor engagement at Accokeek Foundation in Maryland. Her work at the Atlanta History Center was a part of an institution-wide shift in interpretation called "Meet the Past." She holds a BA in communications from Purdue University and a MEd from Georgia State University. Jones can be reached at andreajonesmail@gmail.com.

Martha B. Katz-Hyman is a curator with the Jamestown-Yorktown Foundation, Williamsburg, Virginia. Prior to joining the Foundation in 2012, she was an assistant and associate curator at Colonial Williamsburg from 1985 to 2005, and an architectural conservation project manager from 2005 to 2008. As an independent curator from 2005 to 2012, she worked with historic sites and museums from Virginia to New Jersey. She is coeditor of *World of a Slave: Encyclopedia of the Material Life of Slaves in the United States*, and was awarded the John T. Schlebecker Award in 2013 for service to the Association for Living History, Farm and Agricultural Museums.

Stacia Kuceyeski serves at the director of outreach at the Ohio History Connection (formerly the Ohio Historical Society). With a background in educational outreach, Ms. Kuceyeski has facilitated a variety of educational projects, products, and professional development for educators and museum professionals at the local, state, and national level. Ms. Kuceyeski has a BA in history and an MA in cultural policy and arts administration, both from Ohio State University. She may be reached at skuceyeski@ohiohistory.org.

Wendi Manuel-Scott is director of African and African American Studies and an associate professor of history and art history at George Mason University. She holds a PhD in history from Howard University and teaches both graduate and undergraduate students in a wide range of topics in Caribbean and African American history. She was awarded a Virginia Foundation for the Humanities grant to curate an exhibition titled "Separate and Unequal: Segregation and Desegregation in Buckingham County" and a grant from the National Trust for Historic Preservation to complete an online exhibition, "One Hundred Years of African American Life and Leadership in Falls Church, Virginia."

Michelle L. McClellan is an assistant professor in the Department of History and the Residential College at the University of Michigan, where she also directs the Public History Initiative of the Eisenberg Institute for Historical Studies. She received a BA from Amherst College and a PhD in American history from Stanford University. She teaches courses in public history and historic preservation, Michigan history, and the history of medicine, and has developed partnerships between regional historical organizations and the university. Complete with sunbonnet, McClellan is writing a book about heritage tourism associated with the "Little House" books by Laura Ingalls Wilder.

George W. McDaniel is executive director of Drayton Hall, a historic site of the National Trust for Historic Preservation. An Atlanta native, he earned a BA from Sewanee, a MAT in history from Brown University, and a PhD in history from Duke. He has worked with the Atlanta History Center and the Smithsonian Institution, and has written numerous publications; his book, *Hearth and Home*, won an Honor Award from the National Trust.

Through his publications, presentations, and onsite programs, he has sought to use history museums as inspirational centers for education, historic preservation, and civic engagement.

James DeWolf Perry is the executive director of the Tracing Center. He is a speaker and facilitator on issues of slavery, race, and privilege, and was nominated for an Emmy Award as the principal historical consultant for the PBS documentary *Traces of the Trade: A Story from the Deep North*. He can be reached at jperry@tracingcenter.org.

William Peterson joined the Arizona Historical Society in December 2013 as the Northern Division director in Flagstaff. He was previously in South Dakota where he helped form Deadwood History Inc., an alliance of museums, heritage, and human resources, and in Montana, where he served as the Education and Interpretation Department head of the Montana Heritage Commission. Bill has served as president of the Museums Association of Montana and received the first Save Our History Grant awarded in Montana by the History Channel. He holds a MA in museum studies and a PhD in American culture studies.

Matthew Pinsker holds the Brian Pohanka Chair of Civil War History at Dickinson College in Carlisle, Pennsylvania, where he also serves as director of the House Divided Project (http://housedivided.dickinson.edu/sites), an innovative effort to build digital resources on the Civil War era. Pinsker graduated from Harvard College and received a DPhil degree in modern history from the University of Oxford. He is the author of two books on Abraham Lincoln.

Bernard E. Powers Jr. earned a PhD in American history at Northwestern University. He has been employed in higher education over thirty years and is now professor of history at the College of Charleston. His major work, *Black Charlestonians: A Social History 1822–1885*, published by the University of Arkansas Press, was designated an "Outstanding Academic Book" by *Choice Magazine*. His most recent article, titled "'The Worst of All Barbarism': Racial Anxiety and the Approach of Secession in the Palmetto State," was published in the *South Carolina Historical Magazine*. He is currently researching the rise of black Methodism in South Carolina.

Lynn Rainville is a research professor in the humanities and the founding director of the Tusculum Institute for historic preservation, located at Sweet Briar College. Although her PhD is in Near Eastern archaeology, she has spent the last decade studying historic African American cemeteries, documenting historic, segregated schools and conducting oral interviews with descendants of enslaved communities. Her grant-funded research has produced numerous articles. Dr. Rainville's most recent book is *Hidden History: African American Cemeteries in Central Virginia* (University of Virginia Press, 2014). Her personal website, www.lynnrainville.org, lists additional publications and research interests.

Ana Maria Rea is currently a student at Austin College where she is majoring in International Relations. For her second year in the AmeriCorps NCCC Southern region, she was the Class 19 River 7 team leader. Through AmeriCorps, Rea served in the states of Tennessee,

West Virginia, Virginia, Kentucky, Louisiana, Mississippi, and Texas. She has been active with nonprofits such as the Court Appointed Special Advocates. Originally from Mexico City, her research and career interests are focused on immigration reform.

Julia Rose is the director of the West Baton Rouge Museum. Her primary research interests focus on interpreting difficult histories and documenting historical enslaved plantation communities for museum interpretations. Currently, Rose serves as the chair of the Council for the American Association for State and Local History. She received her PhD from Louisiana State University and her Master of Arts in Teaching from the George Washington University. She has held positions at the Columbia Historical Society, East Tennessee Historical Society, and Magnolia Mound Plantation. Rose also teaches museum studies at Louisiana State University.

Jenny Scanlin has more than twenty years of experience in economic and social development for low-income communities. Currently she is assistant general manager for the City of Los Angeles' Economic and Workforce Development Department, developing and forwarding the city's economic agenda and programs. She previously managed regions and consulted on projects for the redevelopment agencies of the cities of Los Angeles and Long Beach as well as Alameda County. Prior to entering the field of redevelopment, Ms. Scanlin was a policy analyst for a county supervisor and a U.S. congressman and managed two social-service nonprofits.

Amanda G. Seymour currently works for the Thomas Jefferson Foundation at Monticello as the executive assistant to the president and CEO. She has previously worked at the foundation as an intern as well as an historic interpreter, where she co-conducted a training session on the historic interpretation of slavery and has assisted with special programming at Monticello, including the Slavery at Monticello tour. Amanda received her bachelor's degree in anthropology and Italian studies from the University of Virginia in 2010 and completed a Master of Arts in anthropology in 2013 from the George Washington University. She lives in Charlottesville, Virginia, and can be contacted at aseymour@monticello.org.

Ellen Griffith Spears teaches environmental and civil rights history in the interdisciplinary New College program and the Department of American Studies at the University of Alabama (UA). Her book, *Baptized in PCBs: Race, Pollution, and Justice in an All-American Town*, published by the University of North Carolina Press in 2014, recounts the struggles over chemical pollution by residents of Anniston, Alabama, within a larger national story of military-industrial development, regulatory inaction, and race and class inequality affecting toxic towns across America. She has guided UA student and faculty involvement in the Scottsboro Boys Museum University-Community Partnership.

Max A. van Balgooy is president of Engaging Places LLC, a design and strategy firm that connects people and historic places. He works with a wide range of historic sites on interpretive planning and business strategy, from Drayton Hall to Taliesin West. These experiences provide a rich source of ideas for EngagingPlaces.net, where he blogs regularly about the opportunities and challenges facing historic sites and house museums. He serves on the AASLH Council and teaches in the museum studies program at George Washington University, and received his degrees in history from Pomona College and the University of Delaware (Hagley Fellow).

Shelia Washington is the founder and director of the Scottsboro Boys Museum and Cultural Center. The first African American professional staffer at Scottsboro's City Hall, Washington worked for twenty-two years for the city and then served as director of recreation programs for young people in Jackson County. She led the successful effort in 2013 to exonerate the Scottsboro nine and pardon the defendants with standing convictions. She regularly hosts visitors to the museum from across the United States and around the world.

David W. Young is executive director of Cliveden, a historic site of the National Trust for Historic Preservation located in the Germantown section of Philadelphia. Prior to that position, he served as director of the Johnson House Historic Site, a National Historic Landmark of the Underground Railroad. He serves as a lecturer in the Graduate Program in Historic Preservation at the University of Pennsylvania. He has published on Germantown's African American history and on issues related to historic site sustainability. Holding a PhD in history from Ohio State University, his dissertation explored how Germantown's twentieth-century history has been preserved and remembered.